T0271356

The Constitution of Political Economy

The two dominant conceptions of political economy are based on either reducing political decisions to rational-choice reasoning or, conversely, reducing economic structures and phenomena to the realm of politics. In this book, Adrian Pabst and Roberto Scazzieri contend that neither conception is convincing and they argue for a fundamental rethinking of political economy. Developing a new approach at the interface of economic theory and political thought, the book shows that political economy covers a plurality of dimensions, which reflect internal hierarchies and multiple relationships within the economic and political sphere. *The Constitution of Political Economy* presents a new, richer conception of political economy that draws on a range of thinkers from the history of political economy, recognising the complex embedding of the economy and the polity in society. Effective policy-making has to reflect this embedding and rests on the interdependence between local, national, and international actors to address multiple systemic crises.

ADRIAN PABST is Professor of Politics in the School of Politics and International Relations at the University of Kent and Deputy Director of the National Institute of Economic and Social Research.

ROBERTO SCAZZIERI is Professor of Economic Analysis, Department of Economics, University of Bologna, National Fellow of the National Lincei Academy, and Senior Member of Clare Hall and Gonville and Caius College, Cambridge.

The Constitution of Political Economy

Polity, Society and the Commonweal

ADRIAN PABST
*University of Kent, Canterbury, and National Institute of
Economic and Social Research, London*

ROBERTO SCAZZIERI
University of Bologna, and National Lincei Academy, Rome

CAMBRIDGE
UNIVERSITY PRESS

CAMBRIDGE
UNIVERSITY PRESS

Shaftesbury Road, Cambridge CB2 8EA, United Kingdom

One Liberty Plaza, 20th Floor, New York, NY 10006, USA

477 Williamstown Road, Port Melbourne, VIC 3207, Australia

314–321, 3rd Floor, Plot 3, Splendor Forum, Jasola District Centre,
New Delhi – 110025, India

103 Penang Road, #05–06/07, Visioncrest Commercial, Singapore 238467

Cambridge University Press is part of Cambridge University Press & Assessment,
a department of the University of Cambridge.

We share the University's mission to contribute to society through the pursuit of
education, learning and research at the highest international levels of excellence.

www.cambridge.org
Information on this title: www.cambridge.org/9781108831093

DOI: 10.1017/9781108923231

First published 2023

A catalogue record for this publication is available from the British Library.

*A Cataloging-in-Publication data record for this book is available from the
Library of Congress.*

ISBN 978-1-108-83109-3 Hardback

Cambridge University Press & Assessment has no responsibility for the persistence
or accuracy of URLs for external or third-party internet websites referred to in this
publication and does not guarantee that any content on such websites is, or will
remain, accurate or appropriate.

Contents

Tables

Preface

This book develops a new conception of political economy at the interface of economic theory and political thought. Our argument is that political economy covers a plurality of dimensions, which reflect the internal hierarchies and multiple relationships within the economic and the political sphere. We theorise political economy as the interdependence between these two spheres that rests on the web of social relationships in which both are embedded. Policy-making depends on recognising the complex interactions of the economy, the polity, and society.

An overarching theory is needed not only to conceptualise the nature of systemic crises such as pandemics, climate change disruptions, arms races, and struggles for resources facing the world today but also to help design effective policy responses. There are plural and interdependent domains involved in policy-making, which highlight the key role of coordination between local, national, and international actors as a necessary condition to reduce the vulnerability and enhance the resilience of humankind.

The theory of political economy developed in this book considers the economy and the polity as twin spheres arising from the constitution of society in its relatively persistent structure. The economic system and the 'body politic' are closely intertwined within each political economy, which is in turn a sphere whose 'constitution' is identified by specific proportions and an admissible range of transformations. A *constitutional heuristic* is therefore necessary to understand the interplay of persistence and change and to assess the feasibility of policy actions in any given context.

The intellectual strands underpinning our argument are manifold, but two traditions turn out to be central. The constitutional tradition in political theory is a major source of inspiration with its emphasis on the *lex supra regem* principle, which draws attention to the political order of society as a relatively invariant condition independent of the contingent acts of will of a sovereign authority. The structural tradition in economic theory is the other key influence behind our conception of political economy. This tradition emphasizes forms of interrelatedness between economic activities that derive from human actions but not necessarily from human design. Our book combines these two traditions in a unifying framework based on the relative invariance of certain relationships relative to others, and on the 'order of motion' that policy actions should follow under given constitutions of the economy and the polity.

Acknowledgements

This work draws on a scholarly collaboration started almost twenty years ago when Adrian was a PhD student at the University of Cambridge and part of a group of researchers attached to the Centre for Research in the Arts, Social Sciences and Humanities (CRASSH) and Roberto was a visiting fellow at CRASSH, where we were both hosted by its director Ludmilla Jordanova. Our cooperation took shape as part of a collaborative project on 'Migration of Ideas' jointly sponsored by CRASSH and by the Institute of Advanced Study of the University of Bologna and continued shortly afterwards thanks to our joint involvement in the Centre for History and Economics at King's College, Cambridge. In subsequent years, we continued an intense intellectual exchange through a variety of joint writing projects from the history of ideas to the theory of civil society and the theory of political economy.

We owe a debt of gratitude to our respective institutions and scholarly circles. Adrian would like to thank his teachers and colleagues for their wisdom and support, starting at the University of Cambridge with Solomos Solomou who as director of studies at Peterhouse, Cambridge, taught him macroeconomics in a historical perspective; Sheilagh Ogilvie whose teaching on economic history and the first industrial revolution was inspirational; Ha-Joon Chang who emphasised the plurality of state intervention in the economy; Partha Dasgupta whose focus on ethics and ecology was formative; and Willem Buiter who combined scholarly rigour with humour in unique ways during supervisions for the final-year undergraduate dissertation. Adrian is also very grateful to his teachers at the London School of Economics and Political Science, notably John Gray who taught him the meaning of philosophical scepticism and some of the myths of modernity and Paul Kelly who introduced him to modern contractual theory, as well as to Jean-Marie Donegani and Marc Sadou at Sciences Po Paris who broadened his interests in intellectual history.

Adrian would also like to thank numerous colleagues and friends for their generosity and support over many years, including Russell Berman, Simona Beretta, Maxim Bratersky, Leonid Grigoriev, Wayne Hudson, Ron Ivey, Patrick Mardellat, Giovanni Marseguerra, John Milbank, James Noyes, Marcia Pally, David Pan, Catherine Pickstock, the late Pier Luigi Porta, Alberto Quadrio Curzio, the late Roger Scruton, and Larry Siedentop. He owes a special debt of gratitude to Luigino Bruni, Jon Cruddas, Maurice Glasman, Brian Griffith, Andy Haldane, Robert Skidelsky and Stefano Zamagni whose work has been an inspiration over many years. At the University of Kent, he would like to thank Nadine Ansorg, Iain MacKenzie, Richard Sakwa, Ben Turner, Richard Whitman, and David Wilkinson, and at the National Institute of Economic and Social Research Arnab Bhattacharjee, Jagjit Chadha, Peter Dolton, Larissa Marioni, Stephen Millard, Max Mosley, Barry Naisbett and Lucy Stokes. More recently, he has worked closely with colleagues as part of the Productivity Institute, including Bart van Ark, Diane Coyle, Philip McCann, Steve Roper, Tony Venables, and Andy Westwood.

Adrian is also indebted to the institutions that have supported his studies and research, starting with the Faculty of Economics and Peterhouse in the University of Cambridge, the European Institute at the London School of Economics and Political Science, Sciences Po Paris, the Higher School of Economics in Moscow, and the Australian Catholic University where he spent his research sabbatical in 2017–18.

Above all, he is deeply grateful to his parents Reinhart and Brigitte, his wife Elena, and his children Alexander and Katya for their support and patience for so long – especially the evenings, weekends, and holidays spent working on this book.

Roberto is grateful to the teachers, colleagues, and students who have been inspirations and companions in his intellectual journey from Bologna and Oxford to Padua, Cambridge, again Bologna, and in most recent years the Accademia Nazionale dei Lincei in Rome. He is especially grateful to Alberto Quadrio Curzio who prompted his interest in the theory of production and in the history of economic analysis during his formative years at Bologna and has been a continuing intellectual and personal inspiration ever since; to the late Luigi Pasinetti, for his pioneering research on the structural dynamics of production economies and for his exemplary commitment to a lifelong research programme; to Michael Landesmann, the Oxford and Cambridge

friend with whom some of the production analytical tools developed
in this book, and in particular the 'relative invariance' criterion, were
conceived and developed; to Harald Hagemann, for the joint work
on sequentially constrained transitional paths that has been central
to the constitutional heuristic presented in this monograph; to Mauro
Baranzini at Oxford, Cambridge, and Lugano, and D'Maris Coffman
at Cambridge and London, for many years of collaborative research at
the interface between structural dynamics, socio-institutional transformation, and the framing of economic policy; and to Ivano Cardinale
at Bologna, Cambridge, and London, with whom some of the core
ideas behind the theory of political economy presented in this book
were envisioned and developed. Roberto would also like to express his
deep gratitude to the late Paolo Grossi for the enlightening discussions
on matters of constitutional law in historical perspective that have
shaped the final stages of this project.

Among the many colleagues and friends with whom key concepts
of this book have been discussed over the years, Roberto would
like to thank Amartya Sen, David Soskice, Carlo D'Adda, Stefano
Zamagni, Emma Rothschild, Patrizio Bianchi, Lorenzo Ornaghi,
Faye Duchin, Alessandro Vercelli, Silva Marzetti, Jan Kregel, Maria
Carla Galavotti, Bernard Grofman, Douglas Hofstadter, Wang Hui,
Mario Amendola, Albert Steenge, Amit Bhaduri, Sheila Dow, Richard
Arena, Antonio Andreoni, Ha-Joon Chang, Partha Dasgupta, Martin
Daunton, Ian Donaldson, John Morrill, Craig Muldrew, Frank Perlin,
Sophus Reinert, Luisa Brunori, Malcolm Pines, Heinrich Bortis, Lilia
Costabile, Aura Reggiani, Sunanda Sen, Mike Gregory, Marco Di
Tommaso, David Ibbetson, Michele Caputo, and Ajit Sinha. He rec-
ollects with gratitude the inspiring conversations with teachers and
colleagues who have passed away, notably John and Ursula Hicks,
Michael Bacharach, Nicholas Georgescu-Roegen, Francis Seton,
Sukhamoy Chakravarty, Phyllis Deane, Geoff Harcourt, Polly Hill,
Timothy McDermott, Nicola Matteucci, Carlo Poni, Jack Goody,
Ronnie Ellenblum, Izumi Hishiyama, Patrick Suppes, Andrew Skinner,
Istvan Hont, and Pier Luigi Porta.

He would also like to express his gratitude to the institutions that
supported his research in various ways, and primarily the University
of Bologna (Faculty of Political Sciences, Faculty of Economics and
Commerce, and Department of Economics), Linacre College in
Oxford, Clare Hall and Gonville and Caius College in Cambridge,

the Accademia Nazionale dei Lincei, the Bologna Academy of Sciences, the Lombard Institute of Sciences and Letters, the Institute of Advanced Studies and the Interdisciplinary Research Centre in Epistemology and History of Science at the University of Bologna, the Research Center in Economic Analysis and International Economic Development (CRANEC) at the Catholic University of Milan, the Centre for Financial History at Newnham College and Darwin College in Cambridge, the International Interdisciplinary Research Laboratory of the International Balzan Foundation, the Italian National University Centre for Applied Economic Studies, and the Babbage International Policy Forum at the Institute for Manufacturing in the University of Cambridge.

Last but not least, Roberto would like to express his deepest gratitude to his wife Cristina and his son Luigi for their continued support in the long intellectual journey from start to completion of this project.

It has been a great pleasure for us both, as colleagues and friends, to work together on this book.

Introduction
Rethinking Political Economy

The Complex Identity of Political Economy

What is political economy? Contemporary conceptions tend to divide it into separate spheres such as individual actors in an idealised marketplace or the state as an internally undifferentiated actor. In reality, both the economy and the polity are constituted by multiple and overlapping levels of interdependence between actors across the economic and the political sphere. As a result, political economy is a complex object with both static and dynamic characteristics. Its constitution derives from the relationship between two spheres that are distinctly structured and yet are mutually dependent. This means that political economy is subject to mutual constraints generated within the economic and political spheres, and to the mutual influence of sources of change arising within either sphere.

The constitution of political economy is the focus of this book, which builds on both economic and political thought to develop a theory of the relationships between the economic and the political body. Our emphasis is on the body politic considered as a sphere constituted by political actions and agents, which fit some collective condition or purpose that would at a minimum include the (relative) persistence of the body politic itself. Similarly, we consider the economic body as a sphere constituted by economic actions and agents, which fit some systemic condition for material sustenance and welfare that would at a minimum ensure the (relative) resilience of an organized economic sphere.[1]

---

[1] This approach reflects the view of both the economy and the polity as instances of 'organized complexity' (Weaver, 1948; Simon, 1962; Scazzieri, 2021), such that both the economic and political spheres rest on a complex network of interdependencies open to a variety of configurations but subject to systemic conditions of viability and persistence.

Economic and political thinking originally emphasised the dispositional activity connected with governance of the household or of the state but eventually gave way to the consideration of relationships between mutually dependent yet partially autonomous activities, as in the Renaissance literature on civil life.[2] This duality between the dispositional activity of a single individual (or sovereign body) and the relational activities carried out by a plurality of actors in the pursuit of mutually compatible or complementary objectives has remained central to political economy both as an object of investigation and as a field of study.

A consequence of this complex identity is that the long-term historical evolution of political economy shows shifts between a focus on dispositional activities (such as allocation of capabilities or resources) and a focus on material and social interdependencies. This dynamic often makes it difficult to identify the underlying unity of political economy, even if the recurrence of those two perspectives is by itself an indication of the intertwining of actions and structures at its core. The divide between the two opposed conceptions of political economy mentioned above has its roots in reductionist theoretical developments that, both in economic and in political theory, have failed to address the embeddedness and mutual shaping of dispositions and structures at multiple levels of aggregation in the economy and the polity.

The purpose of this book is to develop a new theoretical framework that avoids both types of reductionism by bringing to light the close integration between human dispositions and socioeconomic interdependencies. In our view, avoiding reductionism allows a better understanding of the way in which a given society meets economic needs through principles of direct or indirect governance, that is, how economics meets politics in a given context. In particular, this approach draws attention to the fact that dispositions and structures shape each other at multiple different levels. For example, the pattern of interdependence (say, the pattern of division of labour) at a certain level of aggregation may be the generative mechanism of dispositions that may in turn trigger a certain political arrangement (say, a certain mode of

---

[2] This conception is expressed in Justus Lipsius's definition of civil life as 'what we conduct in the society of human beings to the purpose of common benefit and utility' (Lipsius, 1596, p. 1, as quoted in Ornaghi, 1984, p. 71; see Chapter 5 of the present book).

conciliation of conflicting interests). On the other hand, a different level of aggregation may generate dispositions (and modes of conciliation of interests) that are incompatible with a certain pattern of material interdependence and may trigger a structural dynamic moving the economy from one pattern of division of labour to another.

Beyond the Boundaries of Economics and Politics

This book outlines a theory of political economy that moves beyond the boundaries of economics and politics. Our analysis starts from the observation that contemporary political economy as a field of study and as an object of investigation is divided in two ways: first, the disciplinary divide between economics and political science and, second, a separation between the economic and the political domain that obscures their multiple levels of interdependence. This double division is not merely theoretical but translates into serious shortcomings in policy-making from an economic or from a political perspective, including an excessively short-term outlook, policy and institutional unpredictability as well as the exclusive promotion of sectional interests to the detriment of the 'systemic interest' of the commonweal. As a result, policy makers lack the conceptual tools to understand or tackle systemic challenges within and across regions, nations, and the international community.

By contrast with these dualisms, we argue that the mutual embedding of the economic and political domains suggests a new definition of both domains in terms of multiple and interrelated levels of agency. As a result, the political domain is not limited to a purely 'contractualist' sphere of formal rules and agreements but encompasses a 'constitutionalist' perspective: whereas the former considers how prior interests vie with one another through conflict or compromise, the latter shifts the emphasis to objectives subject to a systemic condition, which gives shape to the interests of different actors. Similarly, the economic domain is not reducible to the micro level of the individual household or to the macro level of the sovereign state but rather is constituted by the relatively persistent relational patterns established at multiple levels of aggregation within a community of actors engaged in division of labour and exchange.

The theory of political economy developed in this book brings to light the fundamental architecture of the economic and political spheres, that is, the relatively invariant structures determining the 'orderliness' (constitutional identity) of either domain. Accordingly, politics cannot be equated with coercive power and the struggle for influence. Rather, the economic features of politics call attention to the complementarities, constraints and possibilities that shape both conflict and cooperation. Likewise, the economy cannot be conceived purely as a collection of rational and self-interested actors interacting with one another under resource constraints on individual opportunities and choices. Instead, the political features of the economy highlight systemic conditions that constrain and orient the division of labour and exchange in the polity if material and social resilience is to be achieved.

Outline of the Book

The argument of this book is developed in a sequence of steps. Part I ('Interdependence and the Economic Constitution') discusses the current state of political economy and develops a theory of interdependence based on social dispositions, technical complementarities, and modes of association. Chapter 1 ('Political Economy in Question') argues for the need to move beyond the duality between micro and macro approaches by focusing on the intermediate units of analysis (such as professional groups, unions, or industrial sectors) that provide the building blocks of an organized economic-political system. The chapter conceptualises political economy as a system of multilayered interdependencies between a plurality of actors. Against this background, the arrangement of actors' relative positions is subject to constraints, opportunities, and affordances that identify what can be described as the 'constitution' of a political economy. This is defined as a relatively stable constellation of relative positions, which includes the relative positional changes that are feasible in a given system without modifying its fundamental identity.

This chapter contrast this 'constitutionalist' conception of political economy with the 'contractualist' view of a deliberate formal arrangement between actors. The chapter also maintains that the constitutionalist approach, by emphasising the context-embeddedness of different actors, provides a bridge between actors' dispositional activities aimed at the provision of needs in a means-ends framework, and the material and social interdependencies that provide a structure to the dispositions and actions of the actors themselves.

Chapter 2 ('Sociability and Interdependence') examines interdependence as both a necessary condition and a consequence of sociability. The latter is a condition of relationality which develops dynamically through a complex interplay between dispositions, actions, and their consequences. Mutual needs (the needs of human beings for one another) give rise to mutual dependencies, from the most elementary relations within the nuclear family to the complex patterns of division of labour in society. On the other hand, mutual dependencies give rise to social dispositions, which induce human beings to rely on one another (or to be opposed to one another) for the satisfaction of their own needs. This chapter considers the reciprocal structuring of interdependence and sociability as the starting point for a theory of social congruence. The continuum between different spheres of mutual needs (from elementary needs to needs of increasing complexity) explains *both* the emergence of distinct affiliations and the likelihood of multiple affiliations for the same individuals or groups.

In particular, the chapter distinguishes between two different approaches to social congruence: the 'analytic' mode and the 'genetic' mode. This distinction can be traced to the work of the seventeenth-century English philosopher Richard Cumberland, according to whom the analytic and the genetic approach entail, respectively, the identification of a general (and fundamental) proportionality condition for congruence, and the reconstruction of the historical process by which a given society ends up with a particular pattern of group affiliations. Cumberland's distinction suggests a way to reconcile the approach to social congruence as the pursuit of an idealized 'perfect republic' (as with the Neapolitan Enlightenment philosopher Paolo Mattia Doria) and its view as an evolutionary process taking shape through history along a plurality of routes (as with David Hume, Adam Smith, and other authors of the Scottish Enlightenment).

In other words, the analytic *versus* genetic distinction emphasises a complementarity between the proportionality conditions for the mutual fitting of dispositions and actions, on the one hand, and the multiple routes by which these conditions can be met depending on context and historical trajectory, on the other hand. The duality between analytical conditions and contexts also allows the identification of the plural ways in which the partial interests of individuals and groups can be accommodated with the proportionality conditions expressing the systemic interest of the political economy as a whole.

Chapter 3 ('Association and the Division of Labour') builds on Adam Smith's theory of division of labour as the mutual fitting of specialised human actions and develops that theory integrating the conditions for the complementarity of specialised technical abilities with the scale requirements arising from the different sizes and capacities of human actors and mechanical tools. This chapter examines the relationship between division of labour and modes of association along the three fundamental dimensions of capabilities, tasks, and materials-in-process. The three dimensions entail distinct association criteria that must eventually find a degree of mutual fitting. Capabilities must combine in executing different tasks (or range of tasks) to deliver a given product or service (or range therefrom). Tasks must 'recognize' one another in the sense of being matching components within the same broad platform of technical operations. The flows of materials-in-process must be satisfactorily synchronized so that the delivery of a certain output at a certain time matches in timing and quantity the need for that output by other processes.

Capabilities, tasks, and materials require modes of coordination eventually integrated with one another within a 'production regime' that entails a network of capabilities, tasks, and materials spanning different levels of aggregation in society. The chapter also analyses the relationship between networks in the production sphere and modes of association of individuals and groups in the social sphere, and it concludes examining ways in which changes of production regime may presuppose and/or induce changes in the social structures of the political economy.

Chapter 4 ('The Constitution of the Economy') develops the conceptual framework of the previous chapters of Part I into a theory of the economic constitution. This chapter argues that the arrangement of economic activities in a society based on division of labour between specialized agents and groups leads to the introduction of interdependencies governed by a principle of relative invariance. This means that the complementarities between activities must be supported by a core set of persistent relationships providing a degree of stability to division of labour beyond the changes that may take place in the modes of coordination between capabilities, tasks, and materials. This material and social infrastructure generates the 'constitution' of a given economy and provides the framework within which patterns of coordination between capabilities, tasks, and materials can change resulting into different schemes of division of labour and sometimes into different production regimes.

This chapter develops a theory of the economic constitution that allows alternative mappings of interdependence between social groups to be compatible with a given fundamental pattern of division of labour. A preliminary step is to identify whether the dominant social infrastructure derives from capabilities, tasks, or materials. A second step is to consider what is the dominant pattern of aggregation for different capabilities, tasks, and materials. A third step is to recognize the dominant constellation of interests in view of the two previous steps. The chapter discusses alternative patterns of complementarity or cleavage depending on whether division of labour is centred on capabilities, tasks, or materials, and on what scheme of aggregation is the dominant one.

A constitutional taxonomy based on the dual distinction between hierarchical *versus* non-hierarchical, and closed *versus* open modes of association leads to the view of the economy as a 'constituted body', in which the relative invariance of certain relative positions allows the feasibility of certain types of transformation while excluding others. Finally, this chapter discusses the constitutional framing of economic policy and suggests that a constitutional heuristic is needed to determine which policy objectives and policy instruments are compatible with the existing economic constitution, and which ones are only feasible provided the existing material and social infrastructure is changed.

Part II of the book ('Political Spaces and Policy Actions') moves to the consideration of the 'body politic' as a system of interdependencies between individual or collective actors reflecting the dominant pattern of division of labour and determining the character of political spaces as domains of complementary or conflicting interests subject to systemic constraints. This point of view is first developed in Chapter 5 ('A Political Economy of the Body Politic'), which starts with the conception of political life as based on the primacy of the relational opportunities, constraints, and affordances involved in social interdependence. This view of politics as inherently associated with the interpersonal embeddedness of human action (Hannah Arendt's *vita activa*) leads to a constitutionalist view of the Body Politic, which is seen as reflecting the human disposition towards mutual recognition and interdependence rather than the mere pursuit of 'influence' through sheer political power or economic wealth.

The chapter develops this constitutionalist view of political life by exploring its links with a complex intellectual tradition which draws on Shaftesbury's and Doria's view of civil life as combination of mutually reinforcing capabilities ('virtues'); Montesquieu, Burke, and Tocqueville's reflections on the primacy of interpersonal association over the actions of individual actors or 'personalized' collective bodies; and Genovesi's conception of the civil economy as the 'political science of the economy and commerce'. This way of conceptualising politics is contrasted with politics as conflict over limited resources, and its development either through struggle or compromise and 'contract' (as in Machiavelli, Hobbes, Locke, and the *Federalist Papers*). On this premise, the chapter outlines a critique of contractualism in its dual expression of the primacy of the state over the economy and society and of the primacy of the economy over society and the polity.

The latter part of the chapter develops the constitutionalist perspective of politics first by exploring its roots in Shaftesbury, Doria, and Genovesi's conception of a 'rational image' of human capabilities and their complementarity in the polity, then by examining the 'evolutionary' approaches followed by Hume, Smith, Beccaria, and Filangieri in their endeavour to root dispositions and social structures in the path dependence followed by modes of association over time, and finally by considering the explorations by Montesquieu, Burke, and Tocqueville into the relationship between social structures and the constitutional development of each polity. This chapter concludes highlighting the openness of the constitutionalist perspective to the plurality of political spaces made possible by multiple layers of interdependence between social actors.

Chapter 6 ('Constellations of Interests and Institutional Architecture') explores the formation of interests in political spaces, the possible recognition of a systemic interest within those spaces, and the emergence of institutional architectures responding to the relative persistence of constellations of interests in a political space. This chapter examines the extent to which the institutional architecture of a polity at a given time is compatible with the existing, or emerging, pattern of division of labour between social groups, that is, with its economic constitution. Interdependencies and their evolution generate different political spaces in which partial interests can be expressed. In turn, this process may lead to alternative mappings of the systemic conditions constraining the pursuit of interests in each political space. This chapter highlights the distinction between a conciliation of interests through compromise or conflict (a scenario close to the contractualist point of view), and a conciliation of interests through the pursuit of partial interests under a systemic constraint (a scenario close to the constitutionalist point of view).

The following analysis in the chapter turns to a discussion of alternative identifications of systemic constraint depending on (i) the dominant pattern of interdependence between social actors, and (ii) the prevailing mapping of interdependence by those actors in a given context. This discussion leads to considering institutional architectures as focal points determining both the patterns of compromise or conflict and the type of systemic interest that may be identified under given conditions. Social dispositions and patterns of interdependence, which are at the origin of institutional architectures, may also be the source of a mismatch between interdependencies and their mapping by social actors. This point introduces the discussion of institutional change as a process influenced by the mutual structuring of changes in the division of labour and changes in actors' dispositions and mapping of interests. Policy-making is a privileged interface between economic interdependencies and political spaces.

Chapter 7 ('Policy Actions in an Embedded Polity') develops a constitutional heuristic aimed at assessing the opportunities, constraints and inducement factors that generate certain policy objectives and policy trajectories while excluding others in a political economy. Our argument in this chapter is that policy actions are carried out at the interface between the economic and the political sphere. The internal structure ('constitution') of the economic body and of the body politic implies that certain policy actions may be compatible, say, with the economic constitution but not with the political constitution, or vice versa. This means that only policy actions compatible with *both* the economic and the political constitution can be carried out without changes in either. In other words, we need a constitutional heuristic as means to evaluate whether a given policy is feasible under the existing constitutional settlement or not.

This chapter outlines a set of policy principles derived from the constitutional framing of the economic and the political sphere developed in the previous chapters. This is done by emphasising that policy actions are designed and carried out in the light of complex patterns of association (division of labour) in the economic sphere and of complex patterns of collective action in the political sphere. The patterns of division of labour and of collective action are not necessarily compatible with each other, and this brings to light the role of constitutional heuristic in evaluating which policy actions are feasible under the existing constitutions of the economic and the political body, and which ones cannot be implemented unless there is a change in either. This chapter then illustrates the above set of principles by examining industrial policy, credit policy, and international trade policy as domains in which the constitution of each political economy makes certain policy actions feasible and others unfeasible under given circumstances. The chapter concludes with a discussion of the conditions for embedded policy making in a political economy facing systemic challenges that may require constitutional changes in the economic or in the political sphere, or in both.

Chapter 8 ('Conclusion') considers possible lines of further research suggested by this book's emphasis on the economic embedding of political activity and the political embedding of economic activity. The distinction between constitutional architectures in the economic and the political sphere may provide a heuristic into the dynamic trajectories open to a political economy and to the policy actions likely to take place within it. Our argument is that constitutional principles entail that persistence and change are closely intertwined: a degree of persistence ensures the identity and stability of a political economy, while openness to transformation is necessary to allow resilience vis-à-vis shocks and adjustment to societal change.

PART I

Interdependence and the Economic Constitution

1 | *Political Economy in Question*

1.1 Political Economy as a Contested Field

The contemporary revival of interest in political economy highlights the coexistence of different and seemingly opposed conceptions among scholars and policy makers when addressing the interface between the economy and the polity. One set of approaches focuses on individual actors in the marketplace or in the public sphere while another set of approaches shifts the emphasis to the state as a self-contained and internally undifferentiated collective actor. Both conceptions result from an oversimplification of the complex, multi-layered configuration that characterises the relationship between the economic and political domains. This chapter outlines a conception of political economy that moves beyond this dichotomy and develops the view of individuals, markets, and states as embedded in a relational field composed of multi-level social interdependencies and institutions.

The first set of approaches mentioned above rests on theories of rational choice driven by the deliberate pursuit of interests (e.g. Shepsle, 1989; McLean, 1991; Petracca, 1991; Green and Shapiro, 1994; Ainsworth, 1999; Persson and Tabellini, 2000, 2005; Weingast and Wittman, 2006; Magni-Berton, 2014; Amadae, 2015). These theories regard politics as a domain of economic decisions, which is itself underpinned by means-ends rationality. Such theories fail to sufficiently incorporate both the non-economic features of political arrangements and the strictly political features of the economy.

The second set of approaches are based upon macro-political theories (e.g. Skocpol, Evans, and Rueschemeyer, 1985; Deane, 1989; Bortis, 1996; Nakhimovsky, 2011; Blyth, 2013; Turchin, 2016; Tribe, 2017; O'Mahony, 2019 [2013]; Streeck, 2019). They conceptualise the state as a collective actor governing the economic system, without directly addressing the state's internal structure as well as its relationship with the plural and interdependent parts of the economy existing at multiple levels of aggregation.

The aim of this chapter is to explore the 'constitution' of political economy, which we identify with the multi-layered and relatively persistent configuration of domains and sub-domains in which economic structures and political actions mutually reinforce or hinder one another, thereby determining the dynamics of social wealth – what we call 'commonweal'. The chapter conceptualises political economy as a relational field resulting from overlapping spheres of social life. On the one hand, it refers to the social relationships that enable the material provision of human needs. On the other hand, it brings to the fore the political dimension of need satisfaction, which involves the balancing and coordination of differentiated interests in society. These dual origins of political economy highlight the interplay between the material and the political dimensions of sociability. Indeed, the meeting of human needs presupposes the existence of patterns of interdependence that are inherently political, in the sense that they require the systemic fitting of differentiated capabilities, interests, and activities. At the same time, political life is grounded in the web of interdependencies that provides material support to the economy. The polity and the economy are mutually intertwined and embedded in society.

This conception has its roots in intellectual traditions that have been either incorporated partially or overlooked altogether in contemporary political economy. It draws on eighteenth-century economic and political writings by figures such as Paolo Mattia Doria (1667–1746), Antonio Genovesi (1713–1769), Adam Smith (1723–1790), Adam Ferguson (1723–1816), Edmund Burke (1730–1797), and John Millar (1735–1801). Common to these thinkers is a focus on the embedding of both economy and polity in social structures and on interdependencies that combine the specialisation of economic activities (division of labour) with the integration of specialised activities in the social domain. Division of labour presupposes specialisation and the modularization of economic activities while at the same time requiring effective coordination. As Ernest Gellner noted,

[i]n one sense, the division of labour has now gone further in industrial society than ever before: there are more distinct and separate jobs. But in another sense, there is less of it and there is far more homogeneity: every

job is carried out in the same style and in much the same spirit [...] Also, specialisms are inter-locking, specialists are obliged to communicate with and understand other specialists, they have to "speak the same language". (Gellner, 1994, pp. 75–76)

Our work builds on these ideas to address the increasing coordination requirements at a time when an ever-greater division of labour in the world economy raises fundamental questions about the material basis of the commonweal.

The origins of political economy lie in the early modern extensions of the classical *oikonomia* (the set of rules for the good governance of the household) to the sovereign rules for the material governance of the polity and, ultimately, to 'the order on which a political body is principally founded' (Richelet, 1785, who refers to the 1694 edition of the *French Academy Dictionary*). The plural character of political economy encompasses a variety of approaches already implicit in its formative stage. For sovereign actions, pursuing the material welfare of the polity involves addressing the relationship between intention and outcome, while the resulting arrangement of economic and political functions suitable to that purpose highlights a structure of interdependencies that can be understood *independently* of the sovereign decision that may be at its origin.

Indeed, that very structure of interdependencies underscores the plurality of spheres whose mutual consistence must be achieved for the economy to be a viable arrangement of activities. This in turn makes it possible to have actors, or constellations of actors, at multiple levels of aggregation capable of mutual adjustment and coordination independently of a single centre of political authority. The historical development of political economy from its origins to its current state encompasses analytical trajectories that have emphasised either the means-ends approach or the structural approach, and that have emphasised either the interdependencies between individual, self-interested actors or the state as the ultimate source of coordination and governance. A macro-micro dichotomy is implicit in either approach. Our argument is that this dichotomy does not reflect the differentiated and multi-layered configuration of political economy as the sphere of actions regarding the provision of material needs in the polity. We argue that a new theory of political economy is needed and that such a theory should overcome the dichotomy between means-ends actions and structures of interdependence. In this light, the reciprocal influence between actions and structures is best investigated by considering the hierarchical arrangement of actions as we move across different levels of aggregation in the polity.

The outline of this chapter is as follows. Section 1.2 discusses the current state of political economy as a contested field in which micro and macro approaches dominate the debate without addressing intermediate levels of analysis and the interplay of actions and structures that takes place at those levels. Section 1.3 introduces the concept of relational embeddedness as a means to overcome the macro-micro duality in political economy. This section builds on John Hicks's distinction between the 'order of doing' and the 'order of being' to develop a framework that encompasses the two principal intellectual traditions in economic theory: one that is exchange-oriented and the other that is production-oriented. Such a framework conceptualises political economy at the interstice between purposive actions and multi-layered interdependencies among individual and collective actors. The section also considers the links between our approach to relational embeddedness and other relational approaches in social theory.

Section 1.4 theorises the 'constitution' of a political economy in terms of the constraints, opportunities, and affordances generated by the interdependence between individual and collective actions across the economic and the political sphere. This web of interdependencies gives rise to constellations of interests that, after compromises or conflicts, may find expression in relatively stable arrangements of the political economy. Section 1.5 contrasts contractualist approaches to political economy with what we call constitutionalist approaches. This section highlights the difference between the contractualist view of a direct relationship between individual actors and the sovereign state (or the transnational market) and the constitutionalist view of a *nested structure* of interdependencies that binds together economic and political relationships within a pre-existing social body. In this perspective, intermediate units of analysis are prior to both micro- and macro-actors, and the interplay of agency and structure that takes place at intermediate levels of aggregation provides a bridge between the means-ends provision of needs and the context-embeddedness of policy actions. Section 1.6 brings the chapter to a close by discussing ways in which the constitutionalist theory of political economy developed in this book overcomes the duality between micro and macro approaches to policy-making through a focus on the existence of a 'constitution' of economic policy involving plural policy domains at multiple different levels of intervention.

1.2 Dichotomies in Economic and Political Theory

Most current research in political economy and public policy-making considers markets, states, and individuals as foundational categories that are more primary than the society they constitute. Such a partitioning of social reality into 'primitive categories' underpins the strict separation of academic disciplines and a process of ever-greater specialisation and the proliferation of new sub-fields. In a 1941 essay, John Hicks anticipated the limitations of an ever-more specialised discipline of economics:

[i]n the field of economics, over-specialisation is doubly disastrous. A man who is a mathematician may live a stunted life, but he does not do any harm. An economist who is nothing but an economist is a danger to his neighbours. Economics is not a thing in itself. It is a study of one aspect of the life of man in society [...]. The economist of tomorrow (sometimes of today) will also know what to advise, on economic grounds; but if, through increasing specialisation, his economics is divorced from any background of social philosophy, he will be in real danger of becoming a dodge merchant, full of ingenious devices for getting out of particular difficulties, but losing contact with the plain root-virtues, even the plain economic virtues, on which a healthy society must be based. Modern economics is subject to a real danger of Machiavellism – the treatment of social problems as matters of technique, not as facets of the general search for the Good Life. (Hicks, 1941, p. 6)

Dividing reality into separate spheres is encapsulated by the split between political philosophy and intellectual history, on the one hand, and the social sciences, on the other hand (Collini, Winch, and Burrow, 1983). A parallel separation has taken place between economic theory and the history of economic ideas (Roncaglia, 2005). In turn, the social sciences are further divided into specialised fields of inquiry according to an ever-greater division of labour. A case in point is the disciplinary divide between political science and pure economics, which deepened following the Marginalist Revolution of the 1870s insofar as both politics and economics were no longer seen as branches of political economy but instead as new sciences in their own right (Collison Black et al., 1973; Dobb, 1973; Blaug, 1997).

Alfred Marshall's argument, which led him to drop the term 'political economy' and to propose 'economics' in its place, is presented in the *Economics of Industry*, which he co-authored with his wife Mary Paley Marshall:

[t]he nation used to be called 'the Body Politic'. So long as this phrase was in common use, men thought of the interests of the whole nation when they used the word 'Political'; and then 'Political Economy' served well enough as name for the science. But now 'political interests' generally mean the interests of only some part or parts of the nation; so that it seems best to drop the name 'political economy', and to speak simply of *Economic Science* or more shortly *Economics*. (Marshall and Paley Marshall, 1879, p. 2)

Henry Sidgwick largely agreed with the Marshalls, although with a significant qualification about the need for continual state enforcement of the division of labour:

[t]his vast system of relations, with all the minutely subdivided organisation of labour which it involves, has been in the main constructed without the direct action of government: though, no doubt, it could not be maintained without the enforcement, through government agency, of rights, of property, contracts, etc.; and though it has been importantly modified – to a varying extent in different ages and countries – by direct government interference. Accordingly, it has been possible for the followers of Adam Smith to separate the study of the industrial organisation of society – under the name of 'Political Economy' – almost entirely from the study of its political organisation: and this separation I should in the main adopt, though I think it is liable to be carried too far. (Sidgwick, 1891, p. 3)

Sidgwick also noted that 'the term "Political Economy" was originally used to denote an *art* rather than a *science* – the theory of right government management of national industry, and not the theory of the manner in which industry tends to organise itself independently of governmental intervention' (Sidgwick, 1891, p. 3*n*).

The private versus public (state) dichotomy, with the consequent split between economics and politics, resurfaced in recent work that builds upon Georg Wilhelm Friedrich Hegel's distinction between state and civil society (Hegel, 1991 [1821]). For example, Agnès Heller emphasises the constitutive role of that distinction, which she considers as a formal guarantor for the existence of a democratic polity (Heller, 1988).[1] From a different but complementary perspective, John Keane has argued that the defence against despotism is the most significant feature of the eighteenth-century transformation of the earlier concept of *societas civilis* into the modern idea of a civil society independent of the state apparatus and protected from its encroachment (Keane, 1988; cf. Pabst, 2018a).

Both contemporary economics and political science continue to significantly differ on the respective role of markets and states or the relative importance of individuals and groups in the allocation and distribution of resources (Coyle, 2020). But this growing disciplinary divide has paradoxically led to the absorption of politics into economics (Lohmann, 2008; North, Wallis, and Weingast, 2010) or else to the absorption of economics into politics (Blyth, 2013).

Connected with this is a growing focus in economics on theories of rational 'means-ends' reasoning, instrumental rationality, and methodological individualism at the expense of the classical analysis of system-wide opportunities and constraints – including the shaping of individual agency by shared interests and norms reflected in institutions and the group affiliations that compose civil society (Scazzieri, 1999a, 2018a). Systemic opportunities and constraints are generally compatible with *different* institutional and organisational patterns that affect the division of labour and exchange arrangements (see also Costabile, 2020). As a result, each system of opportunities and constraints encompasses alternative *political economies*, defined as historically and institutionally specific organisations of the material life of the polity. Seen from this perspective, the rational-choice framework stemming from the Marginalist Revolution has reduced the range of possibilities to a *single* political economy that can accommodate a limited range of policy options (Pabst and Scazzieri, 2012).[2]

---

[1] She also notes that 'the principle of representation ensures the legitimacy of government through the participation of all citizens – further, the right of the representative organs to control those that are not elected. But it reveals nothing of what precedes and what follows the election of the representative organs. As a result of all this, formal democracy leaves open and undecided the problem of the concrete structure of society' (Heller, 1988, p. 130).

[2] Commenting on marginalism, Dobb makes the point that '[e]conomists, becoming increasingly obsessed with apologetics, had an increasing tendency to omit any treatment of basic social relations and to deal only with the superficial aspects of market phenomena, to confine their thoughts within the

The dichotomic approaches to the relationship between the economic and the political order are also unable to conceptualise how and why the respective objects of study (the economy and the polity) are increasingly intertwined with one another. One reason is that the separation of economics from politics prevents a proper conception of political institutions in defining the boundaries of the economic system itself. To quote the political theorist Lorenzo Ornaghi:

> the integrating role of political institutions appears to increase with the degree of complexity and organization of economic action. The relation of political institutions with economic structure then becomes essential for two distinct reasons. First, it provides a better analytical-historical perspective on the links between political economy and 'political order' (the latter is not coincident with the type of 'order' that is associated with the existence of the State). Secondly, it contributes to a 'dynamic' interpretation of the contemporary relations between State institutions and economic order. In turn, this is the only route to an analysis emphasizing the link between order and transformation in a theory of the intersections between economic and political cycle. (Ornaghi, 1990, p. 25)

Thus, the modern separation of economics from political science coincides with a split between economic structures and political institutions, which has reduced the scope of political economy and separated the analysis of both markets and states from the social connections in which they are embedded.

Embeddedness can be understood in terms of the distinct nature of sociability in relation to political society or economic society, which is under-explored in much of contemporary political economy. Its foundations are often grounded in separate spheres that are linked to other domains by formal standards of law or economic contract – not partially overlapping social ties, civic affiliations, or associations in view of a common condition or purpose. In turn, this raises questions about the nature of the structures that shape social relations. Any given *political economy* presupposes a specific organisational structure insofar as it requires the arrangement of human actions in view of a particular objective or set of objectives. At the same

limits of the "fetishism of commodities" and to generalise about the nature of the "exchange economy", until in the end these were made to determine, rather than be determined by, the system of production and production relations' (Dobb, 1973, p. 44).

time, the arrangement of actions in a means-ends pattern generates a set of interdependencies between individual and collective actors quite independent of means-ends (instrumental) rationality. Max Weber's distinction between organisation and association is useful in clarifying this feature of a political economy: '[a]n "organization" (*Betrieb*) is a system of continuous purposive activity of a specified kind', whereas the 'association' (*Verein*) is 'a corporate group originating in a voluntary agreement and in which the established order claims authority over the members only by virtue of a personal act of adherence' (Weber, 1947 [1922], p. 28). A political economy is a specific organisation of purposive activity (*Betrieb*) embedded in a wider space of material and social connections (*Verein*). Max Weber's duality is close to Douglass North's distinction between 'organizations' and 'institutions'. In North's view, '[i]nstitutions are the rules of the game in a society or, more formally, are the humanly devised constraints that shape human interaction' (North, 1990, p. 3). On the other hand, '[o]rganizations are created with purposive intent in consequence of the opportunity set resulting from the existing set of constraints (institutional ones as well as the traditional ones of economic theory)' (North, 1990, p. 5). Michael Oakeshott outlined a different yet complementary perspective with his distinction between 'enterprise association' as a means-ends organisation of social activities and 'civil association' as a practice-oriented pattern of interdependence with no immediate instrumental character (Oakeshott, 1975; see also Section 2.3 below).

Here one can go further than Weber to suggest the idea that different political economies may be rooted in different forms of sociability, and that different forms of sociability give shape to the domains within which markets, states, and individuals interact. For example, and quite separately from the markets versus states dichotomy, we would expect different political economies depending on whether forms of sociability have a predominantly non-hierarchical or hierarchical character (Scazzieri, 1999a; Pabst and Scazzieri, 2012). Either way, it requires moving beyond the strict separation of economics from politics and from other binary opposites such as state versus market, national versus supranational level of analysis, or individual versus collective interest, in the direction of the underlying social relations.

Indeed, a political economy is not confined to the economic or the political sphere but belongs to the wider social domain in which individual or collective actors interact through the material and social structures in which both cooperative and conflictual relationships are grounded (Pabst and Scazzieri, 2012, 2016). That domain encompasses the arranging of different positions and the ordering of different actions needed for the provision of material needs in the polity under consideration (Cardinale and Scazzieri, 2018a, 2018b). As Karl Polanyi (2001 [1944]) maintains, both modern states and modern markets abstract from context-dependent social interdependencies, thereby undermining the complex array of relationships that are at the root of political economies. For this reason, one can suggest that the abstract, formal nature of the modern social contract undermines the complex web of interpersonal ties that embeds the division of labour and the associated patterns of exchange.

Historical and anthropological research indicates that across different societies and cultures, social bonds and intermediary institutions have been more fundamental than formal and contractual ties (Strathern, 1988, 2004, 2020; Godbout and Caillé, 1992). The practices involved in autonomous and self-governing groups and associations often reflect social habits that are rooted in the need for mutual recognition and only indirectly serve private or collective interests (Goody, 2004; Godbout, 2007). As we shall argue below, for these reasons political economy rests on a constitutionalist rather than a formal and contractualist logic.

1.3 Relational Embeddedness and Intellectual Traditions

Michael Oakeshott's above-mentioned distinction between 'civil association' and 'enterprise association' is a useful starting point when addressing the *embeddedness* of purposive activities within the polity. In Oakeshott's view, a 'civil association' is the relationship 'between agents acknowledging themselves to be *cives* in virtue of being related to one another in the recognition of a practice composed of rules' (Oakeshott, 1975, p. 127). Subjects related in terms of a civil association 'are not partners or colleagues in an enterprise with a common purpose to pursue or a common interest to promote or protect. Nor are they individual enterprisers related to one another as bargainers for the satisfaction of their individual wants. They are related in terms of a practice' (Oakeshott, 1975, p. 122). On the other hand, an 'enterprise association' is defined as 'a relationship in terms of the pursuit of some common purpose, some substantive condition of things to be jointly procured, or some common interest to be continuously satisfied' (Oakeshott, 1975, p. 114).

The distinction between 'civil association' and 'enterprise association' is relevant to political economy, seeing that it emphasises the coexistence of non-instrumental conditions determining social interdependencies with the instrumental arrangements guiding social coordination in the pursuit of a particular objective. Instrumental coordination is embedded in an objective order that is not a fixed, predetermined organisation of formal arrangements but is instead a set of relational possibilities that provide the ultimate affordances for social congruence. In this view, most contemporary political economies can be theorised as domains embedding both markets and states and in which socio-economic interdependence reflects *both* an existing set of structural conditions and an arrangement of actions in the pursuit of specific objectives.

This approach is consistent with John Hicks's distinction between an 'order of being' and an 'order of doing' (following Pantaleoni, see Scazzieri and Zamagni, 2008, p. 6) whereby the former is defined as a set of interdependencies that precedes or follows specific goal-seeking practices, while the latter is conceived as a causal structure brought about by practices that aim at particular objectives (but do not necessarily attain their stated purpose). A question raised by this distinction is about intentions for acting versus dispositions to act, and about the complex interplay between actions and outcomes in shaping the unfolding of 'actual causes' in the social world (Pearl, 2000). Here it is instructive to draw on John Broome's emphasis on dispositions in disentangling the ambiguous status of 'acting for a reason' (Broome, 2009). Dispositions are a reminder of the interweaving of deliberate reasoning with habits of which agents may be unaware but which may be central in determining the outcome of actions in a given social context (Drolet and Suppes, 2008). In this connection, uncertainty is important in determining the actual working of interpersonal arrangements that take shape within political economies. Albert Hirschman addressed this point when he highlighted that the outcomes of certain activities 'are so uncertain' that they are 'strongly characterized by a certain fusion of (and confusion between) striving and attaining' (Hirschman, 1982, pp. 84–91, 1985, p. 13).

What these contributions to the literature on political economy suggest is the nature of the relationship between intended and unintended outcomes of actions that are grounded in social interdependencies. The world of practice that characterises the social domain is a complex structure of overlaps between intended and unintended outcomes, and these overlaps capture the constitution of a social realm of subsidiary spheres in which interactions are not solely instrumental (seeing that actors are not only striving for a well-defined aim, such as utility maximization). Within any such domain, social activity is open to a plurality of possible results, and uncertainty is partly a product of the criss-crossing of multiple linkages (Pabst and Scazzieri, 2012). A political economy so configured suggests a fundamental rethinking of economic and political theory. Rather than being wedded to the dichotomy between the economic and the political sphere, which would be governed by the distinction between private and public interest, the approach to political economy focused on natural sociability, and a given 'order of being' views the social domain as the principal locus of the actors' dispositions for cooperation or conflict (Pabst and Scazzieri, 2016).

Our conception of political economy draws upon two main intellectual traditions. First, the primacy of the relational field to which individual and collective actors belong is linked to notions of material interdependence, social mirroring, and cognitive framing as key triggers in establishing division of labour and patterns of exchange according to the tradition of the Scottish Enlightenment, and notably in the work of Adam Ferguson (1966 [1767]) and Adam Smith (1976 [1759], 1976 [1776], 1978 [1762–1762, 1766]). This tradition views both markets and states as *derived* institutional arrangements to be understood in terms of the embedding relational context.

Second, rather than founding political economy primarily on formal rules, rights, and contracts, our conception begins with the prior sociability and mutual dependencies between human beings. Key to this model is the principle of association and the centrality of intermediary agencies in determining the working of both markets and states. Elements of this conception can be found in the works of thinkers such as Montesquieu (1989 [1748]), Benjamin Constant (1818–1819), François Guizot (1839, 1851), and de Tocqueville (1969 [1835–1840], 1856) in France; Edmund Burke (2014 [1790]), Thomas Hill Green (1895), and Leonard Trelawny Hobhouse (1911a, 1911b, 1922) in England; or, before both these groups, the leading scholars of the Neapolitan Enlightenment – in particular, Paolo Mattia

Doria (1729, 1740) and Antonio Genovesi (2013 [1765–1767]) – and the recent reappraisal and extension of this tradition (Bruni and Zamagni, 2004, 2016; Zamagni, 2015; see also Scazzieri, 2012a; Pabst and Scazzieri, 2019). Linking these different thinkers is not just a renewal of ancient, medieval, and Renaissance notions of civic interdependence but also an emphasis on the intermediate spheres of sociability between individual and collective agency. This point of view suggests that association reflects the relational embedding of all actors within multi-level social interdependencies and institutions.

Our conception of the economy and the polity, and of the political economy at their intersection, is also akin to relational approaches in social science, which call attention to the complex nature of individuality within the social domain, and to relationality as an emergent property not reducible to the dispositions of actors involved in generating and maintaining specific relations. In this connection, Marilyn Strathern emphasises, with reference to Melanesian societies, the conception of the 'singular person [...] as a microcosm' which can be considered 'as a derivative of multiple identities' (Strathern, 1988, p. 15). At the same time, Strathern also highlights that such a plural image of personal identity can be overcome, in actual social life, either by 'difference being encompassed or eclipsed' or by 'elimination [...] achieved through detachment' (Strathern, 1988, p. 15). This point of view has far-reaching implications for understanding a system of global interdependencies and acting within it: 'there might [...] be a place for appreciating what it is that divides us, that is, how we may relate to others not by denying difference but through our differences [...] [I]n expanding our horizons we are not limited to acknowledging people insofar as they seem the same as we are. Conversely, perceived difference is not an axiomatic barrier to sustaining relationships' (Strathern, 2018, pp. 87–88).

In a complementary perspective, Margaret Archer emphasises the dynamic processes by which relational goods give rise to something 'in excess of a degree of warmth and some regularity of contact', namely to 'emergent properties [...] that cannot be produced by aggregation and are *also* deemed highly worthwhile in themselves' (Archer, 2012, p. 99; see also Archer, 2000, 2010). Recognition of relationality as emergent property entails 'respect for the relational goods produced and a concern for the preservation and prolongation of this worth that encourages a commitment to fostering the relationship itself' (Archer, 2012, p. 99). This means, as Pierpaolo Donati maintains, that even a simple relationship between A and B involves a *triadic structure*, not only from A to B and from B to A, but also 'the effect of their interaction', which 'can only be examined by taking the relation as the unit of analysis' (Donati, 2010, p. 98; see also Donati, 1991, 2006; Donati and Archer, 2015).

1.4 Constitution versus Contract

Our conception of association is distinct from modern and contemporary accounts committed to a contractualist approach. Contractualism makes two claims. First, the primary units of society are rationally driven individuals who are bound together by formal arrangements as part of the social contract. Second, that all other 'units' are subordinate to the individual and the two institutions that reflect the social contract – the sovereign state and the transnational market. In political economy, this implies that both economics and politics subsume all social relationships under the formal functioning of markets and states (e.g. Buchanan, 1990). Patterns of social interaction at the national and the international levels are subordinate either to political relations within or between states, or to economic transactions in the marketplace. In this manner, the contractualist approach ignores social interdependencies existing at intermediate levels of aggregation as well as across them (Pabst, 2014, 2018a; Milbank and Pabst, 2016).

The alternative approach, which we call *constitutionalist*, focuses on association and the mutual formation of interests. This approach calls attention to the *social body* (the structure of social interdependencies) that underpins both conflict and cooperation (see also Scazzieri, 2020a). Such interdependencies *pre-exist* the emergence of conflict and cooperation and are characterised by 'hybrid' relationships different from the more homogeneous links between members of the same state (its citizens) or between traders in the same market sphere (Pabst, 2014, 2020). Different rules and institutions are grounded in diverse domains of social interdependence. One example is *civil society*, defined as 'the primary constitution of connectivity in which markets and states operate [and which] *embeds* the causal structures determining the relationship between intended and unintended outcomes in any given social domain' (Pabst and Scazzieri, 2012, pp. 337–338). Social bonds straddle several apparent dualisms: first, between the individual and the collective level of agency; second, between instrumental and non-instrumental actions; third, between intended and unintended outcomes. This focus on complex social interdependencies seeks to eschew those dualisms in favour of greater emphasis on 'association' that reflects the multi-layered sociability constituting the domain of political economy (Pabst, 2018a).

In other words, different rules and institutions are grounded in different types of sociability that are variously more hierarchical or more 'egalitarian' and more conducive to cooperation or conflict. The interdependencies that constitute the political-economic domain are a given reality that economics and political science either ignore or subsume under the logic of exchange or the logic of state power.

One possible objection to our constitutionalist approach is that the internal structure of society is so diverse as to produce 'parallel societies' within a given territory and its people. Indeed, there has been much discussion about the growing plurality of late modern societies, including the pervasiveness of fundamental divides (political, economic, social, and ethical) and the inability to overcome such divides by means of rational argument (Hirschman, 1977; MacIntyre, 2000 [1981]). This has led thinkers such as Isaiah Berlin and John Rawls to argue that substantive values are incommensurable and that therefore it is only possible to agree on certain procedural mechanisms such as contractual arrangements backed by the rule of law and ground-rules of fairness (Berlin, 1969; Rawls, 1971).

The conception of association developed in this study seeks to overcome this opposition in the direction of a multi-layered social space in which there can be both disagreement on some substantive choices as well as agreement on others. Even an entrenched diversity of interests is not necessarily incompatible with a stable constitutional order, provided diversity allows for political economies arranged along a plurality of interdependent spheres, which are mutually compatible with a systemic condition for congruence, independently of whether social actors pursue the achievement of this condition or not. This approach rests on a view of political economy that emphasises the relative positions of individuals and groups and the mutual fitting of interdependent economic activities (Quesnay, 1972 [1759]; Romagnosi, 1827, 1835; Stein, 1878).

Classical political economy – both in its original formulations (Smith, 1976 [1776]); Ricardo, 1951 [1817]) and in its modern appraisals and systematizations (Leontief, 1991 [1928], 1941; Sraffa, 1960; Quadrio Curzio, 1967; Lowe, 1976; Pasinetti, 1977) – provides a vantage point from which to develop a theory of political economy based on the multi-layered arrangement of positions and interests. For classical political economy focuses on the formation and distribution of the social product through a system of interdependencies between productive sectors, while also presupposing a system of interdependencies between socio-economic groups (such as workers, capitalists, and rentiers). The former set of interdependencies emphasises complementarities between productive activities that lead to the distribution of the economy's net product between types of income (such as the profit share or the wage share), or to its distribution between investments in productive sectors (such as the agricultural sector or the manufacturing sector). Indeed, the net product shares accruing to certain groups may be inversely related to the shares of other groups, even if there may be a positive relation with the shares going to yet other groups (Quadrio Curzio, 1990; Quadrio Curzio and Pellizzari, 1999). This feature of distribution emphasises the distinction between the interdependencies across groups within the existing social structure and the 'viability conditions' for the persistence of the system (say, a particular polity) embedding those interdependencies. The viability conditions for the economic system to persist over time may be a proxy for the systemic congruence of activities in the economy under consideration, or its 'systemic interest' (see Cardinale, 2015, 2018a, 2019, 2020, 2022).

This perspective highlights the existence of distinct but interlocking conditions (respectively, in the technological and in the socio-institutional domains) that allow the formation of the social product and the persistence of the economic system's productive potential over time. In particular, the technological conditions ensuring the material viability of the productive system ought to be distinguished from the institutional conditions governing the distribution of the social product between groups. Indeed, the entitlements of groups taking part in the distribution of the social product may be incompatible with given technological conditions for viability, and/or with the conditions for persistence of a given socio-economic structure. In the former case, the distribution of the social product may be such as to generate relative prices incompatible with the input requirements of each productive sector for commodities produced in other sectors of the economy.[3] In the latter case, the distribution of the social product may be associated with an accumulation process making the persistence of certain social classes dynamically unfeasible in the long run (Baranzini, 1991; Baranzini and Scazzieri, 1997).

Different representations of economic interdependencies are possible. A fundamental distinction is the one between horizontal representations, which highlight circular relationships between different economic sectors, and vertical representations, which underscore the 'linear' relationship between economic sectors arranged in a hierarchical sequence relative to one another (Pasinetti, 1973; Baranzini and Scazzieri, 1990). For this reason, there are multiple depictions of systemic coherence and therefore of systemic interest. This entails actors' mapping of interdependencies perhaps not being compatible with ongoing transformations of those interdependencies (say, as a result of technological or organisational change). In turn, this underpins the distinction between the space of feasible states within which any given economy may operate and the actual state brought about by the individual or collective actions carried out in that economy. Adolph Lowe addressed the latter issue by distinguishing between two different approaches to economic inquiry, which he calls, respectively, 'structure analysis' and 'force analysis' (Lowe, 1976). The former 'studies the configurations in which the elements of an economic system – inputs and outputs, employment and income, savings and investment, etc. – must be arranged if the transformation of the initial into the stipulated terminal state is to be achieved. These configurations have two aspects: one, physical or technical; the other, social' (Lowe, 1976, p. 17). The latter

raises economics above the level of a mere engineering science by studying the patterns of behaviour and motivation that initiate and sustain the motion of the system along the structurally determined path. These patterns themselves are closely related to the prevailing social structure that defines the institutional framework within which economic activity is to operate (Lowe, 1976, p. 17).

---

[3] A case in point is that of the Russian 'scissor crisis' of the mid-1920s, which may be seen as resulting from the failure of relative prices of agricultural versus industrial products to meet the material viability conditions associated with technology in use (see Seton, 1992, 2000).

More recently, Luigi Pasinetti has introduced a 'separation theorem', which makes the different but complementary distinction between a 'natural' and an 'institutional' level of investigation:

[t]he former type of investigation [...] are aimed at discovering basic relations, which the Classical economists called 'natural', i.e. in their view aimed at determining the economic magnitudes at a level which is so fundamental as to allow us to investigate them independently of the rules of individual and social behaviour to be chosen in order to achieve them [...] This is a stage kept free from specific geographical and historical circumstances. Then, one is able to proceed to a second stage of investigation, which concerns how the economic magnitudes are actually determined, within the bounds and constraints of the institutions characterizing the economy at the time it is investigated. (Pasinetti, 2007, p. 275)

Pasinetti's argument highlights the distinct and specific task of a feasibility analysis considering the economy's structural parameters (in his case, the parameters describing production technology and consumers' average behaviour) relative to the behavioural and institutional conditions that directly influence human actions depending on context (see also Scazzieri, 2012b). Feasibility spaces reflect existing interdependencies between sectors but leave room for a variety of institutional arrangements and behavioural patterns. This, in turn, underscores the point that different patterns of agreement or conflict are inherent to existing structural constraints.

Ivano Cardinale and Michael Landesmann build on this dual character of feasibility spaces to investigate policy contexts in which interdependencies may be differently construed by different sets of actors, thus leading to alternative representations of conflicts of interest. In their contribution 'the analysis of how "sectoral interests" articulate themselves in relation to particular economic variables [...] can lead to interesting insights into the political-economy dynamics [...] when adopting different sectoral decompositions of an economy' (Cardinale and Landesmann, 2017, p. 285; see also Cardinale and Landesmann, 2022). Their approach explores the socio-political dimension of sectoral decomposition and interrelatedness and highlights the possibility of *alternative coalitions* within the same system of interdependencies. This is because potential interest groups are associated with different ways of representing interdependence, so that different policy trade-offs become relevant depending on which type of decomposition is adopted.

The consideration of interdependencies at multiple levels of aggregation brings to light conditions for social congruence within and across different levels of aggregation. This approach moves beyond the macro-micro dichotomy and highlights that the same set of structural parameters may be compatible with different mappings of sectoral interests and systemic interest. For instance, interdependencies between productive sectors can bring to the fore complementarities between activities that a macro approach cannot identify, while macro analysis may detect divisions and conflicts that exist in society beyond the connectivity provided by the material interdependencies of productive sectors. Analysis conducted at intermediate levels of aggregation calls attention to the conditions for potential conflict or potential agreement between different sectors and/or social groups considering the *relative positions* of sectors and/or groups. This approach also suggests a heuristic to assess the likelihood of different divisions and coalitions depending on which group affiliations are dominant in the political economy under consideration.

1.5 The 'Three Bodies' of Political Economy

The constitutionalist conception of political economy developed in this study emphasises the distinctive nature of political economy with respect to *both* economic and political theory. It is widely assumed that both fields are largely self-contained domains independent of a 'thick description' (Geertz, 1975) of the social space. This approach denies political economy an autonomous space of inquiry and leads either to the absorption of politics into economics (North, Wallis, and Weingast, 2010) or to its opposite (Blyth, 2013), as we have already argued above. On the contrary, our argument is that the two spheres are distinct but mutually embedded within a given configuration of social interdependencies. This is what we call the *social body*. Political economy, as a distinct field of investigation, derives from the constraints, opportunities, and dispositions generated by this interdependence between the economic and the political spheres, which – as we develop in the remainder of this section – can be conceptualised, respectively, as the *economic body* and the *political body*.[4]

---

[4] Our conception of the three bodies recalls Ernst Kantorowicz's distinction in his classical work *The King's Two Bodies* (Kantorowicz, 1957), but whereas

Second, we argue that the theory of political economy is primarily a theory about the arranging of different positions and the ordering of different actors' modes of activity, which involve both the economic and the political spheres. Here we draw on the work of John Hicks who clearly distinguishes between economics as a theory of rational market behaviour, which he calls 'catallactics' (following Richard Whately, 1831; Francis Edgeworth, 1881; and Ludwig Mises, 1949), and economics as a theory of the formation and distribution of the social product, for which he reserves the term 'plutology' (Hicks, 1982 [1976]). In the words of Hicks, analysts in the latter tradition 'looked at the economic system primarily from the production angle', whereas 'the catallactists looked at it primarily from the side of exchange' (Hicks, 1982 [1976], p. 10). Hicks's emphasis on the 'social product' as the characteristic field of 'plutology' points to the complex structures of social interdependencies that characterise both the economy and the polity as well as their mutual relationship.

Hicks's distinction between catallactics and plutology finds its roots in his distinction between 'order of being' and 'order of doing', which we discussed in Section 1.3 of this chapter. In fact, plutology brings attention to the objective relational structure that the formation of the social product presupposes at any given time, while catallactics considers the criteria followed (or to be followed) by actors involved in the formation of the social product under specific institutional arrangements. Plutology investigates the interdependencies that *all* human actions generate when involved in division of labour leading to social product formation, whereas catallactics explores which specific actions are generated by rational actors who are allowed some degree of independent choice in the allocation of resources. We maintain that political economy bridges the economic and the political spheres by exploring the *range of conditions* under which the material life of the polity is made possible by the interdependencies generated by human actions in the economic sphere. Hicks's distinction between catallactics and plutology points to a more comprehensive domain in which actions and structures are mutually dependent components of the

he explores the relationship between the king's natural body and the king's representation of the body politic, we study the embeddedness of both the economy and the polity within society as a relational domain.

system determining the material life of a politically organised society, which we may call the *economic body* of the polity.

Third, our conception of political economy presupposes a certain 'constitution of interests' – a structured space that is prior to decisions concerning the allocation of resources or the distribution of the social product between different individual or collective actors. Interests are not simply given but also derive from specific representations of the relative position of any group within society. Such representations presuppose vantage points that organise individual and collective perceptions and provide guidance for social action. Particular interests can only be defined and acted upon in relation to a distinct set of weights (*values*). Values as weights are 'specificators' of interest. This provides a critical device to identify and implement feasible constitutional arrangements. The process of circumscribing different interests requires the consideration of values because values (as weights) attach priority to certain interests over others. Circumscription enables actors to identify which interests are more relevant than other interests. Describing the relative positions and overlaps between interests is central to achieving social coordination, or at least a degree of social congruence, in a polity that encompasses a plurality of partially overlapping and partially diverging values and interests. Circumscribing the interests of different actors is therefore a way by which social interdependence may achieve a pattern of connectivity compatible with an expression of systemic interest, defined as a condition for the *political body* to exist (Cardinale, 2015, 2018a).

This point of view finds expression in several early modern authors, such as Johannes Althusius (1603) and James Harrington (1656), and is central to later contributions to the relationship between the economic and the political orders, such as those by Joseph von Sonnenfels (1765) and Giandomenico Romagnosi (1848). Romagnosi argues that the purpose of economic studies should be to investigate 'the social order of riches' by considering 'the economic functions in their driving motives and in their complex outcomes' (Romagnosi, 1827, pp. 24–27; see also Scazzieri, 2020a). This conception of political economy is different from accounts in both economics and politics that seek to re-embed social relationships in either the economy or the polity (Buchanan, 1990; Vanberg, 2005).

An example of the former is Hayek's attempt to broaden the category of market exchange beyond pure commercial transactions to include all horizontal social interactions – a comprehensive field which Hayek describes as *catallaxy* (Hayek, 1976; Matteucci, 1994). An example of the latter is Pierre Bourdieu's account of the state as not simply an instrumental apparatus for action in the public sphere but as a comprehensive field whose influence goes beyond purely political relations to encompass a wider range of social institutions and interactions (Bourdieu, 2012; Dubois, 2018).[5] Either way, both positions – by expanding the respective fields of economics and politics – end up subsuming the social domain under either the logic of market exchange *or* the logic of decision-making in the space of a polity identified with the modern nation state in its comprehensive sphere of sovereignty.

By contrast, our conception of political economy highlights the multi-layered space that encompasses the economic and political domains. This space, which can be conceptualised as an *economic-political body*, consists of multiple forms of association that have potential for *both* conflict and cooperation and are not reducible to any of the above dualisms or to the binary logic that underpins either of them.[6] In short, we theorise political economy as the embedding of the economic and the political body within the social body.[7] We view economic organisations and political institutions as part of the wider constitution underpinning the economy, the polity, and society.

1.6 Towards a Constitution of Economic Policy

This chapter has outlined a conception of political economy in which multi-layered interdependencies are central. One key implication is that economic-political actors interact, both directly and indirectly, at different levels, which overcomes the conventional distinction

---

[5] This point of view has suggested that, in the interaction between state and non-state actors, the expression of private interests 'cannot merely reflect these interests. It has to be organised following specific rules to translate interests and rationales into a policy that claims to serve the public interest' (Dubois, 2018, p. 47).

[6] Our conception of association draws on traditions stretching back to classical sources like Plato, Aristotle, and Cicero that were developed by medieval, Renaissance, and modern thinkers as diverse as Justus Lipsius, Ralph Cudworth, Giambattista Vico, and Alexis de Tocqueville. Some of the history of ideas that has shaped this account of association is explored in Chapter 5.

[7] Our conception of the 'three bodies' is markedly different from that of contemporary approaches such as Douglass North's who reduces the concept of 'body' to different actors of the organisational type within the institutional domain. In his words, '[o]rganisations include political bodies (political parties,

between micro- and macro-analysis. In fact, what is missing from most conceptions of political economy is a focus on intermediate levels between individual actors and the overall system (such as the state), including meso-level associations and institutions such as industrial sectors, universities, professional organisations, and trade unions. This perspective opens the prospect of policy domains that are located at any one of these levels where economic and political relationships intersect. In turn, the implication is that policy is not reducible to either microeconomic or macroeconomic actions but encompasses multiple spheres of intervention at different levels of aggregation. Either cooperation or conflict may occur depending on the policy domain and on the order of priority between different interests. The circumscription of interests within specialised spheres allows economic actors to focus on a given subset of objectives to the exclusion of others and thereby to identify a hierarchical ordering of priorities. Three policy areas illustrate our argument: first, industrial policy; second, liquidity and monetary policy; and third, international trade policy (see also Chapter 7).

The focus on intermediate levels of aggregation provides a vantage point to assess the effectiveness of industrial policy options dealing with the organisation of activities spanning a range of different production units from individual establishments to industrial networks and complex supply chains. Different aggregation criteria suggest alternative ways to decompose the economic system into subsets of interdependent activities, and each aggregation criterion may highlight different policy options. For example, *aggregation by industries* can identify 'loops' of intermediate product flows and draws attention to the 'horizontal' coordination requirements between those flows. On the other hand, *aggregation by vertically integrated sectors* highlights sequential dependencies between fabrication stages belonging to the same transformation line (say, from primary resources to finished consumption goods), and draws attention to the time synchronisation of

the senate, a city council, a regulatory agency), economic bodies (firms, trade unions, family farms, co-operatives), social bodies (churches, clubs, athletic associations) and educational bodies (schools, universities, vocational training centres). They are groups of individuals bound by some common purpose to achieve objectives [...]. Both what organisations come into existence and how they evolve are fundamentally influenced by the institutional framework' (North, 1990, p. 5).

fabrication stages along the same supply chain and/or to the macro-economic coordination across different supply chains.

Industrial policy measures may be significantly different in the two cases. For instance, the coordination of intermediate product flows may suggest policy actions aimed at facilitating the provision of product components needed across an extensive range of utilisers ('basic components'), while vertical integration may draw attention to actions promoting adequate capabilities or to actions reducing transaction costs between fabrication stages and therefore increasing the speed of productive transformation. This approach highlights the need for differentiated policy actions, which would target the technological and organisational needs of specific clusters of productive activity (Bianchi and Labory, 2018, 2019).

The question of liquidity is another case in point. Provision of liquidity to an economy of interdependent activities is subject to different conditions depending on whether we want that economy to allow full employment and full capacity utilization (a *scale condition*) or the delivery of liquidity at appropriate amounts and times at specific stages of production (a *proportionality condition*) (Cardinale and Scazzieri, 2016). Interdependent activities carried out within the same time period require a type of liquidity that is different from the liquidity needed to coordinate the input and output profiles of different activities over time (Scazzieri, 2017). There is no guarantee that meeting the scale condition would also satisfy the proportionality condition, which highlights a trade-off between the two objectives and a potential conflict of interest between sectors or social groups supporting one or the other option for liquidity policy.

Finally, and consistently with the two previous policy scenarios, the analysis of interdependence between activities at intermediate levels of aggregation highlights the coordination needs of processes related to one another through intra-industry trade networks across different countries. In this case too, policy actions cannot be evaluated independently of the fine structure of interdependencies between activities supplying intermediate inputs to one another in a reciprocal way or delivering inputs to one another along a 'linear' sequence of production stages. For example, an effective trade policy may or may not privilege unrestrained free trade depending on whether transaction costs *between* trading countries are lower than coordination costs *within* each country, or whether the need to maintain certain production stages in a country suggests a degree of protection in lieu of free trade for those stages. This view overcomes the dichotomy between free trade and protection and suggests that interdependencies within and across trading actors lead to differentiated attitudes to trade arrangements depending on which specific goods or services are considered. In short, our approach to the constitution of policy-making, by overcoming the macro-micro duality, highlights not only the links between policy areas but also new targeted actions that focus on the needs and interests of sectors or groups that operate at intermediate levels of association.

To conclude: we argue that political economy cannot be reduced to a single domain or discipline but instead is a *relational field* based on the mutual intertwining of the economic and political bodies and their embeddedness within the social body. As the subsequent chapters will explore, some of the key organising concepts include interdependence, dispositions, and association. Since all social activity presupposes that actors are interdependent, this raises questions about how dispositions emerge from different patterns of interdependence, which in turn lead to multiple forms of association. Such an approach to political economy can make sense of the fundamental structures underpinning both cooperation and conflict in a world that is characterised by contrasting tendencies such as growing interdependencies through trade and international division of labour but also decoupling and a greater focus on systemic resilience at the different levels of world society.

2 | *Sociability and Interdependence*

2.1 Relational Positions within the Social Sphere

This chapter examines the relationship between sociability and interdependence. Sociability describes a fundamental feature of reality, namely the fact that individuals and groups are embedded in mutual relationships and institutions. This embeddedness reflects relational positions within the social domain. Interdependence encompasses both potential and actual ties involving material interests and immaterial dispositions. It works itself out through a process by which dispositions give rise to actions, and actions shape dispositions. We argue that sociability is at once a given condition of relationality and develops dynamically through a complex interplay between dispositions, actions, and their consequences. The outcome of this interplay will tend towards either cooperation or conflict depending on whether different actors' dispositions and actions converge towards a shared objective or not and whether institutions are conducive to more cooperative or more conflictual patterns of action.

In what follows, we explore the relationships between interdependence and congruence conditions in the social domain. Section 2.2 highlights Richard Cumberland's distinction between the study of interdependence *more analytico,* that is, independently of the historical process, and the study of interdependence *more genetico*, which highlights its historical character. Section 2.3 addresses the issue of human dispositions in the light of interdependence and examines which dispositions are compatible with achieving systemic objectives for interdependent activities as an integrated whole. This section builds on the work of thinkers such as Shaftesbury, Paolo Mattia Doria, and Adam Smith to emphasise the relevance of the non-contractualist tradition in investigating interdependence in the social sphere. Section 2.4 outlines a new analytical framework that develops the insights of those earlier conceptions with the aim of integrating the *more analytico* and *more genetico* approaches. This is done by using the method of circumscription, which allows identifying partial similarity amid diversity and on that basis builds patterns of social congruence. Section 2.5 examines the relationship between partial similarity and multiple mappings of interdependence. This will lead us to consider multiple alternative affiliations of individuals and groups and discuss the likelihood of cooperation and conflict in a political economy. Section 2.6 provides some concluding reflections.

2.2 Proportionality and the Social Order of the Economy

Ancient *oikonomia* was concerned with the rules governing the provision of needs but also the production of a surplus which sustains the life of the *polis*. The aim was to develop the capabilities of the household (*oikos*), and of the *polis*, in such a way as to ensure their viability and flourishing (Soudek, 1952; Langholm, 1983; Leshem, 2013). Inherent in this conception is the view that *oikonomia* should achieve the best possible performance of capabilities by maintaining the interdependencies between them that are most conducive to this objective. Capabilities and dispositions are central to the life of the household, so that the latter's welfare presupposes the appropriate functioning of human capabilities ('virtues') and the appropriate 'proportioning' of those capabilities relative to one another. The shift from the household's *oikonomia* (arranging capabilities within the household) to *political economy* (arranging capabilities within the polity) changes the scale but does not fundamentally alter the importance of proportionality conditions that characterize *oikonomia* itself.

This is shown in several early modern writings on the issue of sustaining private economic arrangements in view of objectives relative to the polity as a whole. Antonio Serra's *Brief Treatise* (Serra, 2011 [1613]) is an instance of that approach with its emphasis on the distinction between the general and the specific causes of the wealth within a kingdom. In Serra's analysis general causes highlight proportionality conditions that must be fulfilled independently of historical contingency, whereas specific causes determine the historical trajectory that should be followed by the dynamics of wealth in a given polity. Pierre de Boisguillebert expressed a similar view when he wrote that the two hundred professions that nowadays enter the composition of a prosperous and developed state, starting with the baker and ending with the actor, are not, in general, called forth the ones by the others by anything but the pursuit of pleasure; however, as soon as they are introduced and have taken some kind of roots, they come to be part of the substance of a State, and cannot be disconnected or separated from it without immediately altering the whole civil body (Boisguillebert, 1843 [1707a], p. 404).

In the light of this condition, Boisguillebert maintained that 'right' proportions between productive activities should be maintained to avoid scarcity bottlenecks or commodity gluts: 'it is proportions that make the whole wealth' (Boisguillebert, 1843 [1707b], p. 279; see also Lutfalla,1981).[1]

This emphasis on proportionality requirements resurfaces in the Physiocratic *Tableau économique*, which highlights the interdependencies associated with division of labour and the conditions that have to be fulfilled by inter-sectoral product flows if the economy is to maintain its productive potential over time (Quesnay, 1972 [1759]; Mercier de la Rivière, 1767; see also Lutfalla, 1981). Cesare Beccaria also acknowledged the role of material interdependencies brought about by division of labour when he emphasised that institutional arrangements and cultural beliefs (such as beliefs concerning justice) may often be explained by the organisation of society in the sphere of production and reproduction. Indeed, he viewed social interdependencies as a 'necessary consequence' (*conseguenza necessaria*) of the organisation of actions in the material sphere (Beccaria, 1971a [1770], p. 333; see also Audegean, 2010).

Interdependencies bring to the fore proportionality conditions at different levels of generality. Certain proportionality requirements are compatible with a variety of specific arrangements depending on historical context. On the other hand, not all contingent arrangements satisfy the general proportionality conditions necessary for maintaining collective wealth. Proportionality conditions are central to understanding the relationship between the requirements for a set of proportions that maintain the productive potential (a 'viable' set of proportions) and the historical conditions that match those requirements. Richard Cumberland distinguished two different approaches to analysing

---

[1] '*Ce sont donc les proportions qui font toute la richesse*' (Boisguillebert, 1843 [1707b], p. 279).

proportionality conditions in human society (Cumberland, 1672). One approach, which he called 'analytical' (*more analytico*), is relative to the configuration of any given set of interdependencies without regard to the historical process that generates it. The other approach, which he called 'genetic' (*more genetico*), is relative to the process generating any specific structure and is bound to emphasise the *emergence* of that structure rather than the manifold proportions compatible with any given proportionality condition (and thus the manifold paths of structural transformation compatible with a given viability condition).

The distinction between the analytical and the genetic approach to the study of economic structure provides a clue about the relationship between the proportionality condition that needs to be satisfied by any given economy if that economy is to be sustainable over time, and the *specific* forms that this condition takes in particular historical and institutional contexts. In fact, our approach suggests that a given proportionality condition is often satisfied in a variety of ways. An instance is provided by Adam Smith's analysis of the 'natural progress of opulence' across different economic systems (Smith, 1976 [1776], Book III). This progress is marked by shifting sectoral proportions as the economy achieves maximum growth moving from one stage to another along its dynamic trajectory (Scazzieri, 2012b, 2019).

The 'natural' maximum growth trajectory requires, according to Smith, the development, in a sequence, first of agriculture, then of manufacturing, and finally of international trade. However, this sequence may be reversed (as it was) in the case of commercial city states that developed trade before manufacturing and agriculture. Here we find a reversal of the natural growth trajectory, but that reversal is allowed by the *same* proportionality condition that generates Smith's 'natural progress'. This is because Smith's natural trajectory derives from a proportionality condition that makes maximum growth possible under a plurality of economic structures. For instance, the self-reproduction of a given set of material interdependencies may require the prior development of agriculture depending on whether the supply of primary goods needs to be internally generated or can be provided externally through international trade. Beccaria developed a similar approach when he argued that seemingly unviable economic systems are nonetheless able to maintain themselves over time as long as they are regularly integrated with other complementary systems. In this case, the proportionality condition for reproducibility must express the viability of different economies combined:

the political borders of a state are not always, or almost never, the same as its economic borders [...]. The land of one nation nourishes the industry of another, the industry of the latter fertilizes the land of the former: those two nations, despite having divided sovereignty and being reciprocally independent of their respective political laws, are in fact a single nation closely held together by the strength of physical laws, and dependent of one another in virtue of their economic relationships (Beccaria, 1971b [ms. circa 1769], p. 391). [...] [T]he foreign lands providing the foodstuff that represents the surplus labour of one nation [can be considered as] making a single body with the lands providing subsistence goods in that nation itself. (Beccaria, 1971b [ms. circa 1769], pp. 395–396)[2]

The genetic approach takes a different route: instead of considering the *plurality of proportions* compatible with any given viability condition, it investigates the *specific proportions* adopted under particular conditions, and the sequential process the economy follows in moving from one set of proportions to another. Here we meet the distinction between the type of structural analysis interested in investigating the virtuality of dynamic paths compatible with a given condition (such as the set of proportions consistent with attaining a systemic objective, for instance full employment) and the evolutionary approach addressing the historical trajectory followed by the economy under particular circumstances (Scazzieri, 2018b). The distinction between the structural and the evolutionary approach is akin to the distinction between an investigation in the 'analytical mode' (*more analytico*) and an investigation in the 'genetic mode' (*more genetico*). In this light, Luigi Pasinetti's discussion of a 'separation theorem' distinguishing between the analysis of the fundamental constitutive properties of economic systems and the analysis of their institutionally and historically contingent features emphasises a divide between types of inquiry that reaches back to the formative period of political economy:

a real methodological breakthrough in dynamic economic analysis, which the [Classical Economists] had intuited, can be achieved by adopting what I shall call for simplicity a *separation theorem*. This theorem states that we must make it possible to disengage those investigations that concern the

---

[2] All translations are ours, unless otherwise specified.

foundational bases of economic relations – to be detected at a strictly essential level of basic economic analysis – from those investigations that must be carried out at the level of the actual economic institutions, which at any time any economic system is landed with, or has chosen to adopt, or is trying to achieve. (Pasinetti, 2007, p. 275)

Proportionality conditions are at the root of political economy and explain the meaning originally assigned to the concept of a 'natural state' (Bonar, 1992 [1893]; Scazzieri, 2012b). Pasinetti's separation theorem has brought to light a property of socioeconomic systems that was already implicit in the early investigations following the 'analytical mode'. This property implies that attaining a systemic objective may be compatible with *multiple sets of proportions* rather than with a single proportionality criterion. On the other hand, institutional and historical circumstances can bring about a set of proportions that may not be compatible with the systemic objective.

2.3 Dispositions and the Body Politic

The investigation *more analytico* of interdependent human activities brings into focus a specific approach to human dispositions in the social sphere. This is because dispositions are considered from the point of view of which conditions interdependent activities should meet to realise a systemic objective (such as the self-reproduction of a given household or polity). In other words, dispositions are disentangled from their actual mode of operation in specific contexts and are assessed by asking which proportionality requirements would make them conducive to individual or collective welfare.

The Neapolitan philosopher and political economist Paolo Mattia Doria, who was a contemporary and friend of Giambattista Vico, followed the *more analytico* approach to human dispositions in exploring the conditions of social life in the polity, or what he called 'civil life' (*vita civile*):

since the essence of civil life is the union of those virtues that cannot be held together by a single individual but can be practiced by many in conjunction, it follows that the perfection of the social body consists in the mixing of virtues. As a consequence, the most important rule to be followed in the constitution of a state is to be able to assign the specific virtues of [different] human beings to their appropriate positions, so that a perfect republic can be established. (Doria, 1729, p. 84)

In Doria's 'perfect republic', civil life overcomes 'the almost moral impossibility that human beings hold all virtues individually', and allows 'a mutual support of virtues, and of natural capabilities, which human beings provide to one another in order to attain human happiness; or else a harmony, which consists of particular virtues when they are practiced in support to one another in order to establish a perfect body politic' (Doria, 1729, pp. 82–83). Doria's conception highlights the tension between the ideal proportions among individual affordances ('virtues') that are required in a 'perfect body politic', and the actual proportions in a real polity, which may be quite different from the ideal ones. Doria's attempted solution of this problem consists in acknowledging the central role of passions in orienting human practice while at the same time emphasising the human propensity to construct rational images of passions and the role of those images in determining the concrete expression of passions in specific contexts. In Doria's words:

I do not hope to attain [perfection] but I should not give it up as a goal; for, if I do not try to attain it, the corrupt nature would certainly bring me to its opposite; while as long as I try to attain it, even if I would not make of myself a perfect human being (*uomo ottimo*), I would at least make a good one; while if I were to detach my view from perfection I would make a very bad one. (Doria, 1729, p. 399)

Human dispositions are inherently open-ended, but passions can be harnessed to help pursue perfection if actors succeed in steering the natural course of passions by keeping in sight the proportionality conditions that a perfect body politic requires (see also Torrini, 1983; Scazzieri, 2012a; Milbank and Pabst, 2016; Cardinale, 2018a). The distinction between the ideal and the actual state of the polity is fundamental and constitutive of Doria's approach to civil life, as is his commitment to rational criteria as a means to channel human dispositions, thereby making them compatible with a quest for perfection. Doria's contribution acknowledges the simultaneous existence of different criteria by which interdependent actions may be reciprocally related. This approach implies that the same actions may be reciprocally compatible or not depending on which type of interdependence is considered and on which proportionality condition that type of interdependence is required to meet. An important instance of this situation is Shaftesbury's discussion of the relationship between self-interest and virtue:

[n]ow, if by the natural constitution of any rational creature, the same irregularities of appetite which make him ill to others, make him ill to himself; and if the same regularity of affections which causes him to be good in one sense, causes him to be good also in the other; then is that goodness by which he is thus useful to others, a real good and advantage to himself. *And thus virtue and interest may be found at last to agree.* (Shaftesbury, 1790 [1699], p. 31 [added emphasis])

Shaftesbury's argument follows from the acknowledgement that human actions can be described differently depending on which characteristics of actions are considered. This in turn entails that different patterns of interdependence may be investigated depending on which description of human actions is adopted. Indeed, each pattern of interdependence is associated with a specific proportionality condition determining the most appropriate criterion for the best fitting of actions by different individuals and/or social groups. Shaftesbury's consilience between virtue and interest derives from his consideration of 'interested' motives as the expression of specific action descriptions and of the corresponding proportionality conditions. In this light, self-interest may be differently construed depending on which action description is considered. As a result, 'virtue', defined as the actualisation of capability, is compatible with 'interest' conceptualised as the expression of a proportionality condition allowing the practice of different capabilities in the social sphere. Here self-interest would coincide with the recognition of a proportionality condition allowing the pursuit of virtue, that is, the best performance of one's own capabilities, in a setting characterised by interdependence *within* the set of capabilities of each actor, as well as by interdependence *between* different actors. Shaftesbury's approach to virtue in the social setting highlights the relationship between action description and the conditions for actualising capabilities. It also suggests that different action descriptions are associated with different criteria for the mutual fitting of actions in the social sphere.

Shaftesbury argues that the 'irregularities of appetite' can be avoided by following a proportionality condition that allows both individual actors and the social body to express the best realisation of individual and social capabilities. This point of view has far-reaching consequences for what concerns the emergence of *dispositions* (considered as propensities to action) out of the plurality of passions characterizing individuals and societies. Here the issue of the harnessing of passions is key. Albert Hirschman emphasised the emergence in early modern Europe (starting with Machiavelli, Guicciardini, and Hobbes) of the view opposing 'the *interests* of men to their *passions* and of contrasting the favourable effects that follow when men are guided by their interests to the calamitous states of affairs that prevails when men give free rein to their passions' (Hirschman, 1977, p. 32). In the works of thinkers who followed this approach, the '"interests" of persons and groups eventually came to be centered on economic advantage as its core meaning, not only in ordinary language but also in social-science terms as "class interest" and "interest groups"' (Hirschman, 1977, p. 32).

Shaftesbury's argument expresses a different approach to governing passions that does not rely on a single 'harnessing' force (interest as economic advantage). He suggests instead the alternative route of the *mutual harnessing* provided by passions themselves considered as natural expressions of human capabilities and dispositions once they are balanced against one another according to a proportionality criterion fitting the natures of individual actors and of the social body. Antonio Genovesi built on Shaftesbury's view of 'interest', emphasising the need to avoid a narrow definition of it:

[I] believe it is a delusion to say that the actions of human beings are only motivated by interest, as it is a delusion to deny it [...] And this derives from assigning a greater or smaller extension to the term *interest*. There are people who by interest only mean a *reflective self-love*, and it is untrue that every human being always acts out of this interest, since nothing is clearer in experience than the fact that human beings are *electrical beings*, and that the sympathetic principle is the spring of most human actions. (Genovesi, 2013 [1765–67], p. 34 [author's emphasis])

Shaftesbury's and Genovesi's view of consilience between interests and virtues through the mutual balancing of passions fits the representation of the social body in Doria's *Vita civile* (see above), for consilience between interests and virtues in the social body presupposes a blending of virtues that can only be practiced by groups, not by individuals alone (see Doria, 1729, p. 84 cited above). This proportionality criterion implies that both virtues and people are properly positioned in a well-ordered polity. The consilience view of the relationship between passions and interests through the mutual balancing of the different human drives introduces a bridge between individual and social dispositions. Doria's approach draws upon the acknowledgement of 'habits' (*abiti*) as channels to the mutual balancing of dispositions: 'we have in ourselves certain virtues of the soul, and certain abilities of the body, which all depend on habits, so much so that reflexion, and abstract discourse, become in fact a hindrance to action' (Doria, 1724, p. 67).[3] In a 'perfect republic', the need to achieve right proportions between different social dispositions leads Doria to emphasise the need to adjust the modes of governance to the mixing of dispositions in the social body. Therefore, the rules have to cohere with the 'habits rooted in the mind' of the people because 'rules repugnant to habits are of little or no use' (Doria, 1724, pp. 69–70).[4]

Adam Smith's *Theory of Moral Sentiments* (Smith, 1976 [1759]) presents a comprehensive investigation of social congruence and coordination as a process built on the step-by-step expansion of reciprocal mirroring from the smallest communities of interdependent actors to increasingly large social groups. In fact, Smith's theory of social agency works through the coevolution of actors involved in reciprocal positioning and interacting, and the social situations influencing the way in which such positioning and interacting take place. In Smith's case, agency in the interpersonal sphere presupposes induction by analogy, in which social actors develop dispositions through reciprocal mirroring, while gradually acquiring increasing awareness of the proportionality conditions needed for coordination in the social sphere. Actors make sense of situations by applying a cognitive ability that allows them to identify certain features as salient attributes of the situation in view.

---

[3] Doria draws attention to fencing as an example of the relationship between habit and effective action: '[a]ll habits, which depend on the body, would be poorly executed by us if the mind wants to reflect at the same time as the habits are working. If a fencer wants to reflect on the laws by which he must strike a blow at the same time as he strikes it, the motion will stop in him of those animal spirits, which [are] necessary in order to execute the action with speed, and he would no longer be able to strike the blow' (Doria, 1724, p. 67).

[4] Doria's emphasis on the need to assign habits a central position in the constitution and governance of a well-ordered polity is consistent with Giambattista Vico's view that in a theory of human action rational arguments should be combined with common sense, which is based on verisimilitude rather than truth and is a primary driving motive of social life in the polity (Vico, 1709, pp. 45–50; see also Rosenfeld, 2011).

Such understanding ranges from the merely physical correspondence of feelings to deliberate empathy and the rational reconstruction
of situations in terms of a 'fair and impartial spectator' (Smith, 1976
[1759], III.I.2, p. 110). A characteristic feature of social situations is
the mirroring nature of resemblances, and therefore the indirect route
taken by the discovery of customary connections. Smith takes looking-
glasses to be a necessary tool of self-awareness even at a merely physical level, since 'one's own face [is] the only present object of which
we can see only the shadow' (Smith, 1980 [ms. circa 1777], 'Of the
Imitative Arts', I.17, p. 186). Self-reflection becomes necessary once
human beings attempt to achieve some understanding 'of what other
men feel' (Smith, 1976 [1759], I.i.1.2, p. 9). This is true even for the
most primitive instances of social awareness:

[w]hen we see a stroke aimed and just ready to fall upon the leg or arm of
another person, we naturally shrink and draw back our own leg or our own
arm; and when it does fall, we feel it in some measure, and are hurt by it as
well as the sufferer. The mob, when they are gazing at a dancer on the slack
rope, naturally writhe and twist and balance their own bodies, as they seem
him do, and as they feel that they themselves must do if in his situation.
(Smith, 1976 [1759], I.i.1.3, p. 10)

The reflection of imagined feelings from one agent to another presupposes the perception of distance between the real person and her or his
mirror image. In general, as such distance increases, so does the awareness that the mirrored image bears only an imperfect resemblance to
the real person. This may be clearly seen as we move from the merely
physical correspondence of feelings (as described above) to the more
indirect case of the 'subsidiary sympathy' that may arise when, precisely as a result of perceived social distance, we feel that we ought to
react differently from the person under consideration: 'We blush for
the impudence and rudeness of another, though he himself appears
to have no sense of the impropriety of his own behaviour; because
we cannot help feeling with what confusion we ourselves should be
covered, had we behaved in so absurd a manner' (Smith, 1976 [1759],
I.i.1.10, p. 12).

Mutual sympathy (*fellow-feeling*) presupposes a social mirror one
step further removed from the agents involved in interaction. In this
case, '[w]e suppose ourselves the spectators of our own behaviour,
and endeavour to imagine what effect it would, in this light, produce

upon us. This is the only looking-glass by which we can, in some measure, with the eyes of other people, scrutinize the propriety of our own conduct' (Smith, 1976 [1759], III.1.5, p. 112). With fellow-feeling, persons can understand one another in so far as they can identify a looking glass removed from them and only 'in some measure' coincident with 'the eyes of other people' (see above). In a sense, the stage of fellow-feeling is inherently relational, seeing as it can only be attained, provided all persons are inclined to look at themselves from due distance.[5] Smith's conjecture implies that social distances *among* real actors are reduced precisely when everyone succeeds in attaining a standpoint that is sufficiently removed from *one's own* immediate social experience, and in considering oneself primarily from that point of view.[6]

2.4 Spheres of Interdependence and Patterns of Sociability

The emergence and expansion of fellow-feeling from small to increasingly large social spheres suggest the possibility of addressing the interdependence of human actions by following a stepwise procedure that combines the *more analytico* and *more genetico* approaches. The step-by-step circumscription of action is a distinctive feature of that procedure. In this connection, circumscription is defined as a cognitive operation 'by which some particular aspects of language, such as the

---

[5] Joseph Butler had pointed before Smith to the relationship between distancing and the moral sense: '[t]hat which renders beings capable of moral government is their having a moral nature, and moral faculties of perception and of action. Brute creatures are impressed and actuated by various instincts and propensities: so also we are. But, additional to this, we have a capacity of reflecting upon actions and characters, and making them an object to our thought: and on doing this we naturally and unavoidably approve some actions, under the peculiar view of their being virtuous and of good desert; and disapprove others, as vicious and of ill desert' (Butler, 1834 [1736], p. 316). Charles Griswold recently noted that self-reflection is not always associated with such a prior distancing move. For example, in the case of resentment, self-reflection works through imagination keeping alive immediate feelings and inducing 'the reproduction of anger considerably past the event that occasioned it' (Griswold, 2007, p. 23).

[6] The issue of which type of fellow-feeling (and social congruence) would be brought about when agents have different propensities to look at themselves from a distant standpoint is not directly considered by Smith, but may shed further light on the development of sociability.

domain of individuals or the extension of a predicate, are restricted so that their "coverage" is as small as possible' (Kyburg and Man Teng, 2001, p. 143). This operation is central to detecting partial similarities amid diversity, and it is a means to tackle action descriptions in the social sphere (Scazzieri, 2006).

Circumscription works as follows. Let $\{s_1, s_2, \ldots, s_p\}$, $\{s_1, s_2, \ldots, s_{p-1}\}$, $\{s_{p-1}, s_p, s_{p+1}\}$ be a collection of first-order action descriptions. Partial similarity allows the mapping of the above collection of first-order description into a set of second-order descriptions such as $\{S_1, S_p, S_{p-1}\}$. The latter set turns into a coherent whole a collection of heterogeneous action descriptions by picking up some elements that are common to at least two of the original first-order descriptions. The result is a set of action descriptions that bear partial similarity to first-order descriptions even if the degree of similarity is different depending on which set of first-class descriptions we consider. In the above example, the second-order description is closer (in terms of common elements) to first-order descriptions $\{s_1, s_2, \ldots, s_p\}$ (as $s_1 = S_1$ and $s_p = S_p$ are common) than to the other two sets of first-order descriptions, which have only one element in common with the set of second-order descriptions (as $s_{p-1} = S_{p-1}$ and $s_p = S_p$ are common). It is noteworthy that the expandability of second-order descriptions to new first-order descriptions is inversely related to the former's 'density' (i.e., to the number of included characteristics), for a high-density second-order description, that is, a description that too closely mirrors first-order descriptions, presupposes a degree of completeness that is alien to comprehensive second-order descriptions. In short, a low-density action description is more likely to be inclusive and has a greater likelihood of allowing particulars in a collection of essentials.

Circumscription of one's own and other people's situations is necessary for social coordination to be effective. Successful circumscription presupposes a specific type of reasoning capacity. This is so because human beings need to reach a common ground which allows them to bridge distant and sometimes utterly dissimilar situations. This common ground is prima facie close to Thomas Nagel's 'view from nowhere' (Nagel, 1986). However, effective circumscription differs from Nagel's perspective as it presupposes full awareness of positional differences, and the ability to construct a point of view that is different from anybody's position but is nevertheless precisely located in the social space (Porta and Scazzieri, 2003; Scazzieri, 1999a, 2003a, 2003b, 2008).

The above standpoint derives from an epistemic procedure in which concrete situations are circumscribed and comparisons are made possible. In general, imperfect resemblances become increasingly important as we increase the heterogeneity of agent types. Under such conditions, circumscription identifies the primary elements of social congruence, while imagination provides a sufficiently extended domain in which coordination is feasible. For example, social actors may alternatively approve or disapprove a particular action depending upon (i) the way in which the situation in view has been circumscribed (i.e., described relative to other situations), (ii) the way in which agents' imagination allows them to think of themselves as affected by similar circumstances, and (iii) the way in which agents' reflective sense allows them to consider both their own and other people's circumstances in terms of a uniform set of (higher-order) evaluative principles.

Reasoning stretches beyond the domain of social homogeneity and enables individuals and groups to identify interpersonal benchmarks amid social differentiation.[7] The circumscription of social evidence based upon recognizing imperfect resemblances allows the identification of expanded social domains in which coordination is feasible. The circumscription of situations enables agents mutually to respond to one another in terms of a common rational benchmark. However, this benchmark is not attained by rationality alone, for its identification requires a sophisticated blend of imagination and reasoning. Imagination helps agents to 'fill the gaps' left by imperfect resemblances, while reasoning permits agents to undertake positional inversion to reach a 'view of no one in particular' (Sen, 2002, p. 466), and thus move beyond the constraint of a specific viewpoint. Amartya Sen's discussion of positional objectivity is highly relevant to the analytical reconstruction of Smith's view. In this connection, Sen maintains (in contrast with Thomas Nagel) that 'the objectivity of observations must

---

[7] This feature of circumscribing is remarkably close to Smith's impartial spectator: 'in the Smithian perspective, rationality does not consist of falling into line with any pre-selected motivation, such as self-interested maximization which is often defined as rational behaviour in parts of modern economics, for example, in "rational choice theory". Rather, rationality is seen as reasoned reflection on the nature of the processes involved and the consequences generated, in the light of valuations one has reason to accept. Rationality is an exercise of reasoning, valuation, and choice, not a fixed formula with a pre-specified maximand' (Rothschild and Sen, 2006, pp. 357–358).

be a position-dependent characteristic: not a "view from nowhere", but one "from a delineated somewhere"' (Sen, 2002, p. 464). He goes on to argue that '[o]bjectivity may require interpersonal invariance when the observational position is fixed', while acknowledging that 'that requirement is quite compatible with position-relativity of observations. Different persons can occupy the same position and confirm the same observation; and the same person can occupy different positions and make dissimilar observations' (Sen, 2002, p. 466; see also Sen, 1999a on the multiple dimensions of personal identity).[8]

Both imagination-enriched resemblances and positional inversion are necessary for the circumscription to succeed in providing a prototype of interpersonal comparisons and coordination. Coordination emerges from the *sequence* of stages that characterises effective circumscription in an evolving social context. Sophia Ratcliffe emphasises such a continuum by calling attention to the combination of '"sympathy" (in the sense of empathy) and judgment' in most circumstances requiring the understanding of other people's minds (Ratcliffe, 2008, pp. 42–44). This issue is related to whether the sympathetic reconstruction (in Smith's sense) of human feelings and actions (including one's own) leads to judgments of a normative type. David Raphael has argued against the standard view that 'ought' propositions cannot be derived from statements of fact by maintaining that '[i]f we take the notion of derivation in a broad sense that is not confined to deduction [...] it is not true to say that an "ought" cannot be derived from an "is", or (to put the same point in another way) that an imperative cannot be derived from an indicative' (Raphael, 2007, p. 133), for in such cases 'the grounding is psychological, not logical [...] The normative statement is grounded on fellow-feeling, sympathy' (Raphael, 2007, p. 134). The blending of imagination-enriched identification of likeness and positional inversion provides an entirely new perspective upon the nature and working of social mirrors. This is primarily because it projects a coordination image attained by means of

---

[8] Sen's 'view of no one in particular' (as distinct from Nagel's 'view from nowhere') is close to Stephen Darwall's 'intersubjective stance of someone relating to others as, and reciprocally recognizing his status as, one among others' (Darwall, 2006, p. 102), that is, to 'an *impartially regulated second-personal stance* rather than a third-personal perspective on individuals, oneself included, as simply one among others' (Darwall, 2006, p. 102 [added emphasis]).

deliberate distancing and rational reconstruction: it is a 'distant mirror' allowing a better perspective upon immediate social experiences.[9]

Our point of view suggests that the likelihood of coordination is not increased by a Rawlsian 'veil of ignorance' relative to individual circumstances (Rawls, 1971), but by *deeper knowledge and understanding* of those very circumstances. This point of view is closer to Amartya Sen's view from 'a delineated somewhere' (Sen, 2002, p. 464) than to Thomas Nagel's 'view from nowhere' (Nagel, 1986). The mutual understanding of situations is likely to be more widespread if persons can attain a view from 'a delineated somewhere', making *immediate experiences* comparable with one another. Higher-order social coordination presupposes circumscription by reasoning through adoption of a viewpoint that is sharply different from the merely empathic sharing of emotions. Social coordination in terms of stepwise circumscription of social situations highlights the central role of reciprocal positioning and mirroring as actors watch, and try to adjust to, one another. Such analysis emphasises the coexistence of features of continuity and features of discontinuity as human beings move from one level of coordination to another.

Social mirroring is everywhere of central importance, but the nature of mirroring is sharply different depending on the situation in view. Physical resonance or empathy is clearly distinct from mutual understanding achieved through the point of view associated with Smith's 'impartial spectator'. According to Smith,

[w]e can never survey our own sentiments and motives, we can never form any judgement concerning them; unless we remove ourselves, as it were, from our own natural station, and endeavour to view them as at a certain distance from us. But we can do this in no other way than by endeavouring to view them with the eyes of other people, or as other people are likely to view them. Whatever judgement we can form concerning them, accordingly, must always bear some secret reference, either to what are, or to what, upon a certain condition, would be, or to what, we imagine, ought to be

---

[9] In this connection, John Dwyear notes that '[w]hereas the process of evaluating moral behaviour involves such subjective elements as sensitivity and self-comparison, it requires an even greater degree of objectification. Since the spectator can never hope to understand fully the emotions of the other actor, the latter is forced to present an image, via verbal conversation or the "language of the eyes", which will be acceptable to the former' (Dwyear, 1993, p. 104; see also Dwyear, 2003).

the judgement of others. We endeavour to examine our own conduct as we imagine any other fair and impartial spectator would examine it. If, upon placing ourselves in his situation, we thoroughly enter into all the passions and motives which influenced it, we approve of it, by sympathy with the approbation of this supposed equitable judge. If otherwise, we enter into his disapprobation, and condemn it. (Smith, 1976 [1759], III.1.2, p. 110; see also Raphael and Macfie, 1976; Raphael, 2007)

Mere resonance and empathy are associated with first-order mirroring, such that individuals reflect one another in an immediate way, and influence one another through principles of imitation. Mirroring through a 'third-person' point of view, on the other hand, presupposes higher-order mirroring, such that individuals converge to a mutually shared description of situations, and adjust to one another by means of *indirect reflection* onto an external (and seemingly objective) coordination image. In this case, imagination can exert a moderating influence on passions by lowering the pitch of any passion to the level acceptable to an informed, and internalized, external observer (Smith's 'impartial spectator').

Smith's consideration of the moral judgement through the impartial spectator coming from *self-awareness* (what he called 'the man within') underscores his reliance on the power of rational use of imagination in countering unsocial passions and sustaining the relational structure of the social body. The following passage of Smith's *Theory of Moral Sentiments* makes this explicit:

[i]t is not the soft power of humanity, it is not that feeble spark of benevolence which Nature has lighted up in the human heart, that is thus capable of counteracting the strongest impulses of self-love. It is a stronger power, a more forcible motive, which exerts itself upon such occasions. It is reason, principle, conscience, the inhabitant of the breast, the man within, the great arbiter and judge of our conduct. (Smith, 1976 [1776], III.3.4, p. 137; cf. Scazzieri, 2006)

An interesting implication is that once a 'third person' point of view is adopted, seeming dichotomies in social relationships can be understood as resulting from the consideration of alternative social mirrors. The distinction between 'generalized reciprocity' and 'reverse reciprocity' is a case in point, for generalized reciprocity requires that if A relates to B in a certain way, then B will relate to C in the same way; on the other hand, reverse reciprocity requires that if A relates to B in a certain way, then *C* will relate to *A* in the same way (see Kolm, 2009, p. 78). In general, the dichotomy disappears if social actors are able to attain a 'third-person' viewpoint, for *both* generalized and reverse reciprocity are derived from a 'third-person' standpoint such that *A*, *B*, and *C* relate to one another (pairwise) as the 'third-person' observer would think appropriate.

As we have seen, the detection of social congruence and the actual experience of social coordination presuppose a hierarchy of epistemic steps in which actors attempt to reconstruct one another's circumstances and assess which appropriate actions ought to be taken under those circumstances. In either case, personal attitudes and abilities are shaped in a fundamental manner by the way agents represent one another. The mirror technique is thus an essential component of coordination by reasoning. Such a technique, however, leads to different outcomes depending on the way it is used. At a 'primitive' level, persons are passive receptors of mirrored images, and coordination outcomes are almost entirely dependent on context. At a more advanced level of social understanding, persons become aware that different mirror images are possible, and tend to concentrate their attention upon one image or another depending on their reconstruction of other people's standpoint.

Finally, at the most advanced level, persons make use of what we may consider a multiple-mirroring device. In this case, any given actor first circumscribes other actors' situations as a mirror for one's own, and then makes use of a 'third view' to assess other people's (or even one's own) situations and actions. The change from 'direct reciprocal' mirroring to indirect mirroring through self-reflection is an essential condition if human beings are to move beyond the immediate influence of context.

The mirroring technique becomes an important device for epistemic emancipation within the social sphere. Emma Rothschild notes in this connection that Adam Smith's 'history of the rise of commerce' may be considered 'an epic of the emancipation of the mind' (Rothschild, 2001, p. 10). One reason for this is that trade allows human beings to look at their immediate context *from a distance*, thereby making it possible (in principle at least) to freely interact with one another across differences and over increasingly expanded social domains. The disposition to look at oneself and others from a suitable distance is a necessary condition for moral judgment and spontaneous coordination (see above). The analytical framework of Smith's *Theory of*

Moral Sentiments allows the conjecture that distancing is at the root of epistemic emancipation, both through exchange relationships and otherwise. In a different but complementary perspective, Stephen Darwall emphasises that

> Smith [...] thinks of exchange as an interaction in which both parties are committed to various normative presuppositions [...] All this requires that both be able to put themselves imaginatively into the other's standpoint and compare the responses that one thinks reasonable from that perspective with the other's actual responses, as one perceives them third-personally. (Darwall, 2006, p. 48)

In particular, the mirroring technique sheds light on the complex interactive pattern that thinking as a team ('we thinking') should take to achieve social coordination. A first step in understanding 'we thinking' is to assume that agents are 'in a frame in which first-person plural concepts are activated' (Bacharach, 2006, p. 141), so that any given person 'works out the best feasible combinations of actions for all the members of her team, then does her part in it' (Bacharach, 2006, p. 121).[10] But neither the emergence nor the characteristics of 'we thinking' can be taken for granted. As a matter of fact, 'we thinking' presupposes group identification and the latter is often in a state of flux, so that 'the same person passes through many group identities' in the course of her/his life (Bacharach, 2006, p. 151).

Circumscription analysis disentangles the internal structure of 'we thinking', and calls attention to the *differentiated* reasoning steps that are necessary if social actors are to move beyond the stage of immediate resonance and empathy, to eventually reach the condition of circumscription by a 'third-person' point of view. It is worth noting that the above point of view makes economic coordination subject to the same general rules as social coordination, for 'correspondence of sentiments' becomes the most encompassing criterion by which congruence between persons (or groups) may be achieved (see Sugden, 2005a, p. 101; see also Sugden, 2005b). In this perspective, the ability to reach a condition of fellow-feeling takes precedence over other, more specific, rules of behaviour (which may or may not be compatible with it).

---

[10] According to Raimo Tuomela, 'a proper understanding and explaining of the social world requires [...] a group's point of view, or as I typically will say, the group members' "we perspective"' (Tuomela, 2007, p. vi).

The search for correspondence of sentiments exerts a moderating influence upon agents motivated by self-interest (or altruism) and induces them to 'lower' their original motivation to the level compatible with fellow-feeling (see *TMS* I.i.4.7). This point of view makes self-interested interaction in commercial society socially acceptable, if it is the expression of the 'ability both to abstract oneself from present circumstances, and to attempt to satisfy norms for meaning and truth, rather than just to offer relief to impulses' (Fleischacker, 2005, p. 94). To conclude, the need to achieve a satisfactory degree of fellow-feeling discourages a 'narrow-minded notion of the market', which '[b]y encouraging us to expect the worst of others [...] eventually brings out the worst in us' (Zamagni, 2004, p. 30).[11]

2.5 Aggregation, Systemic Interest, and Conflict

Multiple characteristics lead to a multidimensional structure of human actions, which makes plural patterns of circumscription possible (see Section 2.4). This feature of actions has important consequences for the way actions may be lumped together into coherent wholes that may be mutually fitting or mutually opposed to one another in the social domain. For example, production activities are inherently interdependent once we move from individual production to production in the social sphere. This section investigates productive interdependencies based on different mappings of interdependence and plural criteria of system-wide coherence.

A variety of aggregation patterns are compatible with a given economic structure (see Leontief, 1928, 1941; Pasinetti, 1977, 1980 [1973]). This can be shown by the production flows in a two-industry economy, where any given industry supplies a homogeneous product to the other industry while also using as inputs both the products of the latter and its own product. The above network of inter-industry flows can be represented in Table 2.1.

Table 2.1 shows two different patterns of interdependence simultaneously at work. On the one hand each industry, considered as

---

[11] The characteristics of 'we thinking' are radically different depending on the stage at which mutual responsiveness is achieved. Similarly, 'we thinking' gradually moves away from the immediate sharing of frames and objectives, and gets closer to the sharing of procedures and 'trust responsiveness' as persons approximate the standpoint of the impartial spectator (for a discussion of trust responsiveness see Pelligra, 2007, pp. 294–299).

Table 2.1 *A two-industry inter-connected economy*

	Industry 1 (oil)	Industry 2 (computers)
Industry 1 (oil)	A_{11}	A_{12}
Industry 2 (computers)	A_{21}	A_{22}

supplier *and* user of a homogeneous product, is related to the other industry by a direct product flow: industry 1 delivers oil to industry 2; industry 2 delivers computers to industry 1. On the other hand, each industry appears in a different light if we drop the product homogeneity assumption and allow different sources of supply for, say, computers delivered to industry 1 and computers delivered to industry 2. In the latter case, Table 2.1 represents a pattern of interdependence that is not circumscribed to the economy under consideration if external linkages are the channel by which computers are supplied to either industry 1 or industry 2. In turn, external linkages suggest that lumping together industry 1 (the oil industry) and industry 2 (the computer industry) in the same unit of analysis (say, the same national economy) is not the most effective aggregation criterion, and that aggregation covering cross-border flows is the best way of identifying appropriate units of analysis. This means that multiple aggregation criteria must be considered, and that coordination and conflict take different forms depending on which criterion is most relevant in each context.

The concept of 'viability' is central to studying aggregation criteria in the social sphere. Boisguillebert's emphasis on proportionality conditions for a viable body politic shows awareness of the reproducibility requirements associated with any given pattern of social interdependencies (Boisguillebert, 1843 [1707a], Boisguillebert (1843 [1707 b]); see also Section 2.2). Quesnay's study of the net product (*produit net*) generated by a set of interdependent production and consumption flows highlights the specific features of that interdependence in the case of a circular flow economy, in which commodities are produced by means of other commodities (Quesnay, 1972 [1759]). In Quesnay's circular flow economy, viability requires that at the end of each production cycle (assumed to coincide with the agricultural year), the available quantities of intermediate products be enough to replace the quantities of those products that have been used up in the production processes carried out during that cycle. It is only under that condition that a net product can be identified as the collection of commodities produced over and above what is required for the economy to reproduce itself (see also Leontief, 1928, 1941; Sraffa, 1960; Sinha, 2019). The Hawkins-Simon condition for the viability of intermediate product flows expresses the requirements for a non-negative final output vector to be associated with a vector of non-negative products when the technology of the economy can be represented by a matrix of technical coefficients that is both non-negative and indecomposable (so that all products are intermediates) (Hawkins and Simon, 1949; Nikaido, 2014; Steenge, 2011).

A given configuration of productive interdependencies may be compatible with a variety of approaches to systemic coherence. For instance, a set of interdependent intermediate product flows is associated with a viability condition for its reproducibility (Hawkins-Simon condition) or, alternatively, with a proportionality condition for full employment and full utilization of productive capacity (Pasinetti, 1981, 1993) or, again, with a proportionality condition for maximum growth in the case of intermediate product residuals transferred from one production cycle to another (Quadrio Curzio, 1986; Quadrio Curzio and Pellizzari, 2018). Indeed, the viability condition for reproducibility is generally satisfied by a plurality of proportions between the different industries in an interconnected economy (Sraffa, 1960). This highlights the complex relationship between the proportionality requirements associated with the internal coherence of the whole economy (what we may describe as its 'systemic interest') and the actual configuration of the economy (say, the actual proportions between its constituent industries) at any given time.

In general, we can state three related points. First, different criteria of integration are compatible with a given collection of activities; second, plural identifications of systemic interest are compatible with maintenance of the integrated system; and third, alternative dynamic trajectories are open to the system of interdependencies depending on which type of 'systemic interest' is considered (Cardinale, 2018a, 2022). This suggests the possibility of conflicts between activities (social groups) supporting one or another pattern of integration. For example, there could be conflicts between activities closer to other activities within the same national economy, and activities more closely integrated in the international economy; or conflicts between activities supporting different proportionality conditions (i.e. different views of 'systemic interest') within the same national economy (see Cardinale, 2017, 2022; Cardinale, Coffman and Scazzieri, 2017a; Cardinale and Landesmann, 2017).

Multiple criteria for identifying a 'systemic interest' highlight the possibility of intersecting spheres of interdependence between activities (Pabst, 2017, 2018a). This possibility raises the issue of whether the coexistence of multiple spheres of interdependence is a hindrance or a help towards social congruence. Multiple criteria for interdependence may, under certain conditions, trigger mutual tolerance (if not cooperation) rather than conflict. Individual or group A may be opposed to individual or group B on issue x, but be aligned to group B on issue y, which makes all-out conflict unlikely. On the other hand, excessive fragmentation can make certain alignments difficult to detect, which could trigger a condition of latent or open conflict between individuals or groups. Potential compromise prevails over potential conflict if the two following conditions hold: (a) the number of divisive issues i is less than or equal to ε and (b) for each individual or group j, the distance between the maximum and minimum weight assigned to one's own objectives is greater than σ. This conjecture suggests that compromise is likely to prevail over open conflict provided the number of divisive issues is not too great, and individuals or groups weigh social outcomes in a sufficiently differentiated way across possible social situations. The two conditions taken together denote what we may call the coordination threshold for the polity under consideration (Pabst and Scazzieri, 2016).

2.6 Sociability, Circumscription, and Partial Similarity

This chapter has explored the roots of sociability in a setting characterized by the interdependence of individuals and groups. Building on the non-contractualist tradition in economic and political theory, the chapter outlines an analytical framework based on *circumscription* and *partial similarity*. This framework allows us to study the multiple patterns of convergence or cleavage by which plural interests may aggregate in society. In particular, it is possible to identify cooperation thresholds as dividing lines between individuals and/or groups in social domains structured according to different criteria of affiliation. Modes of coordination are central in a complex social domain, which presupposes an interdependence of different individuals or groups. At the same time, modes of interdependence often lead to relatively persistent configurations of relative positions of individuals and groups, which may significantly influence the dynamic trajectory of a political economy undertaking changes in the division of labour.

The next two chapters of Part I will examine the relationship between forms of interdependence and the organisation of production activities, bringing to light the mutual constitution of specialization of activities and modes of interdependence. Chapter 3, on Association and the Division of Labour, examines coordination in production by distinguishing between interdependence through the association of distinct but non-specialised activities and interdependence through division of labour among specialised activities. The chapter analyses the conditions for the mutual coherence of interdependent activities and the way in which changes in the division of labour may require a change in the mode of integration between production activities, as well as changes in the general mode of social congruence. Chapter 4, 'The Constitution of the Economy', discusses how existing relative positions may stimulate or thwart structural transformation. Division of labour is closely interlinked with social congruence. This means that institutional conditions, as an expression of social congruence, stimulate certain patterns of division of labour while thwarting others. This chapter will outline a framework for investigating changes in the material structure of a political economy in its relationship with the configuration of interests in society.

3 | Association and the Division of Labour

3.1 The Association of Interdependent Activities

As we have seen in Chapter 2, interdependence is a necessary condition of association. Mutual engagement under a given congruence condition and/or in the pursuit of shared objectives presupposes capabilities and dispositions whose *relative positions* and possible *relative contributions* are identifiable and mutually recognized. This reciprocal recognition is not based on a convergence of individual wills, as would be the case with notions of 'social contract', but rather on the fitting of mutual dispositions and interests. However, interdependence is merely virtual unless it gives rise to *actions* that are reciprocally coordinated *ex ante* or reciprocally influential *ex post*. This chapter explores the conditions for the association of activities in the pursuit of mutually consistent objectives in the production sphere. Section 3.2 builds upon Adam Smith's approach to social interdependence as the mutual fitting of specialised human actions by analysing the relationship between the division of labour considered in the *Wealth of Nations* (Smith, 1976 [1776]) and the social mirroring aspect of human association in the *Theory of Moral Sentiments* (Smith, 1976 [1759]).

This reconstruction of Smith's argument is followed by a reappraisal of Edward Gibbon Wakefield's distinction between 'simple cooperation' and 'complex cooperation', which inscribes division of labour within the wider sphere of the organisation and functioning of human dispositions in a relational setting (Wakefield, 1835–1843). With simple cooperation, actors associate with one another in performing the same tasks. With complex cooperation (division of labour), actors bring about patterns of coordination between specialized activities that involve different dimensions of the production process such as capabilities, tasks, or materials-in-process. In fact, complex cooperation in the production sphere requires the coordination of actors performing actor-specific tasks by making use of different capabilities and generating a complex network of materials-in-process and intermediate products that are transferred from one producer (or set of producers) to another. Charles Babbage (1835) developed Smith's insights by emphasising the operational requirements of multi-dimensional complex cooperation and addressing in particular the coordination requirements that are necessary *within* individual establishments as a result of the different operational needs for various elements of the production process.

Section 3.3 examines the consequences of complex cooperation along the three fundamental dimensions of capabilities, tasks, and materials-in-process. Complex cooperation between *capabilities* is the simplest and most visible case of division of labour: it requires actors to combine in executing different tasks to make the same product. Complex cooperation between *tasks* tends to be more elusive but is also essential to an effective division of labour: it requires different operations to fit one another, that is, to be mutually matching components of the same arrangement of technical and organisational activities. Complex cooperation between *finished or semi-finished products* highlights the material side of interdependence: the availability of a certain product at a certain time may be a necessary condition for other products to be made at the same time or at different times.

Section 3.4 discusses proportionality conditions at the level of capabilities and at the level of tasks in light of Babbage's criteria for complex cooperation in manufacturing (Babbage, 1835 [1832]; Scazzieri, 1993, 2014a). This section also addresses proportionality conditions for interdependent products or materials-in-process in view of the Hawkins-Simon viability conditions for a self-reproducing economy (Hawkins and Simon, 1949). The section concludes by evaluating the respective roles of Babbage's proportionality criteria and Hawkins-Simon's viability conditions in determining the feasibility and effectiveness of modes of association in the production sphere. One important conclusion of this section is that changes in the internal structure of the production process can trigger changes in the proportionality conditions governing the association between capabilities, tasks, and materials-in-process in the production sphere. This highlights the existence of an important link between production regimes and division of labour at different levels of analysis, which may encompass individual productive establishments, different collections of establishments (such as industries or vertically integrated sectors), and eventually the economic system as a whole.

Section 3.5 considers alternative *production regimes* (here defined as alternative arrangements of capabilities, tasks, and materials-in-process) and examines the conditions under which the switch between production regimes entails switching from one mode of association to another, as well as from one set of proportionality conditions to another. This section introduces a broad classification of production regimes based on the distinction between *straight-line* and *job-shop* forms of production organisation. We illustrate this distinction by comparing the straight-line structure of steam-engine technology with the job-shop structure of the Jacquard-loom technology at the time of the First Industrial Revolution. In light of that distinction, the section also examines current developments in manufacturing technology and organisation. Production regimes are characterised by networks of capabilities, tasks, and materials-in-process spanning different levels of aggregation in society.

Section 3.6 examines the relationship between the structure of networks in the production sphere and the modes of association between individuals or groups in the social sphere. The concluding section 3.7 examines the relationship between *structural dynamics* (defined as change in the proportionality conditions governing interdependence at the level of capabilities, tasks, and materials-in-process) and the transformation in the prevailing *modes of division of labour*. This section discusses the way in which structural dynamics may change the *material constitution* of a polity and its evolution over time, in the sense that changes in the proportionality conditions between capabilities, tasks, and materials-in-process may bring about changes in modes of association, which in turn may trigger or thwart further structural change. The appendix provides a set of analytical tools for investigating the fundamental elements of production structures and their arrangements into networks of interdependent activities.

3.2 Modes of Association, Division of Labour, and Levels of Activity

The concept of association implies that interdependence is instrumental to achieving a common objective. In Johannes Althusius's words, association is the bond that allows the mutual exchange 'of things, works, and laws' (Althusius, 1932 [1614], I.31, n.1) and therefore the orderly life of the polity.[1] Althusius's *communicatio* describes the blending of relative positioning and interacting that is at the root of human association. Smith's *Theory of Moral Sentiments* (Smith, 1976 [1759]) explores the emergence of relationality from relative positioning, which presupposes social mirroring but also the ability to see one's own specificity in the light of other people's positioning and gazing, and ultimately from a 'third-person' standpoint (Smith, 1976 [1759], III.2.31–32; Raphael, 2007; Scazzieri, 2006; see Chapter 2). Satisfaction of material needs is fundamental to the polity and highlights the importance of modes of association necessary to the provision of goods.

Edward Gibbon Wakefield, building on previous contributions on division of labour, investigated those modes of association by introducing the distinction between 'simple cooperation' and 'complex cooperation'. In simple cooperation, 'several persons help each other in the same employment' (Wakefield, 1835–1843, I, p. 26), while in complex cooperation 'several persons help each other in different employments' (Wakefield, 1835–1843, I, p. 26). John Stuart Mill took up Wakefield's distinction, arguing that 'Mr. Wakefield was […] the first to point out that a part of the subject had, with injurious effect, been mistaken for the whole; that a more fundamental principle lies beneath that of the division of labour, and comprehends it' (Mill, 1965 [1848], I, p. 116). In Mill's view, this 'more fundamental principle' should be identified with 'combination of labour', which he finds at work behind both simple and complex cooperation (Mill, 1965 [1848], Chapters 8–9). Combination of labour brings to light the role of *scale dimensions* as a factor governing associations in the material sphere. Simple cooperation provides the most immediate instance of the scale conditions for material association. However, the same principle also governs complex cooperation (division of labour), as the latter involves a minimum scale constraint for implementing any given pattern of specialisation between interdependent actors.

---

[1] This view of human association enters Althusius's definition of political theory: '*subjectum politicae sunt praecepta de communicatione quarundam rerum, operarum et iuris, quae ad […] commune commodum vitae socialis conferimus*' [the subject of politics is the principles concerning the exchange of things, works, and laws, which […] we follow in view of the shared advantage of social life] (Althusius, 1932 [1614], I.31, n.1).

The minimum scale condition provides a common ground between different modes of association in the production sphere. This condition highlights the existence of a systemic element behind complex cooperation: the minimum scale at which specialised actors can be employed depends on the overall level of activity across different specialised processes in the economy. The minimum scale condition also reflects a link between the technical and the social aspect of the division of labour, as the minimum scale can also derive from indivisibilities associated with institutional and/or organisational bottlenecks. Adam Smith hints at the systemic condition governing division of labour when arguing that the degree of division of labour depends on the 'extent of the market' (Smith, 1976 [1776], I.iii.1).

After Smith, Charles Babbage emphasised the internal structure of constraints facing manufacturing production, showing that effective manufacturing implies a proportionality condition, which in turn makes the process dependent on scale and scale variation:

the master manufacturer, by dividing the work to be executed into different processes, each requiring different degrees of skill or of force, can purchase exactly that precise quantity of both which is necessary for each process; whereas, if the whole work were executed by one workman, that person must possess sufficient skill to perform the most difficult, and sufficient strength to execute the most laborious, of the operations into which that art is divided. (Babbage, 1835, pp. 175–176)[2]

Babbage's 'law of multiples' derives from his reformulation of Smith's theory of the division of labour:

[w]hen the number of processes into which it is most advantageous to divide [the production process], and the number of individuals to be employed in it, are ascertained, then all factories which do not employ a direct multiple of this latter number, will produce the article at a greater cost. (Babbage, 1835, p. 211)

---

[2] Babbage mentions that he had discovered this principle 'after a personal examination of a number of manufactories and workshops devoted to different purposes' but that he had later found that the same principle 'had been distinctly pointed out in the work of Gioja, *Nuovo prospetto delle scienze economiche*, 1815, tom. I, cap.iv' (Babbage, 1835, p. 176, with reference to Gioja, 1815–1817, p. 100). The same proportionality advantage from division of labour within the establishment was also noted in Friedrich von Hermann's *Staatswirthschaftliche Untersuchungen* (Hermann, 1832).

The analysis of complex cooperation (division of labour) and of its scale conditions brings to light a hierarchy of constraining and/or enabling factors operating across different levels of aggregation of productive units. For example, Smith's 'extent of the market' requirement is an aggregate condition that produces effects at lower levels of aggregation down to the most elementary units of production. On the other hand, Babbage's law of multiples is a micro-condition that must be satisfied at the level of elementary production units (productive establishments). However, it is likely also to produce effects at intermediate levels of aggregation (say, at the level of constellations of productive units or of the industrial sector) and at the level of the whole economy.

J. S. Mill's 'combination of labour' highlights a unifying criterion linking modes of association and scale constraints/opportunities at different levels of aggregation. As a result, the aggregate 'extent of the market' condition makes certain patterns of division of labour economically feasible and others unfeasible. On the other hand, the Babbage condition makes certain patterns of variation of production scale feasible and others unfeasible depending on whether the law of multiples is satisfied. There is no guarantee that a certain pattern of division of labour is consistent with the Babbage requirement that scale is varied by discrete steps. However, what cannot be achieved at a given level of aggregation could possibly be achieved at other levels of aggregation. For example, production units that individually satisfy the Babbage condition but not Smith's 'extent of the market' condition might be able to satisfy the latter condition in the aggregate, provided one moves from an output-based to a process-based definition of scale.[3] Similarly, a constellation of productive units that individually satisfy Smith's 'extent of the market' condition but not Babbage's proportionality condition might be able to satisfy the latter at the level of the whole economy, provided there are organisational devices allowing the switch of capabilities (say, of workers and productive equipment) from one productive establishment to another within the set of productive units as a whole.

---

[3] A set of simultaneously performed tasks within a single productive unit, or within a set of interdependent productive units, can be associated with a large *process scale* independently of the size of individual productive units. For example, if the production process is seen as an arrangement of different productive tasks, there is no reason to think that a large process scale should necessarily be associated with a large quantity of any particular type of output produced within the productive unit (Scazzieri, 1993, p. 35).

3.3 Process Balancing and Extent of the Market: Routes to the Division of Labour

Division of labour is subject to different proportionality conditions depending on whether we consider Babbage's law of multiples or Smith's 'extent of the market' principle. As we have seen in Section 3.2, there is no guarantee that the two conditions can be simultaneously met. This suggests that a pattern of division of labour compatible with Babbage's law of multiples may not find the extent of the market that would allow a full (or at least satisfactory) utilisation of different specialised capabilities. For example, the extent of the market may not allow a productive establishment to follow a path compatible with the expansion by integer multiples that Babbage's law requires. For any given productive unit there can be a trade-off between the proportionality requirement associated with Babbage's law and the effective demand requirement associated with Smith's law. Indeed, Babbage's law and Smith's law bring to light different conditions depending on whether we consider specialisation at the level of actors, tasks, or material products. Each dimension of productive activity is associated with a Babbage condition and a Smith condition specific to it. For example, actor specialisation is subject to Babbage and Smith conditions independently of the proportionality and effective demand requirements relative to tasks and material products.

Similarly, there can be one pair of Babbage-Smith conditions that apply to task specialisation and another pair of those conditions that apply to specialisation of material products (and in particular to specialisation of intermediate products). Again, there is no guarantee that fulfilling the Babbage and Smith conditions for a particular dimension of productive activity means fulfilling those conditions for other dimensions of production. Different dimensions of productive activity bring to light different proportionality conditions and different 'extent of the market' requirements. This entails different modes of association depending on which dimension of productive activity is most prominent in a given production arrangement. A production organisation centred on the interdependence between human capabilities is likely to give prominence to Babbage and Smith conditions relative to specialised actors and their connectivity. Similarly, a production organisation centred on the interdependence between productive tasks is likely to give prominence to Babbage and Smith conditions relative to specialised tasks and their mutual relationship. Finally, a production organisation centred on the interdependence between material products or materials-in-process is likely to give relevance to Babbage and Smith conditions relative to the proportionality between material flows and to the extent of the market needed to sustain those flows, to the relative neglect of the interdependence between labour capabilities and tasks.

There is a hierarchy of organisational layers in the production process, and feasibility conditions may change as we move from one layer to another. Depending on which layer is dominant (actors, tasks, materials), the Babbage and Smith conditions require different organisational arrangements and different types of matching between the organisation of productive activity and the composition of effective demand. For example, a production organisation centred on actors' capabilities and on the interdependence between capabilities brings to light a Babbage condition centred on proportionality between labour specialisms and a Smith condition centred on 'concentration of demand' for products classified by their relative requirements for each type of labour specialism. In this case, fulfilment of the Babbage condition for different labour specialisms may or may not be compatible with the required distribution of demand across different products. A similar argument applies to production organisations centred on tasks and task interdependence, and to production organisations centred on materials entering one another's production.

To sum up: shifts from one form of production organisation to another are likely to change the relative importance of actors, tasks, and materials. It follows that fulfilling the Babbage and Smith conditions is profoundly different across different production organisations. This underscores the need for in-depth analysis of each organisational form as a prerequisite for assessing how likely the fulfilment of Babbage and Smith conditions is in different contexts.

Nevertheless, there are important common features across different forms of production organisation. This is true for the formal structure of the Babbage proportionality condition at different levels of aggregation of productive units, and for the formal structure of Smith's 'extent of the market' condition at different levels of aggregation of effective demand. Societal modes of association are shaped in a fundamental way by forms of production organisation. However, the Babbage and Smith conditions express requirements that may vary significantly across different forms of production organisation and levels of aggregation. Association is subject to a *plurality* of constraints. At the same time, the fulfilment of combination requirements is made easier by the variety of aggregation levels in the 'complex cooperation' (division of labour) case. Conditions that are impossible to fulfil at a given level of aggregation may be met by productive units at lower or higher levels of aggregation.

3.4 Production Regimes and Proportionality Conditions

Production regimes are modes of association in the production field characterised by a relative degree of persistence across a plurality of production arrangements. Any given production regime can be defined as a specific integration of actors' specialisms, tasks, and materials-in-process. Each production regime involves a specific way in which the Babbage condition and the Smith condition may be fulfilled at the different levels of aggregation of productive units in the economy.

The history of production regimes since the First Industrial Revolution provides insights into the variety of integration patterns of actors' specialisms, tasks, and materials-in-process that characterise production organisation in industrial economies. Despite their variety, the different production regimes are different ways of addressing the integration of actors' specialisms, tasks, and materials-in-process under the constraints expressed by the Babbage condition and the Smith condition (see Section 3.3 above). For example, the *mass manufacturing regime* associated with the Ford-Taylor organisation of production is an attempt to simultaneously address Babbage's proportionality requirements and Smith's concentration of demand requirements. In this production regime, the implementation of Babbage's condition is associated with the economies of large-scale production made possible by a specific demand concentration consistent with the requirements of manufacturing organisation (Chandler, 1977, 1990).

The *flexible manufacturing regime* that superseded mass manufacturing in the latter part of the twentieth century is an attempt to overcome the difficulties arising on the demand side once the 'smoothing out' of differences between demand requirements from different production processes by the aggregate management of effective demand ceased to be possible (Ranky, 1983; Rathmill, 1986). Flexible manufacturing allowed reshuffling of the integration pattern of agents, tasks, and materials-in-process so that production organisation could reflect a Babbage condition whose satisfaction in turn depended on the way demand was distributed between different production processes. A characteristic feature of the flexible manufacturing system, as shown, for example, in several automotive manufacturing establishments, is its use of a number of different and interrelated multi-skilled machines that are flexibly allocated to productive tasks to cope with changes in demand levels for individual products as well as with changes in the composition of the product bundle manufactured in each establishment (Landesmann and Scazzieri, 1996, pp. 283–289; see also Ranky, 1983; El-Maraghy and Caggiano, 2014; El-Khalil and Darwish, 2019).

Differently from flexible manufacturing, in the *mass customisation regime* the Babbage condition does not require concentration of demand on specific goods. In this case, production organisation overcomes *both* the division of actors' specialisms, tasks, and materials-in-process (required in the mass manufacturing regime) and the utilisation of multi-skilled actors, versatile tasks, and multiple-utilisation materials-in-process (required in the flexible manufacturing regime). The mass customisation regime allows production organisation to switch to the utilisation of *general-purpose* agents, tasks, and materials-in-process. In this case, production organisation is based on 'high-level' simple cooperation (rather than complex cooperation), in which agents are endowed with general-purpose capabilities (rather than with a single specialised capability, or with multiple specialised capabilities), tasks are identified in the most general and fundamental way, and the customisation of materials-in-process is left open-ended until the finishing stages of fabrication (Bianchi and Labory, 2019).

The mass customisation regime entails the switch to a 'high-level' Babbage condition by which line balancing within each productive unit is achieved through a proportionality condition that applies across general-purpose (rather than single-purpose, or multiple-purpose) agents, tasks, and materials-in-process. It is likely that once 'the number of processes into which it is most advantageous to divide [production], and the number of individuals to be employed in it, are ascertained' (Babbage, 1835 [1832], p. 212), it would still be true that 'all factories which do not employ a direct multiple of this latter number, will produce the article at a greater cost' (Babbage, 1835 [1832], p. 212).

However, the split between the requirements for production organisation and the concentration of demand for specific products implies that changes in the composition of the product mix and in the levels of production of *differently customised products* are compatible with a range of different levels of output for different products. A continuous, or semi-continuous, change in the product mix of customised products becomes possible within productive units of given size. In this way, fulfilling the Babbage condition gets detached from fulfilling Smith's condition. Identifying and implementing the most effective coordination of capabilities, tasks, and materials-in-process within a given productive unit can be done independently of Smith's requirement of a minimum concentration of demand ('extent of the market') for specific products. Variations of output levels become irrelevant, provided the changes in levels of output are compatible with the size of the productive unit under consideration.[4]

3.5 Straight-Line versus Job-Shop: A Fundamental Duality in Production Regimes

The above analysis highlights the different association principles characterising production regimes as we move from mass production to flexible manufacturing, and from flexible manufacturing to mass customisation. This section outlines a general framework for analysing production regimes in terms of a fundamental duality between the flexible versus the rigid coordination of capabilities, tasks, and materials-in-process. The prototypical flexible coordination regime (*job-shop* coordination) is characterised by: (i) 'universal' or versatile capabilities (i.e. capabilities that can be employed in a wide range of tasks), (ii) processes associated with different precedence patterns of tasks within the same productive unit, and (iii) fixed sequences by which capabilities can perform any given task in different processes (Scazzieri, 1993, p. 88).[5] The prototypical rigid coordination regime

---

[4] This condition for mass-customised productive units is a special case of the size condition for productive units following the job-shop prototype of production organisation (Scazzieri, 1993, pp. 86–90; Landesmann and Scazzieri, 1996, pp. 253–261; see also section 3.5).

[5] The latter property reflects the difference between the precedence patterns of tasks in the processes carried out within the productive unit. For example, in a productive unit that conducts process A requiring task τ_1 to be performed before task τ_2, and process B requiring task τ_2 to be performed before task τ_1, not all sequences in which capabilities can perform tasks are compatible with the continuous utilisation of capabilities.

(*straight-line* coordination) is characterised by: (i) specialised capabilities (i.e., capabilities that can only be employed to perform a single task or a small number of tasks), (ii) processes associated with the same precedence pattern of tasks within a given productive unit, and (iii) a plurality of sequences by which capabilities can perform the same task in different processes (Scazzieri, 1993, p. 87).

The distinction between the job-shop and the straight-line coordination of capabilities, tasks, and materials-in-process reflects two different approaches to the relationship between division of labour and provision of needs at the societal level. Certain activities provide 'instruments of action', while other activities provide 'instruments of production' (Aristotle, *Politics*, I.II.5). Instruments of production allow human beings to *make* – rather than simply to *do* – something, while the opposite is true with instruments of action. This distinction is clearly expressed by Aristotle, who writes that 'from a shuttle we get something else beside the mere use of the shuttle, but from a garment or a bed we get only their use' (Aristotle, *Politics*, I.II.5, p. 17). A production process delivering instruments of action, such as 'a garment or a bed' (Aristotle, *Politics*, II.ii.5), is more likely to be directly affected by sudden changes of taste (say, a change of fashion) than would be the case with production processes delivering instruments of production. Production arrangements more directly responsive to changing human needs and desires tend to be *more unstable* than production arrangements more distant from the immediate satisfaction of needs and desires.

Production regimes whose internal structure is compatible with a plurality of arrangements of capabilities, tasks, and materials-in-process are better equipped to deal with changing needs and desires than are production regimes whose internal structure presupposes a fixed arrangement of capabilities, tasks, and materials-in-process. Job-shop coordination provides the template for production regimes compatible with unstable and unpredictable demand structures, while straight-line coordination provides the template for production regimes organised on the assumption of stable and/or predictable demand. A production system centred on final goods and services *and* based on job-shop coordination may be more resilient than a production system centred on intermediate goods (and services) *and* based on straight-line coordination. Production activity may alternatively exert a stabilising or destabilising influence depending on whether capabilities, tasks, and materials-in-process are organised according to a flexible or a rigid mode of coordination.

The economic history of industrialisation illustrates this duality. In Britain, the First Industrial Revolution was associated with steam engine technology and eventually led to the appearance of 'endogenous' industrial cycles (Tugan Baranovsky, 1894; Deane, 1980; Kindleberger, 1978; Landes, 1965, von Tunzelmann, 1995). In France, industrialisation was originally associated with 'largely traditional' organisation and methods (Crouzet, 1990, p. 26). However, a central feature of French industry was the utilisation of a light and flexible weaving technology (the Jacquard loom), which made it possible to combine mechanisation with the ability to cope with sudden changes of fashion and production programmes (Poni, 1998, 2001).

The British case illustrates the essential features of a straight-line production regime. In this connection, David Landes notes that

[t]he technological changes that we denote as the "Industrial Revolution" implied a far more drastic break with the past than anything since the invention of the wheel. On the entrepreneurial side, they necessitated a sharp redistribution of investment and a concomitant revision of the concept of risk. Where before, almost all the costs of manufacture had been variable – raw materials and labour primarily – more and more would now have to be sunk in fixed plant. The flexibility of the older system had been very advantageous to the entrepreneur: in time of depression, he was able to halt production at little cost, resuming work only when and in so far as conditions made advisable. Now he was to be *a prisoner of his investment*, a situation that many of the traditional merchant-manufacturers found very hard, even impossible, to accept. (Landes, 1965, pp. 275–276 [added emphasis])

The case of French flexible manufacturing was very different, and points to the possibility of an alternative trajectory of industrial growth. In his study of the Lyon silk industry, Carlo Poni (1998, 2001) called attention to the fundamental role of annual changes of fashion as a powerful instrument by which the merchant-manufacturers of Lyon could control a market by making it *deliberately* volatile. In this case, the production structure was a *space of possibilities* (a probabilistic structure), which enabled the merchant-manufacturer to use his workshop (and the whole industrial district) to strengthen competitive edge. Contrary to the standard industrialization case described by Landes, the entrepreneur was *not* a prisoner of his investment.

Indeed, he turned the 'liquidity' of his capital (working capital rather than fixed capital) into a source of flexibility and competitiveness.

British steam-engine technology and French silk-fabric technology illustrate the fundamental duality between straight-line and job-shop production regimes. In one case (steam-engine technology), innovation brings about a concentration of effort and utilisation of resources by means of an increasing size of productive establishments, the task-specialisation of workers and tools, and the fabrication of a commodity mix such that task-sequencing is the same for all production processes in the same establishment. In the other case (flexible silk-fabric technology), innovation is associated with dispersion of complementary works, versatility of workers and tools, and effective utilisation of capabilities by means of adaptability and redundancy. Watt's steam engine and Jacquard's loom suggest two alternative paradigms of industrial growth. In either paradigm, industrial variety is possible. But variety has a different meaning in the two cases.

The steam engine 'bundles together' production processes that are homogeneous from the technological point of view (same task sequencing). This condition has far-reaching consequences. In particular, the tasks executed by each workstation (worker-and-tool) are rigidly determined in terms of sequencing and duration. An important consequence of this arrangement is a 'tight' economy of time, that is, a production structure in which tasks and processes are expected to have definite duration and to follow one another along a rigid sequence. This technological set-up is compatible with considerable diversity of the product mix, for there may be several product specifications compatible with the same pattern of sequencing between tasks. However, product variety is limited by technological uniformity: the proportions between different product types may be varied, but a continuous (or 'satisfactory') utilisation of productive elements presupposes the same (or a 'similar') task sequencing between production processes.

The flexible technology associated with the Jacquard loom suggests an entirely different production regime. This is because a Jacquard loom substitutes a set of *virtual* production arrangements for a specific 'implemented' structure. In this way, heterogeneity of technical practices is 'built' into the machine, and task sequencing may be varied (by means of automatic control) between different fabrication lines. The following description of the Jacquard loom gives an idea of the way in which a far-reaching innovation could be developed within the apparently traditional framework of Lyonnaise silk technology:

[i]n Jacquard's loom, all threads were attached to hooked wires, which were in turned linked to pins in a central control device. A series of punched cards controlled the operation of the loom according to prespecified patterns of thread, with each card corresponding to the arrangement of threads required at each pass of the shuttle. The system was essentially digital, using binary logic [...]. [A] hole in the card permitted a pin to pass, which lined up a wire to be lifted and, with it, the appropriate thread [...]. Each set of cards corresponded to a prespecified cloth pattern; they were linked together in an endless chain and fed into the central control to actuate the pins and automatically put the loom through its paces. To change the pattern, *it was only necessary to change the set of punched cards; the machine remained the same.* (Noble, 1986, p. 148 [added emphasis])

The Jacquard loom made product differentiation the very reason of its existence. Once in operation, it would be compatible with a virtually boundless variety of designs. This result was achieved by means of the 'programmable mechanization' (Noble, 1986, p. 147) of the weaving process. The weaving stage could be split into several operations of predetermined duration. On the other hand, the duration of human tasks could, to a certain extent, remain variable:

[t]he programming of the machine [...] involved only the preparation of the cards and this was done in a formal and tedious process. The desired finished pattern was first drawn in magnified detail on graph paper and the appropriate thread configuration for each shuttle pass was determined. This information was then punched into the cards, which were linked together in the proper sequence to control the loom automatically. (Noble, 1986, p. 148)

The flexible manufacturing achieved by the Jacquard loom is consistent with a variety of human capabilities and tasks. It did not presuppose a 'tight' sequencing of human operations, nor a continuous flow of material transformations. Flexible manufacturing made it possible for Lyon merchant-manufacturers to stick to 'traditional' organisation and methods despite high scale and speed of production. This result was achieved by bundling together production processes according to a pattern different from the one associated with steam-engine technology.

In the early years of the nineteenth century, the focal point of the manufacturing process in Lyon silk workshops was the Jacquard loom.

This meant that capabilities, tasks, and material transformations were clustered around a mechanical source of *multiple and independent* motions. Any given loom was in fact a *space* of technical opportunities, which could be 'activated' by a suitable impulse stemming from art and invention (a new design). Technical coordination was central to the structure of the Jacquard loom but could be implemented through a *variety* of task sequences. Each set of punched cards corresponded to a specific cloth pattern, and simply changing the set of punched cards could change the coordination mode.

Steam-engine technology is fundamentally different, for the focal point of the manufacturing process was a *common motive force* associated with coordinated motions and tasks. This means that, contrary to the Jacquard loom, steam-engine technology (and the factory system associated with it) could not allow a quick and non-disruptive change-over from one production structure to another. David Ricardo had this technology in mind when he wrote that machinery could make economic systems especially vulnerable to a change in the composition of final demand:

[i]n rich and powerful countries, where large capitals are invested in machinery, more distress will be experienced from a revulsion in trade, than in poorer countries where there is proportionally a much smaller amount of fixed, and a much larger amount of circulating capital [...] It is not so difficult to withdraw a circulating as a fixed capital, from any employment in which it may be engaged. It is often impossible to divert the machinery which may have been erected for one manufacture, to the purposes of another. (Ricardo, 1951 [1817], p. 266)

Steam engine technology is compatible with a variety of production structures, but *not* with a swift change-over from one structure to another. Capabilities, tasks, and materials-in-process are clustered around a motive force that induces continuity, regularity, and synchronisation. In other words, steam-engine technology increases the effectiveness of technical practices by clustering productive elements around a common source of motion but is not by itself conducive to flexible industrial organisation.

Steam-engine technology and Jacquard-loom technology illustrate the fundamental duality between straight-line and job-shop production regimes. In steam-engine technology, the production regime is associated with the source of motive power. This makes the steam engine an effective tool of coordination for capabilities, tasks, and materials-in-process, but leaves flexibility aside. Jacquard-loom technology makes a different technological universe possible. Here manufacturing is *defined* by the flexible organisation of tasks and fabrication stages. The Jacquard loom brings change-over processes to the core of manufacturing organisation and turns the production structure into a space of virtual production arrangements.

The duality between straight-line and job-shop production has resurfaced in recent developments in manufacturing technology and organisation. The flexible manufacturing systems (FMS) and just-in-time (JT) organisations that characterised the manufacturing regimes of the late twentieth century are ways to implement responses to a volatile demand for products by following, respectively, the straight-line and the job-shop models. In FMS, capabilities are clustered around flexible instruments of production (primarily flexible machinery), so that flexible productive equipment may switch from one production line to another as required by changes in demand composition. In the JT system, the production process is arranged according to a plurality of production lines simultaneously active in the productive establishment. Flexibility is *embedded* in the internal structure of the process. Differently from the FMS, human actors and machines are not necessarily multi-purpose but must be ready to switch from one production line to another as need arises. Distinctive features of this form of manufacturing organisation are: (i) the need to reduce or eliminate waiting times when shifting workers, tools, and machinery between different production lines; (ii) the need to maintain a mix of production lines compatible with the capabilities of existing workers, tools, and machines; (iii) the need to allow waiting times for the materials-in-process to move from one fabrication stage to the next in each production line; and, finally, (iv) the need to reduce or eliminate the formation of stocks of yet-to-be delivered final products. The Covid-19 pandemic of the 2020s has illustrated the systemic weaknesses of JT systems, particularly the lack of stocks in relation to critical medical supplies.

The so-called Fourth Industrial Revolution of the early twenty-first century (*mass customisation regime*) integrates artificial intelligence (AI) and information communication technology (ICT) by moving from automation *within* the productive establishment to information networks in which both the formation and the utilisation of products are parts of the same network of interdependencies (Bianchi and Labory, 2019). This manufacturing regime entails a shift to 'intelligent production lines' in which (i) production equipment in the establishment takes the form of a network of interdependent components, (ii) production lines can be easily reconfigured as different needs arise, and (iii) establishments respond to changing economic conditions through 'predictive maintenance' rather than 'reactive maintenance'. Flexibility is at the core of this manufacturing regime, as it had been with FMS and JT, but in this case the versatility of production organisation moves beyond individual productive establishments (and even beyond clusters of individual establishments) and extends to the *whole network* of the producers and users of products and services.

Perhaps for the first time since the First Industrial Revolution, a pattern of coordination compatible with the interdependence of markets *but quite distinct from it* has been made possible by developments of production and organisation technology. Pervasive coordination becomes the hallmark of production interdependencies within and across productive establishments. As a result, the modes of association between producers (or groups of producers) take a degree of fluidity that makes them different from the patterns of division of labour which characterise previous manufacturing regimes. The straight-line and job-shop principles get combined in the attempt to overcome *at once* the types of rigidity characterising either form of production organisation. The law of multiples constraining the variation of *process scale* in straight-line production is satisfied by making materials-in-process flow 'at spot call' from one work unit to another within and across establishments. Workers, tools, and machinery can be in continuous use independent of the indivisibilities associated with traditional straight-line arrangements of production organisation.

On the other hand, the law of multiples constraining variation of *establishment size* in job-shop production is satisfied by making *size itself* vary through adjustment of the pool of capabilities embedded in the individual establishment. This is different from the traditional job shop (such as the artisan workshop), which is constrained in size by the need to encompass a sufficiently heterogeneous combination of production lines corresponding to different sequences of fabrication stages (Bücher, 1968 [1893]; Scazzieri, 1993). Here, by contrast, the establishment size can be adapted to requirements of both users and customers. The law of multiples constraining job-shop production can be satisfied by taking advantage of flexible combinations of capabilities and by making size itself *endogenously determined* within the network of interdependent capabilities, tasks, and materials-in-process.

To conclude: recent manufacturing processes point to the possibility of shifts in production interdependencies from materials-in-process within and across production units to capabilities-in-connection within the social domain. This shift highlights a situation of enhanced mutual dependence between patterns of connectivity in the production sphere and modes of group affiliation in the social sphere. Division of labour turns into arrangements that tend to exert a deep influence upon modes of association in the polity, while being in turn profoundly influenced by them.

3.6 Production Regimes and Social Structures

As we have seen, production regimes are characterised by the interdependence between capabilities, tasks, and materials-in-process. This interdependence not only characterises the internal structure of any given process but it is also a central feature of the coordination between *different* processes at the level of each industry, or of each supply chain, or of the socioeconomic system as a whole. For example, tasks need to be coordinated with one another not only in a given process but also *across* the different processes that deliver the intermediate products leading to final outputs. The same is true for the coordination of capabilities and materials-in-process needed to support a given system of interdependent activities. In short, capabilities, tasks, and materials-in-process form closely knit networks, which in turn are part of a wider nested structure spanning production units of varying size. For this reason, the interdependencies between capabilities, tasks, and materials-in-process at different levels of analysis (say, the individual establishment, the industry, or the economic system as a whole) presuppose certain socioeconomic structures and are incompatible with others. Any given pattern of division of labour involves an overlap between the 'technical' organisation of work within individual production processes and the overall division of labour in society. In turn, this highlights that Smith's 'extent of the market' constrains not only the internal division of labour within the workshop but also the degree of specialisation of activities at the societal level.[6]

The mode of association required by a certain production regime may be incompatible with the existing size distribution of productive units, or with the existing institutional arrangements regulating the mode of utilisation of resources. On the other hand, the introduction of a new production regime may be a powerful factor in triggering new social structures and new institutional arrangements. For example, forms of manufacturing organisation such as the FMS presuppose an approach to the complexity of productive tasks in which the description of individual tasks 'has an intermediate rather than an extreme degree of precision' (Kochen, 1980, p. 16). In turn, this situation may be associated with a reshuffling of the capabilities of workers and machines that emphasises versatility and the ability to switch between multiple tasks (Bessant and Haywood, 1986, p. 472). Finally, it is possible to detect attempts to make the sequence of fabrication stages of materials-in-process independent of too detailed specifications of finished products. This in turn involves (i) the possibility to shape materials according to producers' needs (which is an important characteristic of so-called new materials; see Cohendet, Ledoux, and Zuscovitch, 1988a, 1988b; Willinger, 1989) and (ii) the possibility to 'just-in-time' pull materials-in-process from one production stage to another within a given establishment, or a network of interrelated establishments (Deleersnyder et al., 1989). These transformations of production organisation presuppose social structures compatible with tasks and capabilities identified in a much looser way than in a traditional Taylorist factory, as well as a pattern of interdependence between supply chains allowing for multiple arrangements of production flows under the same broad organisational framework.

---

[6] This situation brings to mind what Polly Hill noted when referring to traditional forms of division of labour in West Africa: '[w]hereas in medieval Europe and imperial China there were in the villages specialist artisans, such as cobblers and builders, who did no farming, this is not so in West Africa, where most rural blacksmiths aspire to be farmers. In Hausaland in northern Nigeria, which is surely not anomalous in this way, there is a very strong tendency for the most successful farmers to have the most remunerative non-farming occupations and *vice versa*. Non-farming occupations, *which may be pursued at any time*, provide farmers with some insurance against the unreliability of the climate' (Hill, 1989, p. 10 [added emphasis]).

A matrix representation of the capability network (which we may call *capability matrix*) provides a visual picture of the interdependencies between capabilities and of the hierarchical relationships that may exist between capabilities at different levels of aggregation (see Appendix).

A capability matrix highlights the *relative positions* of capabilities within the economic system and shows which patterns of intertwined capabilities are feasible on that basis. It emphasises the existence of networks of capabilities and makes it possible to distinguish between the contexts in which capabilities or groups of capabilities may be disconnected from one another and the contexts in which capabilities are so closely intertwined as to generate sets of capabilities whose functioning may be very different from that of individual capabilities separately considered.

Capabilities perform tasks that carry certain materials-in-process from one production stage to another. There is not always a one-to-one correspondence between capabilities, tasks, and materials-in-process. Certain materials are processed by using a plurality of tasks, and certain tasks are executed on a plurality of materials, depending on which form of production organisation is adopted (see above). A matrix representation of task networks and material networks (which we may call, respectively, *task matrix* and *material matrix*) shows the interdependencies between tasks and between materials-in-process (including intermediate products) and the hierarchical relationships that may exist between tasks and between materials at different levels of aggregation (see Appendix).

Capability matrices, task matrices, and material matrices provide a bridge between individual capabilities and materials on the one hand, and their utilisation in production structures on the other hand. Individual capabilities or materials may be useless or even dysfunctional if they are not integrated in a system of interconnected capabilities, tasks, and materials, for it is the integrated system of capabilities, tasks, and materials that turns specialisation into a viable division of labour between activities. The functioning of individual capabilities or sets of capabilities is significantly enhanced or hindered depending on whether the capability matrix allows a positive or negative connectivity between capabilities or sets of capabilities (Scazzieri, 1993, 1999b). For example, a capability matrix facilitating close connectivity between capabilities may generate a closely integrated pattern of division of labour. Networks of canals at the time of the First Industrial Revolution (Deane, 1980) and big data hubs in the contemporary world (Wamba, Akter, Edwards, Chopin, and Gnanzou, 2015) provide examples of the fundamental role of 'connectors' in allowing the association of potentially complementary capabilities to achieve coordinated results in the production sphere.

On the other hand, a capability matrix allowing loosely connected capabilities points to a division of labour in which certain specialisms may disappear without seriously affecting the viability of the overall system.

In the former case, the capability matrix can be described as an *indecomposable system* in which positive or negative shocks directly affect the whole pattern of division of labour. In the latter case, the capability matrix describes a decomposable or nearly decomposable system, in which positive or negative shocks only influence the capabilities directly affected by the shock (*decomposable systems*), or initially influence the capabilities that are directly affected by the shock and subsequently all other capabilities (*nearly decomposable systems*; see Simon, 1962, 2002; Scazzieri, 2021, 2022).

The internal structure of the capability matrix highlights important features of division of labour in each social and institutional context. In particular, the structure of the capability matrix is important in explaining the different functioning of capabilities under different modes of coordination. The same set of capabilities may be associated with different modes of utilisation (*conversion functions*) depending on differences in the structure of the capability matrix. For example, loosely connected capabilities are likely to lead to levels of functioning that are critically dependent on connections *external* to the social context under consideration, as shown by the critical role of material or immaterial infrastructures in the examples above. On the other hand, closely integrated capabilities may reinforce one another, leading to effective but 'inward looking' systems of division of labour. The structure of the capability matrix is conducive to different modes of integration of specialised activities and thus to different trajectories of increasing returns as growing specialisation leads to a cumulative process of 'improved proportionality' between productive inputs, reduced waste, and producers' learning (Smith, 1976 [1776]; Babbage, 1835; Young, 1928; Stigler, 1951; Kaldor, 1967; David, 1994; Scazzieri, 2014a; Szirmai, 2012; Andreoni, 2014; Andreoni and Scazzieri, 2014).

In fact, division of labour is either 'outward looking' or 'inward looking'. In the former case, the introduction of increasingly specialised activities leads to improved functioning of capabilities on the condition of increasing external connections (i.e. increasing connections between capabilities internal to the system and capabilities external to it). In the latter case, the improved functioning of capabilities presupposes an increase in connections between capabilities internal to the system. The structure of the capability matrix exerts a significant influence on the degree and type of responsiveness of any given system of capabilities when positive or negative shocks affect the production structure. A loosely integrated (decomposable or nearly decomposable) system of capabilities may be less responsive to factors of change that could potentially make it more effective (e.g. by triggering a cumulative process of increasing returns). Also, a decomposable or nearly decomposable capability matrix can make the system of capabilities less vulnerable to negative shocks (e.g. by halting or slackening a process of decreasing returns). On the other hand, a closely integrated (indecomposable) capability matrix may be more responsive to factors of change, triggering increasing returns through greater division of labour and increased connectivity. However, an indecomposable capability matrix may be more vulnerable to disruption, as shocks affecting parts of the economy are likely to spread across the whole system of interdependent capabilities.[7]

Capabilities are used to perform tasks on materials, transforming the latter and moving them from one production stage to another. This process leads to the formation of networks of interdependent flows of materials-in-process (including intermediate products), which provide material support to an economy based on division of labour. Each network of interdependent material flows is sustainable (i.e. capable of self-reproduction from one period to the next), provided it satisfies the so-called viability condition (Hawkins and Simon, 1949). A material network highlighting complete interdependence of all materials-in-process (the case of a 'circular flow' economy) (Leontief, 1991 [1928])

---

[7] See Simon (1962, 2002) for a discussion of the respective dynamic properties of indecomposable, decomposable, and nearly decomposable systems. The relationship between the internal configuration of a system and the persistence of certain structural features amid a dynamic process is discussed in Dagum (1969) and Scazzieri (1998). Alternative patterns of vulnerability and resilience depending on system structure are examined in Cardinale (2022).

may generate a closely integrated pattern of division of labour. On the other hand, a material network allowing partial and/or asymmetrical interdependencies between materials-in-process brings to light a division of labour in which certain production processes may disappear without affecting the viability of the overall system (Quadrio Curzio, 1986, 1996).

A 'circular flow' economy highlights full interdependence and the mutual connections of all materials-in-process with one another. On the other hand, *partially* interdependent subsystems of materials-in-process highlight the existence of cleavages between subsystems, and call attention to the possibility of partial or non-synchronized transformations of different parts of the economy (this economy would behave as a decomposable or nearly decomposable system). Each material network may exert an important influence on the pattern of division of labour that prevails in a given social and institutional context, but it is also substantially influenced by it. The same materials may be associated with certain production stages and not with others depending on the structure of the materials-in-process matrix. A fully integrated ('circular-flow') materials-in-process matrix is independent of external sources of supply and is therefore less likely to take advantage of international division of labour in the provision of intermediate products. On the other hand, a loosely integrated materials-in-process matrix is open to external supply sources and more likely to be integrated in cross-systems supply chains.

3.7 Modes of Association and Structural Change: The Material Constitution of a Dynamic Polity

This chapter has investigated the dual constraints affecting modes of association in the production sphere. One is the 'internal' proportionality constraint expressed by the Babbage condition, and the other is the 'external' concentration of demand constraint expressed by the Smith condition. As we have seen, the Babbage and Smith conditions have different implications depending on which production regime one is considering. The mass production (Fordist) regime aims at the joint fulfilment of the Babbage and Smith conditions by the aggregate management of consumer demand. The flexible manufacturing regime aims at the joint fulfilment of the two conditions by a reshuffling of production organisation that adjusts the Babbage condition to the changing concentration of demand between different products. The mass customisation regime aims at fulfilment of the Babbage and Smith conditions by switching to general-purpose capabilities, tasks, and materials. This allows differently customised products to be simultaneously made within a given productive unit, thereby relaxing the need for a 'narrow' implementation of the Babbage and Smith conditions. In this case, general-purpose capabilities, tasks, and materials bring to light a 'looser' Babbage proportionality requirement by which multiples of the minimum effective size of the productive unit occur at *larger intervals* than in the case of mass production or flexible manufacturing.

On the other hand, products may be customised to individual needs, so that Smith's concentration of demand condition is no longer a central requirement for effective production organisation. Here, the matching between production organisation and demand conditions requires substituting versatile for specific capabilities, tasks, and materials. However, production organisation can match demand conditions, provided there is *enough variety* of the product mix (combination of differently customised products). From this point of view, customisation must be substantial (and possibly increasing) for the mass customisation regime to be feasible.

In the mass customisation regime, the productive unit can fulfil the Babbage condition specific to it, provided its own mix of customised products allows the continuous or semi-continuous utilisation of capabilities and materials. In short, production organisation in this regime is *incompatible* with excessive concentration of demand on specific products, as the latter is likely to disrupt the production organisation of specific units of production. Alternatively, the output levels of specific products may increase beyond the range compatible with productive units of a given size by switching to productive units of greater size (subject to the Babbage condition for versatile capabilities, tasks, and materials-in-process).

The changes in production organisation associated with the switch from one production regime to another entail changes in the *mode of association* between individuals and/or social groups in the economy. In the mass production regime, the specialisation of capabilities, tasks, and materials privileges a modular pattern of association supported by an adequate concentration of demand across different productive units. This production regime is compatible with a high degree of specialisation of capabilities, tasks, and materials in each productive unit as well as with the splitting of each production process between production units delivering different product parts in productive units of different sizes (Young, 1928; Ames and Rosenberg, 1965; Scazzieri, 1993, 2014a).

In the mass production regime, the overall consistency between production organisation and concentration of demand between processes can be achieved by aggregate demand management (see above). In a flexible manufacturing (FMS) regime, the Babbage condition becomes dependent on the concentration of demand *across* different products, seeing that capabilities, tasks, and materials can be shifted from one specialised use to another as the shifting conditions of demand require. This production regime involves the combination of different specialisms in each productive unit, *or* in each integrated system of production units (as industrial districts, or other types of interdependent establishments). In the absence of aggregate demand management, the consistency between the Babbage proportionality condition and Smith's concentration of demand condition can be achieved, by reshuffling different specialisms within productive units comprising multi-purpose capabilities, tasks, and materials. In a mass customisation regime, Smith's concentration of demand condition is *reversed*, seeing that the demand for specific products *cannot* be heavily concentrated on specific products for any productive unit of given size. This production regime involves the combination of productive units of different sizes to address different types of customisation requirements. In a situation of increasing demand for specific products beyond their respective organisational boundaries, productive units are constrained to *either* increasing their sizes by discrete and often significant 'jumps', *or* to increasing their ability to address more detailed customisation opportunities at their existing size. The latter condition may involve a re-bundling of specialisms and a reduction of technical division of labour within productive units and at the societal level.

Complex cooperation (division of labour) makes interdependence at the level of capabilities, tasks, and materials-in-process a necessary condition for the production of goods and the provision of services. Interdependence at the level of capabilities, tasks, and materials-in-process presupposes precedence relations that make their availability a necessary prerequisite for the functioning of other capabilities, the performance of other tasks, and the transfer of materials-in-process from one fabrication stage to another. These precedence relations may take a different form depending on whether we consider capabilities, tasks, or materials-in-process. In the case of capabilities, the precedence relations concern the functioning of certain capabilities to enable other capabilities to exist or to function (examples could be the surgeon teacher's capability to make another surgeon's capability to exist, or the nurse's capability to enable the surgeon's capability to function). In the case of tasks, the precedence relations concern the performance of certain tasks as a requirement for other tasks to be executed (an example could be wood cutting as prerequisite for wood assembling in the making of furniture). In the case of materials-in-process, the precedence relations concern the availability of certain materials as prerequisite for other materials to be processed (examples could be standard cases of intermediate product utilisation).

Precedence relations complicate interdependence and may introduce feedback mechanisms that could make certain sub-systems of capabilities, tasks, or materials-in-process relatively self-contained and independent of other subsystems in a production structure. Self-contained material subsystems highlight production as a circular flow subject to the reproducibility condition for intermediate inputs (Hawkins and Simon, 1949; Morishima, 1964, pp. 15–17). The viability condition identifies which proportions of production sectors are compatible with the 'balance of input and output for all goods be satisfied only for outputs all positive' (Morishima, 1964, p. 14), by this means allowing the maintenance of networks of materials-in-process. It is important to note that this condition is necessary but not sufficient for the feasibility of any given network of production processes in the complex cooperation case, for the implementation and maintenance of any material network presupposes the coordination of that network with the corresponding networks of capabilities and tasks. Each mode of association in the complex cooperation case requires a hierarchy of different feasibility conditions. First, each capability, task, and material network must be *individually* feasible. Second, there must be a feasible mode of integration (i.e. a feasible form of production organisation) that connects the capability, task, and material networks in a coherent way. Production arrangements that satisfy the above hierarchy of conditions may be effective to a higher or lesser degree and may to a higher or lesser degree be compatible with the concentration of demand condition between different products or services. The Babbage and Smith conditions highlight the general requirements for the effectiveness *and* demand adequacy of complex cooperation. However, the Babbage and Smith conditions should also be compatible with each other.

An economy undergoing structural change may be associated *both* with the transformation of its productive structure (and thus with the transformation of its capabilities, tasks, and material networks) and with changes in the relative proportions between different products or services. This means that structural changes are likely to modify the prevailing mode of association in the polity by changing the coordination requirements at the level of capabilities, tasks, and materials. This process is also likely to modify the concentration of demand for specific products and services. In short, structural dynamics changes the *material constitution* of society both on the production and on the demand side. At the policy level, this complex process entails the need for adopting *ad hoc* coordination devices, which are different at every single step of societal transformation.

Appendix: Capabilities, Tasks, and Materials in Production Structures

As we have seen in this chapter, each production regime is identified by a specific organisational architecture determining which arrangements of capabilities, tasks, and materials-in-process are feasible and which ones are not. This appendix provides a matrix representation of capabilities, tasks, and materials-in-process to depict their relative positions within a system of interdependencies in the production sphere (a production network). Relative positions are essential to identify the internal hierarchies of capabilities, tasks, and materials-in-process that characterise production regimes in each institutional and organisational context.

Let capability matrix C represent the capabilities of individuals or groups in their relation to tasks. Any element c_{ij} of matrix C denotes the functioning of capability i ($i = 1, ..., n$) in the performance of task j ($j = 1, ..., m$). Thus, for example, c_{11} denotes the functioning of capability 1 in the performance of task 1, c_{21} denotes the functioning of capability 2 in the performance of task 1, and so on. In matrix C below, any given capability can perform all tasks from 1 to m, and any given task can be executed by any capability from 1 to n.

$$C = \begin{matrix} c_{11} & c_{12} & \cdots & c_{1m} \\ c_{21} & c_{22} & \cdots & c_{2m} \\ \cdots & \cdots & \cdots & \cdots \\ c_{n1} & c_{n2} & \cdots & c_{nm} \end{matrix}$$

In practice, however, not all capabilities perform all tasks, nor can all tasks be executed by all capabilities. The case in which there is a one-to-one correspondence between capabilities and tasks (and all tasks need to be executed) can be represented by the diagonal matrix C' below:

$$C' = \begin{matrix} c_{11} & 0 & \cdots & 0 \\ 0 & c_{22} & \cdots & 0 \\ \cdots & \cdots & \cdots & \cdots \\ 0 & 0 & \cdots & c_{nm} \end{matrix}$$

It is also possible for the capability matrix (such as matrix C'' below) to be partitioned into a number of *partially overlapping* sub-matrices $(C_1, C_2, ..., C_k)$, such that, for example, submatrix C_2 includes capabilities suitable to executing tasks 1, 2, ..., m as well as tasks $m + 1$, ..., $m + l$, while also including capabilities that are *not* suitable for tasks 1, 2, ..., m, as well as capabilities *only suitable* for tasks $m + l + 1$ to $m + l + k$:

$$C'' = \begin{matrix} c_{11} & \cdots & c_{1m} & 0 & \cdots & 0 & \cdots & 0 & \cdots & 0 \\ c_{p1} & \cdots & c_{pm} & 0 & & 0 & \cdots & 0 & \cdots & 0 \\ c_{q1} & \cdots & c_{qm} & c_{qm+1} & \cdots & c_{qm+l} & \cdots & 0 & \cdots & 0 \\ \cdots & & \cdots & c_{sm+1} & \cdots & c_{sm+l} & c_{tm+l+1} & \cdots & c_{tm+l+k} \\ 0 & \cdots & 0 & c_{zm+1} & \cdots & c_{zm+l} & \cdots & c_{zm+l+1} & \cdots & c_{zm+l+k} \end{matrix}$$

In the capability structure represented by matrix C'', the introduction of additional capabilities and tasks (which may result from increasing division of labour and task specialisation) may induce *greater flexibility* of the production arrangement, provided sufficiently 'thick' and semi-independent sub-matrices of versatile and mutually substitutable capabilities are maintained in the system. This would be the case if capability matrix C'' could be partitioned into the sub-matrices C_1'', C_2'', and C_3'' as shown below:

$$\mathbf{C_1}'' = \begin{matrix} c_{11} \cdots c_{1m} \\ c_{p1} \cdots c_{pm} \\ c_{q1} \cdots c_{qm} \end{matrix}$$

$$\mathbf{C_2}'' = \begin{matrix} c_{qm+1} \cdots c_{qm+l} \\ c_{sm+1} \cdots c_{sm+l} \\ c_{zm+1} \cdots c_{zm+l} \end{matrix}$$

$$\mathbf{C_3}'' = \begin{matrix} c_{tm+l+1} \cdots c_{tm+l+k} \\ c_{zm+l+1} \cdots c_{zm+l+k} \end{matrix}$$

In each capability sub-matrix $\mathbf{C_1}''$, $\mathbf{C_2}''$, and $\mathbf{C_3}''$, there are capabilities that can be substituted for one another. For example, capabilities c_1 and c_p may both execute task 1 in sub-matrix $\mathbf{C_1}''$, and capabilities c_s and c_z can both execute task $m + l$ in sub-matrix $\mathbf{C_2}''$. On the other hand, the three capability sub-matrices are not completely separate from one another: capability c_q may execute tasks not only in capability sub-matrix $\mathbf{C_1}''$ but also in capability sub-matrix $\mathbf{C_2}''$, while capability c_z may execute tasks not only in capability sub-matrix $\mathbf{C_2}''$ but also in capability sub-matrix $\mathbf{C_3}''$.

Tasks are related to capabilities, but interdependence between tasks gives rise to distinct network properties, which may in turn reveal operational features relevant to the functioning of capabilities.

Let matrix T represent the tasks to be carried out by the activation of capabilities in the productive unit under consideration. Any element t_{ij} of matrix T denotes that task i ($i = 1, \ldots, n$) is performed by activating capability j ($j = 1, \ldots, m$). Thus, for example, t_{11} denotes that task 1 is performed by activating capability 1, t_{21} denotes that task 2 is performed by activating capability 1, and so on. In matrix T below, any task from 1 to n can be performed by any capability from 1 to m.

$$T = \begin{matrix} t_{11} & t_{12} & \cdots & t_{1m} \\ t_{21} & t_{22} & \cdots & t_{2m} \\ \cdots & \cdots & \cdots & \cdots \\ t_{n1} & t_{n2} & \cdots & t_{nm} \end{matrix}$$

In practice, tasks may not be performed by activating any capability, and there will be a degree of capability specialisation in the performance of tasks. The case of extreme specialisation of tasks and capabilities, in which there is a one-to-one correspondence between capabilities and tasks, is represented in the diagonal matrix T' below:

$$T' = \begin{array}{cccc} t_{11} & 0 & \cdots & 0 \\ 0 & t_{22} & \cdots & 0 \\ \cdots & \cdots & \cdots & \cdots \\ 0 & 0 & \cdots & t_{nm} \end{array}$$

In task matrix T', tasks are capability specific in the sense that for each task there is a single capability whose activation allows its performance: in matrix T', task 1 can only be performed by capability 1, task 2 can only be performed by capability 2, and so on. In general, however, there is some degree of 'task versatility', so that a given task can be performed by different capabilities, often in a variety of different combinations. In this case, the task matrix (say, T'') can be partitioned into a number of *partially overlapping* sub-matrices $(T_1, T_2, ..., T_k)$, such that, for example, submatrix T_2 includes tasks that can be performed by activating capabilities 1, 2, ..., m as well as by activating capabilities $m + 1$, ..., $m + l$, while also including tasks that are *not* suitable for capabilities 1, 2, ...,m, as well as tasks that can only be performed by capabilities $m + l + 1$ to $m + l + k$:

$$T'' = \begin{array}{ccccccc} t_{11} \cdots t_{1m} & 0 \cdots & 0 & \cdots & 0 & \cdots & 0 \\ t_{p1} \cdots t_{pm} & 0 & 0 & \cdots & 0 & \cdots & 0 \\ t_{q1} \cdots t_{qm} & t_{qm+1} \cdots t_{qm+l} & \cdots & 0 & \cdots & 0 \\ \cdots & t_{sm+1} \cdots t_{sm+l} & t_{tm+l+1} & \cdots & t_{tm+l+k} \\ 0 \cdots 0 & t_{zm+1} \cdots t_{zm+l} & \cdots & t_{zm+l+1} & \cdots & t_{zm+l+k} \end{array}$$

An increase in the number of tasks of matrix T'' may induce *greater flexibility* of production structure, provided the greater number of tasks is associated with a sufficient number of sub-matrices of tasks that can be performed by different capabilities. If this is the case, matrix T'' can be partitioned into sub-matrices T_1'', T_2'', and T_3'' as shown below:

$$T_1'' = \begin{array}{c} t_{11} \cdots t_{1m} \\ t_{p1} \cdots t_{pm} \\ t_{q1} \cdots t_{qm} \end{array}$$

$$T_2'' = \begin{array}{c} t_{qm+1} \cdots t_{qm+l} \\ t_{sm+1} \cdots t_{sm+l} \\ t_{zm+1} \cdots t_{zm+l} \end{array}$$

$$T_3'' = \begin{array}{c} t_{tm+l+1} \cdots t_{tm+l+k} \\ t_{zm+l+1} \cdots t_{zm+l+k} \end{array}$$

In each sub-matrix T_1'', T_2'', and T_3'' there are tasks that can be 'shifted' from one capability to another. For example, tasks t_1 and t_p may both be performed by activating capability 1 in sub-matrix T_1'', and tasks t_s and t_z may both be performed by capability $m + 1$ in sub-matrix T_2''. On the other hand, the three sub-matrices are not completely separate from one another: task t_q may be performed by capabilities in sub-matrix T_1'' but also in sub-matrix T_2'', while task t_z may be executed not only by capabilities in sub-matrix T_2'' but also by capabilities in sub-matrix T_3''.

The above argument entails a distinction between the specialisation/versatility of capabilities and the specialisation/versatility of tasks, and shows that the former does not involve the latter (nor vice versa). In fact, there are situations in which a given capability may perform a plurality of tasks, while any one of those tasks can be performed only by activating that specific capability. On the other hand, there are also situations in which a given task may be performed by a plurality of capabilities, while any one of those capabilities can perform only that particular task. In other words, versatility of tasks relative to capabilities does not involve versatility of capabilities relative to tasks. Different production regimes are likely associated with different arrangements concerning the versatility of capabilities and tasks, and thus with different modes of association depending on which pattern of specialisation of capabilities and tasks prevails in each context.

Materials-in-process (which include intermediate products) provide yet another dimension of interdependence in the production sphere. They provide the material basis to the activation of capabilities in the performance of tasks, and they bring about material networks that may in turn influence in a fundamental way which patterns of interdependence between capabilities and tasks are feasible under given conditions.

Let a materials-in-process matrix M represent materials in their relation to fabrication stages (see also Scazzieri, 1997, pp. 233–239). Any element m_{ij} of matrix M denotes the physical quantity of material i that enters fabrication stage j in the productive unit under consideration (which may be, say, the productive establishment, the industry, or the economic system as a whole). The rows of matrix M correspond to different materials, while the columns of matrix M correspond to different fabrication stages. In matrix M no material is redundant in the sense that all materials are needed in all fabrication stages and all fabrication stages need all materials:

$$M = \begin{matrix} m_{11} & m_{12} & \cdots & m_{1m} \\ m_{21} & m_{22} & \cdots & m_{2m} \\ \cdots & \cdots & \cdots & \cdots \\ m_{n1} & m_{n2} & \cdots & m_{nm} \end{matrix}$$

The case represented in matrix M is that of a pure circular economy, in which all that is produced is fed back into the system to make further production possible (Leontief, 1991 [1928]; Pasinetti, 1977; Cardinale and Scazzieri, 2019).

Here, no material is redundant, as all materials are needed for the completion of the m fabrication stages. The case in which there is one-to-one correspondence between materials and fabrication stages can be represented by the diagonal matrix below:

$$M' = \begin{matrix} m_{11} & 0 & \cdots & 0 \\ 0 & m_{22} & \cdots & 0 \\ \cdots & \cdots & \cdots & \cdots \\ 0 & 0 & \cdots & m_{nm} \end{matrix}$$

There may also be cases of partial substitutability of materials for one another. For example, we may have material structures in which materials are substitutable within specific subsystems of materials but not in general. This is shown by matrix M'' below, which represents a material structure decomposed into the partially overlapping sub-matrices $(M_1, M_2, ..., M_k)$, such that, for example, submatrix M_2 includes materials suitable to fabrication stages 1, 2, ..., m as well as to fabrication stages $m + 1, ..., m + l$, while also including materials that are *not* suitable for fabrication stages 1, 2, ..., m, as well materials suitable for fabrication stages $m + l + 1$ to $m + l + k$:

$$M'' = \begin{matrix} m_{11} \cdots m_{1m} & 0 & \cdots & 0 & 0 & \cdots & 0 \\ m_{p1} \cdots m_{pm} & 0 & \cdots & 0 & 0 & \cdots & 0 \\ m_{q1} \cdots m_{qm} & m_{qm+1} & \cdots & m_{qm+l} & 0 & \cdots & 0 \\ \cdots \quad \cdots & m_{sm+1} & \cdots & m_{sm+l} & m_{sm+l+1} & \cdots & m_{sm+l+k} \\ 0 \cdots 0 & m_{zm+1} & \cdots & m_{zm+l} & m_{zm+l+1} & \cdots & m_{zm+l+k} \end{matrix}$$

As we have seen with the capability matrices considered above, the material structure in M'' shows that when additional materials and/or fabrication stages are added to the system, the system may acquire greater flexibility if semi-independent blocks of versatile and mutually substitutable materials are maintained in the system.

4 | *The Constitution of the Economy*

4.1 Constitution and Interdependencies

The concept of 'constitution', which is central to this study, has applications in a variety of fields. In the study of society, the legal application is the most prominent one, where 'constitution' refers to the fundamental architecture of a polity, in so far as the polity is an organised collective structure that encompasses multiple levels of agency and a variety of plural institutions beyond the state. From this point of view, a constitution provides the polity with a set of principles determining what is a necessary condition for its existence and what could be changed without putting its survival at risk.[1] Starting from this premise, two questions arise: first, is the concept of 'constitution' relevant for our understanding of the economy, and, second, how does it relate to an analysis of the material arrangements that are necessary for the polity to exist?

Our argument is that the constitution of an economy reflects the existence of a relatively invariant set of interdependencies between its elements, which determine whether that economy may or may not be capable of subsisting over time. For example, a given constitution of the economy may allow the relative proportions between its sectors to change within a certain range of variation but not within others.

---

[1] The word 'constitution' originates from the Latin word *constituere*, which has the meaning of '*aliquid erigere, locare, aedificare, fundare, construere*' [to erect, locate, build, found, construct something] (*Thesaurus Linguae Latinae*, vol. iv, p. 512). In other words, 'constitution' refers to the 'action of constituting, making, establishing' (*Oxford English Dictionary*, 1989, vol. III, p. 789), as well as to '[t]he way in which anything is constituted or made up' in terms of 'the arrangement or combination of its parts or elements' (*Oxford English Dictionary*, 1989, vol. III, p. 789). This means that a 'constitution' is not just a given state but also a dynamic process. Constitutional principles are subject to changes that may happen independently of any formal recognition in written, or otherwise validated, law. In certain cases, these changes allow the constitution to maintain its fundamental identity, while in other cases they involve shifting to a different system of constitutional principles.

Changes of relative proportions outside that range would be incompatible with the persistence of that polity under the given economic constitution. The notion of economic constitution is central to the application of a constitutional framework to the discussion of economic matters, in particular to an appraisal of economic policies against the benchmark of the fundamental institutional and legal order of the polity.

The structure of this chapter is as follows. Section 4.2 outlines a conceptual framework for analysing the economic constitution in terms of the constellation of dispositions and economic interests characterising the polity. Section 4.3 highlights that such constellations give salience to one or another mode of association between socioeconomic groups, and that any given economic constitution is identified with a relatively persistent mode of association connecting individuals or groups. This point of view suggests that a given constitution is consistent with a limited range of variation of the prevailing pattern of group affiliation, while more radical changes of group affiliation might take the economy away from the existing constitutional arrangement. Section 4.4 discusses constitutional arrangements associated with alternative patterns of group affiliation, which are related to the prevailing aggregation/decomposition criterion within the existing division of labour. Section 4.5 builds on the previous argument, developing the conception of 'economic body' as an instance of organised complexity arising from the network of relative positions and feasible motions within the economy and determining the role of intermediate structures at different levels of aggregation within it. This section investigates the way in which alternative arrangements of intermediate structures influence the response patterns of economic constitutions to factors of change, and the trajectories of constitutional development that are most likely in each case. Section 4.6 brings the chapter to a close by discussing how the existing constitution of the economy provides a heuristic for identifying feasible policy options, as well as feasible structural change trajectories open to the economic-political system under given circumstances.

4.2 Modes of Association, Dispositions, and Interests

Interests are inherently relational, as the Latin root of the word 'interest' (*inter-esse* or 'to be between') suggests. However, the notion of 'interest' is ambivalent, as it may express either the sharing of a particular common goal between individual and/or collective actors or the existence of divergent objectives (Ornaghi and Cotellessa, 2000, p. 21). In particular, 'interest' denotes at the same time relationality relativity to others as well as distinctiveness from them (Ornaghi, 1984, p. 2). Johannes Althusius brought this duality of meaning to the fore when he emphasised that the existence of 'something particular' ('*quid peculiare*'; Althusius, 1932 [1614], II.1.20) is a necessary condition of human association in the pursuit of 'common advantage' ('*commodum commune*'; Althusius, 1932 [1614], II.5.21). In its manifold applications, the concept of 'interest' denotes a relationship between the objectives of certain actors and the objectives of others, independently of the degree of convergence or opposition between them. Even 'self-interest' presupposes patterns of interdependence between individual or collective actors in the light of a relational structure, although this structure may result from a shared concern for the protection of individual safety and entitlements (Hume, 1998 [1751]; Tuck, 1993, 2016).

Value systems often express the balance between betweenness and non-betweenness in a given social domain. The ambiguous character of interests makes them a privileged field of investigation when discussing the constitution of the economy, for it is reasonable to assume that the economic constitution primarily reflects the way in which modes of association in the material sphere (and related patterns of division of labour) are projected into the sphere of dispositions and goal-setting. Therefore, they become enmeshed with the dispositions and modes of association that make the division of labour stable and predictable within what can be a relatively extensive time horizon.

The aim of this section is to explore some of the ways in which modes of association in the material sphere (such as the modes of association between capabilities, tasks, and materials-in-process) constitute dispositions and constellations of interests across individuals and/or social groups. At the same time, modes of association are in turn affected by those dispositions and interests once the latter become entrenched in the polity under consideration. As we have seen in Chapter 3, the multi-dimensional character of production highlights plural criteria by which capabilities, tasks, and materials-in-process may be clustered together (or split from one another), and give rise to production networks (see the appendix to that chapter). It is important to realise that in most cases one pattern of aggregation/decomposition does not exclude the simultaneous possibility of other such patterns. For instance, a system of industries defined by the transfer of materials-in-process (including intermediate products) from one industry to another *does not exclude* the possibility of representing the same system of material transfers in terms of vertically integrated sectors cutting through the different industries and highlighting the one-to-one linkages from stocks of materials-in-process and intermediate products to specific final products of the consumption or investment type (Pasinetti, 1980 [1973]; Scazzieri, 1990; Landesmann and Scazzieri, 1993; Cardinale and Scazzieri, 2019).

However, it is reasonable to assume that in each economy, one pattern of aggregation/decomposition will prevail over the others, and that this criterion will significantly influence the mode of association between socio-economic groups in the polity. A polity whose material life gives prominence to its own 'internal' system of industries is likely to be associated with dispositions and interests giving prominence to the coalescence between 'internal' industrial interests rather than to alternative group affiliations. As shown in Chapter 3, alternative patterns of aggregation/decomposition are possible not only for networks of materials-in-process but also for networks of capabilities and networks of tasks. This means that aggregation/decomposition criteria should be given a central role in investigating the emergence or disappearance of modes of association in the material sphere, which in turn highlights the importance of aggregation/decomposition criteria for investigating constellations of dispositions and interests in the economy.

The economic constitution results from the interplay of the prevailing mode of association in the material sphere with the dispositions and interests coherent with that mode of association. This means that any specific mode of association is likely to generate a specific set of individual and group objectives, which in turn supports that mode of association, and/or allows it to change by following certain trajectories but not others. For the purpose of investigating the relationship between modes of association and objectives, we may distinguish between (i) the horizontal interdependencies between industries delivering *mutually needed* intermediate products and (ii) the vertical interdependencies between *sequentially related* production stages leading to a given final output. This distinction provides an example of the relationship between modes of association on the one hand and constellations of dispositions and interests on the other hand.

If horizontal interdependencies prevail in the production sphere, we may expect a mode of association in which dispositions and interests develop under the constraint that the existing system of industries must remain within the range that makes that system sustainable (in the sense of it being capable of replication over time). This notion of interdependence is clearly expressed in the view of the economic system as a 'circular flow', in which all production and consumption activities are mutually dependent and mutually needed. François Quesnay, writing in mid-eighteenth century France, expressed this view in his *Tableau économique* (Quesnay, 1972 [1759]), which represents in a visually explicit way the 'zig-zag' character of the interdependencies brought about by the flows of products delivered by agricultural and manufacturing activities, and re-entering the economic system either through the 'necessary consumption' needed to replace the means of production in those activities or through the luxury consumption of unproductive socio-economic groups (see also Coffman, 2021).

In the later work by Wassily Leontief (Leontief, 1941), which was inspired by Quesnay's *Tableau*, the horizontal character of the interdependencies generated by product flows from one industry to another is explored in the context of a modern industrial economy characterised by a core set of interdependent industries delivering intermediate products to one another (the inter-industry core of the economy). This core set of industries is surrounded by industries that need intermediate inputs provided by the core industries but whose products are not needed in the latter's self-replication. A horizontal system of industries suggests a mode of association in which a hierarchical constellation of interests and dispositions is possible. Activities making up the inter-industry core of the economy are likely to generate a constellation of interests that is compatible with the self-replacement (replicability over time) of the core, and therefore of the whole economic system. On the other hand, the same horizontal structure makes it possible to have multiple 'second-order' constellations of interests associated with the activities that are external to the inter-industry core. In this case, multiple constellations of dispositions and interests reflecting alternative configurations of final demand can be compatible with the self-replacement of given core activities. Interests associated with the core set of industries take precedence over interests generated by alternative configurations of final demand. In short, the interdependencies within the 'horizontal' inter-industry core generate a constellation of *fundamental interests* that circumscribes the cleavages and conflicts that may arise out of the 'peripheral' configurations of final demand.

If, on the other hand, we consider a situation in which vertical linkages prevail in the production domain, we expect a different mode of association, in which dispositions and interests would develop around semi-independent supply chains rather than around mutually dependent activities. In this case, the coherence between the different vertical sequences into which the production system may be decomposed can be achieved through a macroeconomic condition, such as full employment resulting from public expenditure, or full employment generated by diffusion of expenditure flows from certain vertically integrated sectors to the rest of the economy. This situation is one in which (differently from the 'horizontal' case) constraints arising from within the network of productive interdependencies are less prominent, which can make it more difficult for individual supply chains to adjust to a systemic condition of coordination. However, it may still be the case that the interests of individual supply chains (vertically integrated sectors) are contained within a range of systemic feasibility thanks to an external source of purchasing power or to purchasing power generated by one or more vertically integrated sectors but flowing from them to the remaining sectors of the economy.

Vertical linkages can generate dispositions and interests that are remarkably different from those resulting from interdependencies of the horizontal type. In the vertical case, a hierarchy of dispositions and interests is also possible, but it may be completely different from that associated with horizontal interdependence. For example, the decomposition of interests into separate clusters corresponding to different supply chains could be more visible than the aggregation of interests *across* different supply chains. Luigi Pasinetti has argued that in the case of a collection of vertical sectors making use of labour only in the production of final consumer goods (the case of a 'pure labour economy'), coherence between vertical sectors can be achieved through a full employment condition, which in turn may be obtained either by fluke or by direct external policy intervention (Pasinetti, 1993, 2007). It follows that the vertical mode of association can trigger powerful reconfigurations of dispositions and interests depending on context. As we have seen, a constellation of vertical sectors may depend for its maintenance either on the existence of a 'higher order' layer of interests allowing public intervention (say, public expenditure) in support of systemic coherence, or on the working of a trickle-down effect from leading sectors to 'peripheral' sectors. In the latter case, the production structure generates a hierarchical configuration of dispositions and interests that may lead to full employment for the whole economy.

However, it is also possible that certain vertical sectors follow a trajectory independent from that of other sectors, and that the particular interests of the different sectors would sharply diverge. In this case, systemic coherence is difficult to achieve. For instance, the export sector(s) of an export-led economy may have little in common with the 'peripheral' sectors of that economy, which would make the full employment condition across vertical sectors (either by public intervention or trickle-down effects) more difficult to achieve. In this case, it is important to realise that systems of vertically integrated interests *may* or *may not* arise from the same ('horizontal') system of mutually dependent industries. In the former case, the viability condition for the corresponding horizontal system of industries still acts as a powerful 'centre of gravitation' for the prevailing mode of association and the corresponding configuration of interests (see Bianchi and Labory, 2019). Here, conflicts may arise between different 'vertical' interests, but the viability condition for the replicability of the underlying system of industries may act as glue constraining the conflicts between vertical sectors (supply chains) within the range compatible with the viability condition. In the latter case, the vertical sectors may result from lumping together activities distributed across *different* horizontal systems of industries (e.g. across systems of industries belonging to several countries). In this case, plural centres of gravitation may vie with one another, and we can no longer presume that divisions and conflicts will be contained within the range compatible with the replicability of any given system of industries considered in isolation.

4.3 Group Affiliations and Constitutional Arrangements

The previous section of this chapter examined the relationship between the modes of association in the material sphere and the constellations of dispositions and interests that may arise jointly with them. The aim of this section is to analyse the ways in which dispositions and interests related to modes of association can constrain and, at the same time, empower constitutional arrangements in the economic domain. As we have seen, the constitution of a given economy identifies the conditions(s) for the persistence of that economy over time, while also identifying which economic arrangements may be feasible and which ones should be excluded. The forms of interdependence arising from material life are varied, as they encompass a plurality of connectivity patterns at the level of capabilities, tasks, and materials-in-process (including intermediate products) (see Chapter 3). Alternative modes of aggregation/decomposition of capabilities, tasks, and materials-in-process highlight the possibility of *alternative modes of association* corresponding to different criteria of aggregation or decomposition. In turn, alternative modes of association are related to different constellations of dispositions and interests, which may eventually result in different types of group affiliation depending on which mode of association is salient in each context.

This argument entails a step-by-step chain of reasoning. First, it is necessary to identify which *dimension of material organisation* is the dominant one in each context, for modes of association are likely to be different depending on whether they derive primarily from coordination of capabilities, tasks, or materials-in-process. Second, it is necessary to detect which *mode of aggregation/decomposition* is the dominant one in the system under consideration. Third, it is necessary to recognise which *constellation of dispositions and interests* is the dominant one in view of the two previous steps. At this level of investigation, it is important to examine which lines of separation are associated with the dominant mode of association, as those separations would generally determine the economic constitution of the system. This argument reflects the view that interdependencies of production activities are a dominant feature of material life, especially when those activities presuppose an extensive division of labour (Durkheim, 1902). At the same time, prevailing divisions of labour shape to an important extent the dominant group affiliation in society (Simmel, 1955 [1922]). However, both divisions of labour and group affiliations take shape along a plurality of dimensions. Division of labour tends to involve interdependencies at the level of capabilities, tasks, and materials-in-process, while group affiliations reflect the *relative positions* of actors depending on which dimension of interdependence is considered. This greatly complicates the identification of dominant (or most visible) group affiliations in each context. As Georg Simmel noted, "[T]he larger the number of groups to which an individual belongs, the more improbable is it that other persons will exhibit the same combination of group-affiliations, that these particular groups will intersect once again [in another individual]" (Simmel, 1955 [1922], p. 140). Simmel adds that 'as the individual leaves his established position in one primary group, he comes to stand at a point at which many groups "intersect"' (Simmel, 1955 [1922], p. 141).

This feature of group affiliation in a society based on extensive division of labour has important consequences for the relationship between organisation of material life and group affiliation. The position of each actor (or group of actors) relative to other actors (or groups of actors) is different depending on which dimension of activity we consider. For example, the relative positions of actors when performing tasks can be different from their relative positions when we consider the capabilities to be used or the materials to be processed. As we have seen in Chapter 3, capabilities, tasks, and materials-in-process may cluster into subsets that are fully *or* partially overlapping (see the appendix to that chapter). This means that in many contexts interdependencies between capabilities are not fully replicated by interdependencies between tasks and by interdependencies between materials-in-process. This situation highlights the possibility of *alternative* modes of affiliation, depending on what the dominant (or most visible) pattern of interdependence is. As we have seen, any given pattern of interdependence is associated both with complementarities and cleavages between capabilities, tasks, and materials-in-process. This means that the organisation of material life gives rise to association as well as to separation between individuals or groups. Consequently, constellations of dispositions and interests may arise or dissolve depending on the structural dynamics affecting interdependencies within production networks. A given economic constitution determines which modes of association are feasible and which ones are not under the prevailing constellation of dispositions and interests.

This view of the economic constitution is related to the conception of 'material constitution' outlined by the legal scholar Costantino Mortati, who defined it as the result of 'social forces, historically determined, which provide a sufficient guarantee that limitations [in the exercise of power] will be satisfied' (Mortati, 1998, p. 204). Mortati also highlighted the intrinsically dynamic character of a material constitution, which he saw as presupposing 'compromises between opposing principles' (Mortati, 1998, p. 207). This means that a change involving a modified balance between these principles may lead to a change 'in the working of the original constitution' and should be considered 'as the expression of the introduction of a different constitutional arrangement' (Mortati, 1998, p. 207; see also Goldoni and Wilkinson, 2018; Rubinelli, 2019, 2020).[2]

Our conception of the economic constitution builds on Mortati's conception of material constitution, while extending it beyond the consideration of opposed 'social forces' to that of the prevailing mode of association, and of the cultural frames and dispositions characterising human beings in a given social context. This approach is close to the view of law as 'an *ordering framework* rather than an *expression of will*' (Grossi, 2007, p. 15; see also Grossi, 2010 [2007], Grossi, 2021). As Grossi points out,

[t]he distinction between the two ways of describing law is not purely nominal. The former denotes a bottom-up emergence of law and is characterized by the primacy of objective reality in determining the legal order, which otherwise would not be an effective ordering framework but violence and artifice. The latter highlights the expression of a superior will, which descends top-down and may even exert violence on objective reality, being the expression of arbitrariness and artifice. In the view of law as ordering framework, law is custom itself that, when it is considered a value for human association, is generally followed and therefore becomes a social constraint; [law] is no longer the expression of power, but rather the expression of the plurality of forces in a given social set-up. (Grossi, 2007, p. 15 [our translation])[3]

---

[2] Lucia Rubinelli emphasises as follows the coexistence of relative invariance and openness to transformation in Mortati's conception of material constitution: '[i]n aiming for its own maintenance, the material constitution stabilizes itself through the formal constitution, that crystallizes the equilibrium of social forces through institutional structures and protects it through legal procedures. Yet the material constitution also opens itself up to revision and minor changes, to absorb and integrate potentially competing forces and draw them closer to the dominant *fine politico* [political aim]' (Rubinelli, 2019, p. 528).

[3] We may add that, according to Grossi, 'the human being is a subject who, even if embedded in structures and finding in them possible constraints, [is] nonetheless capable to build', and therefore 'to overcome structural impediments' (Grossi, 2018, p. 49 [our translation]). More recently, Grossi has emphasised this viewpoint, arguing that '[t]he constitutional dimension [...] is not a block that has been fixed once [and] for all in its immobility' (Grossi, 2021, p. 172).

An economic constitution can be considered the result of 'compromise' between different modes of association related to clusters and cleavages at the level of capabilities, tasks, and materials-in-process. The dispositions and interests corresponding to different modes of association may give rise to a social space in which several *different* patterns of interdependence are feasible. A given economic constitution is generally compatible with plural cleavages across different group affiliations, provided those cleavages are contained within a range allowing the persistence of the constitution itself. In a nutshell, a given economic constitution is defined in terms of the affiliations and cleavages compatible with that particular balance between different modes of association.

For example, an economic constitution may derive from compromise between aggregation/decomposition modes such that a degree of underutilisation of certain capabilities is allowed, provided the viability condition for reproduction of the materials-in-process network is satisfied. This economic constitution rests on a compromise between (i) interests arising from mutually dependent industries providing one another with intermediate inputs and (ii) interests associated with the system of mutually dependent capabilities. Such an economic arrangement is compatible with a plurality of production structures if they allow for the persistence of the underlying compromise. This could entail a degree of underutilisation of certain capabilities (say, a certain level of labour unemployment), provided that is made acceptable by the availability of unemployment benefits and/or other social welfare provisions. According to some analysts, cleavages are more likely to be compatible with maintaining a given pattern of accommodation between different interests if they are of the 'cross-cutting' type. In this view, group affiliations may be such that individual (or group) *A* has a conflict of interest with individual (or group) *B* on issue *x* but has a common interest with *B* on issue *y*. This case exemplifies the 'cross-cutting' condition that may help to identify a constitutional compromise in a fragmented social domain (Lijphart, 1975 [1968]; Rae and Taylor, 1970; Scazzieri, 1999a, 2003c; Mutz, 2002, 2006; Pabst and Scazzieri, 2016).

According to Arend Lijphart, cross-cutting cleavages have been one important reason for the congruence of Dutch society since the time of the United Provinces (Lijphart, 1975 [1968], 1977). In the framework of our discussion of the economic constitution, one example could be a production economy in which the network of capabilities C is split between a subset C_1 of high-level capabilities and a subset C_2 of low-level capabilities while the network of materials-in-process M is split between a core set of materials M_1 entering one another's transformation and a 'peripheral' subset of materials M_2 entering the production of final consumer goods only. Here we may distinguish between (i) a situation a, in which all processes requiring high-level capabilities require and transform materials belonging to core set M_1, while all processes requiring low-level capabilities C_2 only require materials in subset M_2, and (ii) a situation b, in which processes requiring and transforming materials in M_1 require the low-level capabilities in C_2 while utilisation of the high-level capabilities in C_1 is concentrated in processes requiring materials in M_2.

Situation a gives rise to an economic constitution in which cleavages are *completely overlapping*, so that the cohesion of the whole economic system may require a compromise involving transfers from the high-skilled to the low-skilled processes. The subsistence over time of this economic constitution is likely to depend on the system's ability to maintain transfers from one time period to another. On the other hand, situation b gives rise to an economic constitution in which cleavages are *cross-cutting*, so that the cohesion of the system as a whole may be achieved by a compromise *internal* to the production network, that is, without external interventions balancing the asymmetries between different groups of producers. In the latter case, the sustainability of the economic constitution depends on the balancing achieved by cross-cutting. For example, the switch to a context in which too few high-level capabilities in C_1 require materials in M_2 could make the existing economic constitution unsustainable and may require the introduction of a new constitutional arrangement.

4.4 A Constitutional Taxonomy

As we have seen, the economic constitution can be defined as the relatively stable compromise between modes of association that allows economic interdependencies to have a degree of persistence despite changing weights between the different components of the economy. The previous section highlighted the distinction between horizontal vs. vertical modes of association as well as the distinction between internal vs. external compromises supporting the economic constitution. The two distinctions generate the set of constitutional possibilities set out in Table 4.1.

Table 4.1 *A taxonomy of economic constitutions*

	Internal balance	External balance
Horizontal association	Closed non-hierarchical	Open non-hierarchical
Vertical association	Closed hierarchical	Open hierarchical

The types of economic constitution shown in Table 4.1 arise from different combinations between modes of association and patterns of constitutional settlement. The economic constitution that combines the horizontal mode of association with internal balance highlights a settlement in which the reciprocal dependencies between activities make the socioeconomic network a self-contained system whose replicability over time presupposes the reproducibility of materials-in-process, the maintenance of capabilities, and the replicability of tasks.[4] The horizontal mode of association can also be combined with a constitutional settlement external to the network. In this case, the maintenance conditions internal to the network are no longer in the foreground, as capabilities and materials-in-process may be obtained from outside the network. Here the economy comes to depend on the existence of an external economic settlement that guarantees the outsourcing of capabilities and materials-in-process through international exchanges or other forms of cross-system transfer of goods and services. In this case, the internal coordination of capabilities, tasks, and materials-in-process presupposes the working of an 'external' arrangement with outside actors.

The distinction between internal and external constitution is also relevant for vertical modes of association. A socioeconomic network in which the vertical mode of association is the dominant one is likely to generate a constellation of interests that may be conducive either to an internal or to an external settlement. In the former case (internal settlement), the mutual fitting of production activities may be achieved through an *internal agency*, ensuring that the proportions between

---

[4] Reproducibility of materials-in-process is guaranteed by the Hawkins-Simon 'viability' condition (Hawkins and Simon, 1949), maintenance of capabilities may be achieved through maintenance of capability funds (such as a society's infrastructural endowment), and replicability of tasks may result from maintenance of capability funds combined with the reproduction of materials-in-process needed for task performance.

vertically integrated sectors (as defined above) are compatible with a condition of systemic coherence (for instance, with full employment).[5] In the latter case (external settlement), the mutual fitting of vertical sequences of fabrication stages may be achieved through an *external agency* ensuring the availability of the capabilities, tasks, and materials-in-process needed in each vertically integrated sector independently of whether the commodity stocks in each sector are produced in the same 'horizontal' system of interdependent industries. In this case, a working economic constitution presupposes one or more international supply chains able to deliver to internal sectors the required capabilities and materials-in-process (which would enable capabilities to perform the required tasks). This type of economic constitution is compatible with asymmetric coordination of the requests and procurements of capabilities and materials-in-process across different economic systems. In this case, successful requests and procurements presuppose a degree of mutual fitting between the internal constitution of each production network and the external settlements sustaining the wider system in which those networks are embedded.

4.5 The Economy as a 'Constituted' Body

The argument of the previous section draws on the idea that group affiliations are central to the working of the economy. The modes of association that determine the way in which goods and services are provided reflect the prevailing patterns of group affiliation while at the same time being a critical influence in determining the way in which affiliations can change over time. The coevolution of group affiliations and modes of association in the material sphere gives shape to the economy as a 'constituted body', in the sense of a system of mutually dependent practices defined by relationships of complementarity and by a given hierarchy of motions between its elements.

---

[5] Luigi Pasinetti highlights in this connection a 'fundamental macroeconomic condition' ensuring full employment under changing technical coefficients for labour utilisation (l_is) and changing per capita consumption of consumer goods (c_is). This condition ($\Sigma c_i l_i = 1$), which is obtained mathematically by solving the system of equations corresponding to a set of n productive sectors in the absence of inter-sectoral linkages, highlights the strictly macroeconomic character of the association between the different sectors, seeing that the condition holds independently of the number of sectors in the economic system under consideration (Pasinetti, 1993, pp. 20–22).

The *economic body* of a given polity is a complex system of inter-dependent activities whose properties cannot be derived from the consideration of individual activities only, nor from the consideration of direct interactions between them. Rather, the activities within the economic body are arranged in a system defined by a particular *hierarchy* of relationships and by a particular *sequence* in which the different activities can change in content, direction, and intensity.

The economic body is a system of interdependent actors and processes for whose investigation the principles of *organised complexity* provide a useful analytical benchmark. Economic actors are not such that 'each [...] has a behaviour which is individually erratic, or perhaps totally unknown' (Weaver, 1948, p. 538). On the contrary, actors are 'interrelated in a complicated, but nevertheless not in helter-skelter, fashion' so as to form 'an organic whole' (Weaver, 1948, p. 539). A distinctive feature of organised complexity is that 'complexity frequently takes the form of hierarchy, and that hierarchic systems have some common properties that are independent of their specific content' (Simon, 1962, p. 468; see also Baas, 1994; Barabási and Albert, 1999; Barabási, 2007; Scazzieri, 2021). The economic body is an instance of organised complexity, since actors and processes are mutually dependent according to a relatively persistent hierarchical pattern. Actors interact with one another in ways that reflect their persistent or mutable identity, dispositions, and membership in particular groups within the economic body. This multi-layered, hierarchical structure makes the material life of the polity reflect the coexistence of strong and weak connections between individual or collective actors.

Actors are responsive to factors of change according to sequential patterns that reflect their respective positions within the economic body. At any given level of hierarchy, actors are likely to respond to a given dynamic impulse and to one another's reaction to it. On the other hand, the *timing* of their response is constrained by the responses of actors who belong to other layers of the hierarchy. Responses may be different depending on the character of each dynamic impulse, but will always be consistent with the relative positions of actors in the hierarchy of possible motions and with their degree of rigidity relative to one another. The relative persistence of the condition of certain actors relative to others generates a specific 'order of sequence' in the repercussions of any dynamic impulse as it works itself through the internal structure of the economic body (see also Myrdal, 1939, p. 27).

The relative invariance of certain elements relative to others plays a central role in the organised complexity of the economy and makes its 'constitution' open to changes along certain directions while excluding others. The reason is that, given relative invariance, any trajectory triggered by a dynamic impulse must belong

to a *limited set of feasible transformations* [...] [T]he impulse from which the original state of the economy is modified may be purely exogenous but the actual process of transformation can be explained in terms of the "dynamic" characteristics of the existing structure (that is in terms of the specific paths of the feasible transformations that are compatible with [the system's] description). (Landesmann and Scazzieri, 1990, p. 96 [added emphasis])

This property entails a specific ranking of the *relative motions* of individual and collective actors within the economy. Such ranking does not necessarily affect the direction and speed of transformation of those actors but does constrain which actors can move first and which ones can move later. In short, the mutual conditioning of motions 'identifies a virtual sequence of transformations that must be followed whenever the system under consideration is subject to a source of change' (Landesmann and Scazzieri, 1990, p. 96). This principle of *relative structural invariance* is a 'general postulate' in the analysis of economic structures whose state may be changed by exogenous impulses but whose 'actual process of transformation [is to be] explained in terms of the "dynamic" characteristics of the existing structure (that is in terms of the specific paths of feasible transformations that are compatible with [the system's] description' (Landesmann and Scazzieri, 1990, p. 96).

The above argument has far-reaching implications for the dynamic trajectories that are possible within the economic body, for any 'constituted' body will be associated with a given distribution of invariances across individual or collective actors. There is a close relationship between the economic constitution of a given polity and the distribution of invariances among its individual or collective components. This means that each economic constitution is distinguished by the particular set of feasible transformations that are open to it. An important consequence is that any 'constituted' economic body will be flexible with respect to transformations compatible with it, and rigid relative to transformations that would require a different constitutional settlement. The relationship between the *variety* of relative positions compatible with the constitution of the economic body and the *constraints* on those relative positions, which that constitution generates, is at the source of the relationship between the partial interests of particular stakeholders and the 'systemic interest' of the overall economy.[6]

For example, a given economic constitution is compatible with changing relative weights between industries within the range that is compatible with the viability condition linked to the technology in use (see Chapter 3). However, other structural dynamics may drive the economy away from the range of variation in industrial weights compatible with the viability condition of the political economy under consideration. This would be the case if the political economy is moving to a different constitution, or even if it is in the process of losing its distinctiveness by entering a domain shaped by the ordering principles of an external settlement, for example, joining a currency union and adopting its shared set of rules.

Relative structural invariance is key to the intertwining of persistence and change that characterises the constitution of political economies, for the ordering principles defining a political economy shape the types of motion that take place within its structure. At the same time, these ordering principles determine which elements of the economy (such as industries or vertical supply chains) are more persistent than others and may therefore work as 'attractors' when a dynamic process starts displacing the political economy from its given constitution, opening way to the embedding of different ordering principles. This last point characterises the dynamics of hierarchically ordered systems. As noted by Herbert Simon, a system in which there are relatively stable 'subassemblies' of elements at intermediate levels of aggregation (what Simon calls 'stable intermediate forms') is more likely to persistently embed transformations than systems in which all elements are immediately responsive to dynamic impulses (Simon, 1962; see also Venkatachalam and Kumar, 2021). In a complementary perspective,

---

[6] The relationship between partial interests and 'systemic interest' is different from what would be a relationship between partial (or sectoral) interests and collective interest, particularly as the 'systemic interest' is a structural condition that is not necessarily translated into an objective (Cardinale, 2017, 2018; see also Cardinale and Coffman, 2014).

the mathematician Michele Caputo emphasised the role of 'memory' in dynamic system behaviour, pointing out that memory can work as an attractor so that in a system including several economies, the economies with the longest memory (these would be the more persistent 'stable intermediate forms' in Simon's theory) tend to attract the 'short memory' (least persistent) economies (Caputo, 2019; see also Scazzieri, 2020b).

The character and distribution of relative invariances within each economy give rise to the response pattern of that economy to dynamic impulses. Simon's conception of 'stable intermediate forms' and Caputo's conception of 'memory' are relevant in this context, for the relative invariances within the economic body generate constellations of actors that are *at the same time* capable of withstanding disturbances and of making the economy 'reboot' after a shock.[7] An economic constitution whose internal composition shows strong invariances of certain intermediate structures (sub-systems) relative to others is *at the same time* less vulnerable to negative shocks (disturbances would primarily and/or initially have a local effect) and more receptive to positive shocks (e.g. innovations may be introduced gradually without requiring the immediate and system-wide overhaul of relative positions and practices). Differently from this pattern, an economic constitution whose internal composition does not have relatively persistent intermediate structures (sub-systems) would be more vulnerable to disturbances (an initial disturbance may lead to the immediate disruption of the whole system) *and* less receptive to deep transformations (as these transformations would require the overhaul of relative positions and established practices across the economy) (see also Cardinale and Scazzieri, 2019).

To conclude on this point: differences in relative invariances between components of a 'constituted' economic body entail sharply different patterns of transformation in the relationship between the whole economy and its intermediate structures as the latter respond to dynamic triggers (see also Kauffman, 1990; Reggiani, 2013; Caputo, 2019; Scazzieri, 2020b, 2021). In the case of relatively persistent intermediate structures, the dynamic impulses may be 'contained'

---

[7] It is for this reason that 'stable intermediate forms' allow structures to evolve 'much more rapidly if there are intermediate stable forms than if there are not' (Simon, 1962, p. 473).

within the existing constitution. A disturbance would not abruptly modify a pre-existing trajectory of constitutional changes: negative shocks may be gradually absorbed while positive shocks may lead to the gradual transformation of all elements of the economic body along a path in which sudden ruptures can be excluded. Economic bodies constituted by relatively persistent intermediate structures (such as resilient group affiliations or productive sectors) are likely to follow a relatively smooth path of transformation. On the other hand, economic bodies whose intermediate structures are weaker and less developed tend to be more immediately responsive to dynamic impulses, and are therefore more likely to experience sudden ruptures and/or divergences from past trajectories (see also Di Tommaso et al., 2020).

The constitution of economic bodies can be widely different depending on the role performed by intermediate structures between the micro and macro levels. As we have seen, intermediate social structures must have a degree of 'self-containment', making them relatively stable within the system embedding them. A condition for their relative invariance is the long-term character of the relations between individual or collective actors independent of contingent occurrences, or even disagreements and conflicts. In the legal field, relational contract theory has brought to light that the web of relations between actors 'has become a minisociety with a vast array of norms beyond the norm centered on exchange and its immediate processes' (McNeil, 1978, p. 901; see also McNeil, 1980, 1985, 2000; Lake, 1999; Maskin and Tirole, 1999). The contribution of intermediate structures (akin to Simon's 'intermediate forms') to the stability of the economy as a 'constituted' body is consistent with the relational character of the constitutionalist approach to the body politic and is far removed from the 'discrete transaction' approach of contractualism (see Chapter 5 below; see also Pabst, 2014, 2018a).

The relationship between the 'economic body' and the body politic is central to the structure and working of a political economy and can take a variety of forms. A broad classification of political economies can be useful in this connection. We will distinguish three fundamental types of such a relationship. First, there are political economies whose constitution privileges the complementarities between internal actors and the viability condition for replicating the interdependencies between those actors. In these economic constitutions, the economic body coincides with the body politic, and the identification of stable intermediate forms is likely to reflect the distinction between actors and activities belonging to a core set of essential ('strategic') intermediate structures on the one hand, and 'peripheral' actors and activities on the other hand. This condition is typical to division of labour within the city state or the nation state. In this case, the economic constitution is a scheme of interdependencies reflecting the pattern of specialisation between workers or workers' groups who are also members of the same body politic, and it is politically regulated by the same jurisdiction. Anthony Black argued that in the case of medieval city states, intermediate structures had a fundamental role in creating a sense of community that gradually developed into a more general allegiance to the whole political unit:

a distinctive and clearly defined notion of community developed during the take-off period of the urban movement, and was applied indifferently to towns of all sizes, to villages and to guilds. Popular and official opinion in towns appears to have regarded such a community as by its very existence having a moral right to corporate status, to juridical personality, to the ownership of collective property, and also a moral right to elect its own rulers and govern its internal affairs. This was part of the secret behind the rapid spread of the word universitates to describe such groups. (Black, 1984, p. 45)

Indeed, 'in German cities, and in Italian cities which escaped despotism, the council remained the centre of government, to which later on craft guilds clamoured for admission' (Black, 1984, p. 48). At the root of this process Black finds a 'politicization of guild values': '[a guild] was no longer "brotherhood" in the sense of a commitment to specific persons [...] but rather a readiness to be friendly to others just because they are one's fellow citizens. It was a social relationship under the rule of law' (Black, 1984, p. 77). However, this development from economic to political allegiance cannot be taken for granted, as in certain cases membership in intermediate institutions was considered as more primary than membership in political and legal structures (Gierke, 1900, especially pp. 1–100; Gierke, 1973, especially pp. 143–160; Maitland, 2003; Böckenförde, 1982).

In a second type of political economy, the economic constitution privileges the complementarities between internal and external actors. In this case, a viability condition is less visible, and the interdependence between actors is associated with a criterion of

'comparative advantage'. This criterion primarily reflects the allocation by transfer of resources or final products between polities engaged
in international trade. Intermediate structures can arise also in this
type of economic constitution, but they are circumscribed to actors
specialising in trade activities, organised in trade guilds, and following
a set of norms specific to them (the so-called *lex mercatoria*, or the
Law Merchant; see Trakman, 2003). Intermediate structures of this
type may link otherwise distant individuals or groups. The knowledge of a common language, or the sharing of a common culture, may
facilitate the emergence of such intermediate structures, as was the
case of twelfth-century Maghribi traders exchanging goods and establishing marriage ties with traders in Malabar (see Goitein 1967, vol. I,
pp. 167 and 169; see also Chauduri, 1985). Other examples are medieval long-distance trade along the Silk Road (de La Vaissière, 2004)
and contemporary global commerce (Sassen, 2001) (see also Pabst and
Scazzieri, 2012). In this type of political economies, the relationship
between the economic body and the body politic remains open-ended.
In certain cases, the body politic aims to promote comparative advantage in international trade by promoting internal competition and
international free trade. In other cases, the sovereign authority takes a
proactive attitude towards comparative advantage and tries to achieve
favourable terms of trade by power politics and monopolistic actions
(Hont, 2010, 2015). Here, the economic constitution reveals complementarities based on the international division of labour and generating intermediate structures across polities involved in interdependent
activities. In this case, viability may again be important, but it is often
associated with intermediate cross-polity structures rather than with
the activities carried out in any particular polity of the 'cosmopolis' in
question.

Karl Polanyi examined a third type of economic constitution when
investigating patterns of internal and external trade embedded within
a dense network of social and political relationships (Polanyi, 1957a,
1957b). This conceptual framework is compatible with a plurality of
trading practices, including gift trade, administered trade, and market trade, and highlights '[p]olitical, social, and administrative factors, insofar as they channel the movements of goods (and have an
influence on price formation)' (Rotstein, 1970, p. 126). Explicit or
implicit tributary systems can be considered as instances of partially
'marketless' trading combining features of gift trade, in which 'the

organization of trading is [...] usually ceremonial, involving mutual presentation; embassies; [and] political dealings between chiefs or kings' (Polanyi, 1957b, p. 262), with features of 'administered trade' whose foundation is 'in treaty relationships that are more or less formal' (Polanyi, 1957b, p. 262). A tributary system can be considered a means to implement a pattern of division of labour that combines the vertical mode of association with the viability linked to the external procurement of capabilities and materials-in-process (Fairbank, 1941; Buzan and Little, 2000; Yongjin and Buzan, 2012; Wang, 2014; Chochoy, 2015).

These three types of economic constitution differ widely in terms of the working of intermediate structures in driving constitutional dynamics. Constitutions of the first type allow trajectories compatible with changes in the proportions between activities that are compatible with the viability condition for a polity-bound economic body. Constitutions of the second type allow constitutional changes independent of viability conditions and tied to conditions for the efficient allocation of given resources between trading polities. Constitutions of the third type may prompt trajectories of constitutional change guided by a viability condition encompassing all polities involved, or a limited collection of them. The dynamics of economic constitutions of this third type are characteristically open. A plurality of intermediate structures may develop across different political bodies. If enough intermediate structures are developed across polities and the lines of separation between them are cross-cutting (Rae and Taylor, 1970; Lijphart, 1977, 2012; see also Section 4.3 above), it is likely that no political body will be fully hegemonic or entirely powerless. This is a situation in which an economic constitution encompassing several political bodies may gradually evolve into a corresponding political constitution. However, it is also possible that intermediate structures will be undeveloped, or that lines of separation will *not* be cross-cutting. In this case, the formation of an encompassing political constitution is less likely, or it may generate strongly asymmetrical structures.

Dynamic impulses can have very different responses in the three cases above. In a polity-bound economic body, impulses can be contained within the system as long as they do not disrupt the intermediate structure at the core of the economy. In a cross-polity economic body, intermediate structures do not arise beyond the polity level, except for cross-polity structures (such as the World Trade Organisation) that are set up to regulate trade activities. In economic bodies constituted by intermediate structures encompassing several different polities (such as different states), the propagation of dynamic impulses is characteristically open ended: it may be contained within certain structures, or uniformly spread across structures, or even differently distributed between structures. It is reasonable to conjecture that the pattern of propagation within intermediate structures spanning different jurisdictions would reflect the extent to which coordinated policy actions can be carried out across different polities. Polities able to coordinate are more likely to share the 'advantage' of stable intermediate forms, both by containing negative shocks and by ensuring that positive impulses (such as innovation waves) are distributed to activities external to the intermediate structures directly affected. On the other hand, lack of coordination is likely to generate propagation patterns characterized by an uneven distribution of gains and losses across jurisdictions.

4.6 The Constitutional Framing of Economic Policy

A given economic constitution provides the framework in which different modes of association may coexist, giving rise to a relatively stable constellation of dispositions and interests, and to a relatively stable division of labour between individuals, as well as between social groups. One important feature of economic constitution is its *potentially dynamic* character. Any given constellation of dispositions and interests is generally compatible with several coordination arrangements of capabilities, tasks, and materials-in-process. It also identifies the range of transformations in division of labour compatible with a particular economic constitution, while also identifying which patterns of division of labour would *not* be compatible with it.

The intertwining of modes of association (patterns of division of labour) and constellations of dispositions/interests is central to the character of the economic constitution and its dynamics over time. Here it is useful to distinguish between two types of constraints: one type related to constellations of dispositions and interests and the other related to modes of association. Under certain conditions, dispositions and interests have a degree of persistence that entrench the prevailing mode of association, making it difficult to change the coordination arrangements for capabilities, tasks, and materials-in-process. Under other conditions, it is the prevailing mode of association that has a degree of persistence, which could make it difficult to map possible changes in the dispositions and interests of individuals or groups. In general, however, both the prevailing mode of association and the dominant constellation of dispositions and interests have a degree of flexibility that may allow, respectively, some variability in dispositions and interests for any given mode of association and some variability in mode of association for any given constellation of dispositions and interests.

Starting with a given mode of association (a pattern of division of labour entailing a given coordination of capabilities, tasks, and materials-in-process), it may be possible to reshuffle the existing constellation of dispositions and interests, making it possible for individuals and groups to envisage, and eventually to implement, a transformation in the coordination of capabilities, tasks, and materials-in-process (a structural dynamic of the production network). Alternatively, starting with a given constellation of dispositions and interests, it may be feasible to reshuffle the existing mode of association (the existing pattern of coordination between capabilities, tasks, and materials-in-process), making it possible for individuals and groups to shift to a different constellation of dispositions and interests (a change of the economic constitution).[8]

The resilience of modes of association and constellations of dispositions and interests is a central element in explaining the institutional conditions for changes in the production network, and the material conditions for changes in dispositions and interests. The economic constitution results from intertwining a mode of association (or combination of different modes of association) with a particular constellation of dispositions and interests. A situation in which plural modes of association coexist in the same economy is likely to be compatible

---

[8] The distinction between 'progressive' and 'regressive' coalitions (Bianchi and Miller, 1996) is relevant to the above discussion of the relationship between mode of association and constellation of interests. Entrenched interests (either because of the prevailing mode of association or because of ossified relative dispositions) are likely to lead to regressive coalitions, while situations in which constellations of interests are flexible (either because of flexible relative dispositions or because of an accommodating pattern of division of labour) are likely to lead to coalitions of the progressive type.

with several constellations of dispositions and interests, while a single mode of association is likely to show features of rigidity in the associated constellation of dispositions and interests.

The open relationship between mode of association and constellation of dispositions and interests is at the root of the constitutional framing of economic policy. Economic policy may be defined as the conceiving and implementing of collective actions concerning the material life of the polity (Tinbergen, 1952; Amable, 2018; Dubois, 2018). The constitutional character of economic policy derives from the consideration of policy-making as an exercise that goes beyond the setting of a desired state of the economy subject to constraints (e.g. setting the objective of employment maximization in an economic system subject to a balanced State budget condition) by also encompassing the setting of an 'acceptable' trajectory that the economy should follow in order to reach that desired state.

This means that, from a constitutional perspective, there will be threshold values associated with the different policy tools as well as threshold values associated with the different dimensions of the end state of the economy. These threshold values reflect the constitutional settlement of the economy at any given time. For example, an economic constitution characterised by flexible coordination of capabilities, tasks, and materials-in-process, and by a correspondingly flexible constellation of dispositions and interests, could allow a higher 'socially acceptable' rate of unemployment than a constitution characterised by a relatively invariant coordination of capabilities, tasks, and materials-in-process and by a correspondingly invariant constellation of dispositions and interests. In any given economic constitution, we may find that the attainment of certain policy objectives (say, the maximization of the macroeconomic growth rate) is subject to boundary values for certain policy variables (such as the macroeconomic rate of inflation or the ratio of public debt to gross domestic product) (Tinbergen, 1952; Marzetti Dall'Aste Brandolini, 2011, pp. 318–320; Pabst and Scazzieri, 2016, pp. 351–354; Cardinale and Landesmann, 2017, 2022).

Certain policy tools may or may not be feasible, depending on the existing economic constitution. For example, a given policy tool may presuppose the dominance of the horizontal *or* the vertical mode of association, and it may require that the mode of association be of the internal *or* the external type (see Section 4.4 of this chapter).

An economic constitution characterised by a horizontal mode of association (horizontal division of labour between interdependent activities) and by non-hierarchical interdependencies of the 'internal' type may be more receptive to policy measures aimed at achieving a fully integrated socioeconomic network independent of external trade relationships than would be the case with a constitution characterised by a horizontal mode of association and non-hierarchical interdependencies of the 'external' type. On the other hand, the latter may be more receptive to policy measures aimed at furthering the integration between the internal production network and the external procurement of goods and services. Alternative approaches to industrial policy may provide an instance of the above duality: in the former case, policy measures may directly support domestic industries and their reciprocal procurement requirements; in the latter case, policies may privilege 'universal' incentives supporting the improvement and diffusion of capabilities, and making the internal production network more responsive to external procurement conditions.

PART II

Political Spaces and Policy Actions

5 A Political Economy of the Body Politic

5.1 The Human Condition of Sociability

This chapter outlines a political economy of the body politic based on the primacy of association, which we define as the network of relational opportunities, constraints, and affordances involved in social interdependence. Our conception of the body politic focuses on the older sense of *oikonomia*, that is to say, an organised plurality of actors who are governed by ordering principles that aim to achieve correct proportions between the different levels of agency and thereby ensure the viability of the body politic over time. We contrast this 'constitutionalist' conception with 'contractualist' conceptions of the body politic, which emphasise the formal arrangements between individual or collective units of society. Paolo Grossi describes the contrast as one between 'the unitary subject of natural law, an a-historical and thus merely virtual subject, a model of human being, and nothing more' and 'an intrinsically *relational* [original emphasis] entity, fully embedded in a cultural, social and economic context, seen in conjunction with the other, the others, and connected to them by necessary and close-fitting bonds' (Grossi, 2010, p. 617; see also Grossi, 2021, pp. 166–167).

By contrast with the contractualist conceptions of the body politic, we argue that association and the constitution of interests are plural and hybrid (Pabst and Scazzieri, 2016). This point of view differs from the contractualist tradition primarily because of an alternative approach to individuality and agency. Our approach accentuates the interdependencies and institutions in which individuals and/or social groups are embedded, whereas contractualism emphasises individual preferences and transactions. The difference between association and contract has far-reaching implications for the issue of political agency in the context of the plural spaces of debate, decision, and action that constitute the polity. Our argument is that the plurality of spaces in which political decisions and actions are made rests on diverse forms of human association. These forms give rise to intermediary bodies that are the sources of political agency. Such bodies are constituted by social and intergenerational ties, which are more open ended and view informal norms as more primary than legally enforceable commitments whereas contractual arrangements tend to be time-bound and privilege legal enforcement over social constraints. As such, intermediary institutions embody a human disposition to pursue shared ends by way of collective action over time and space – spanning different generations as well as places. The set of intergenerational and cross-spatial arrangements reflects the idea of a partnership based on relationships embedded in societal structures rather than the notion of a purely formal social contract between 'virtual' individual actors beyond space and time.

The latter can be based on an a-social 'state of nature' in which original disorder or even violence is regulated by the will of a single sovereign – of which Hobbes's *Leviathan* is emblematic (Hobbes, 1998 [1651]). Or else it can rest on a conception of a social condition of humankind, as for Rousseau, who argued that individuals are born free but 'everywhere live in bondage' (*Du contrat social*, Rousseau, 1997 [1762]). The reason is that life in society inevitably leads to interpersonal comparison, rivalry, and ultimately conflict with other individuals. As Rousseau writes, '[i]n a word, there arose rivalry and competition on the one hand, and conflicting interests on the other, together with a secret desire on both of profiting at the expense of others' (*Discours sur l'origine et les fondements de l'inégalité parmi les hommes*, Rousseau, 1923 [1755], p. 218). This can only be regulated by a consensus that emerges from the aggregation of individuals – exemplified by Rousseau's *volonté générale*. Either way, the contractualist tradition views the body politic as being constituted by a collective person (Leviathan) or by a collection of individuals (Rousseau) rather than by persons or groups embedded within linkages and bonds at multiple levels of association.

Contrary to the contractualist tradition, we argue that association of individuals and/or groups is part of the human condition (Arendt, 1958): human actions and thoughts are intrinsically social by virtue of human beings living in a humanly made environment and by virtue of the disposition to associate around deliberately or implicitly adopted shared ends. As Hannah Arendt argued:

[t]he *vita activa*, human life in so far as it is actively engaged in doing some-thing, is always rooted in a world of men and of man-made things which it never leaves or altogether transcends. The things and men form the envi-ronment for each of man'activities, which would be pointless without such location; yet this environment, the world into which we are born, would not exist without the human activity which produced it, as in the case of fabricated things; which takes care of it, as in the case of cultivated land; or which established it though organization, as in the case of the body politic. No human life [...] is possible without a world which directly or indirectly testifies to the presence of other human beings. (Arendt, 1958, p. 22)

Political life involves sociability. In turn, it presupposes a type of sociability that makes association a condition for the pursuit of ends. However, these ends are always contested, which involves both coop-eration and conflict. The complex interaction of rights and obligations involved in social and political relations requires more than legal-contractual ties because trust and cooperation cannot be mandated by law or enforced through coercive means, as Ralph Cudworth con-tended *contra* Hobbes (Cudworth, 1743 [1678]). Human sociability is a necessary condition for the formation of personal identity and the common building of a society, polity, and economy.

One focus in this chapter is on the human disposition towards *mutual recognition* rather than the mere pursuit of 'influence' through political power or economic wealth. Mutual recognition implies that humans are relational beings, embedded in relationships that enable them to organise social, political, and economic associations. Therefore, the conception of human being that underpins the idea of association emphasises the relational nature of human beings and overcomes the idea that humans are either isolated individuals or subsumed under a single collective body. In other words, humanity is a complex compact of relational beings bound together by a common outlook – a natural desire for mutual recognition and prosperity shared within smaller or larger groups, which encompasses a hierarchy of different social spheres and eventually strives for, or adjusts to, a collective aim of the polity as a whole (the 'public good'). The following passage from Antonio Genovesi's *Lezioni di economia civile* expresses this conception well:

[e]very person has a natural and intrinsic obligation to study how to procure his happiness; but the political body is made of persons; therefore the entire political body and each of its members is obligated to do his part, i.e. all that he knows and can do for common prosperity, as long as that which is

done does not offend the rights of the other civil bodies. This obligation, from the civil body, with beautiful and divine ties, returns to each family and each person for the common pacts of the society. Each family and every person are under two obligations to do that which they can to procure public happiness: one comes from within nature, and the other comes from the subsequent pacts of communities. A third obligation can be added, that of one's own utility. That which Shaftesbury [*Inquiry of Virtue and Merit*] said will be eternally true: he said that the true utility is the daughter of virtue; because it is eternally true that the great depth of man is the love for those with whom he lives. This is the love that is the daughter of virtue. (Genovesi 2013 [1765–1767], pp. 30–31; see also Shaftesbury, 1790 [1699])

Section 5.2 of this chapter presents a critique of contractualism in contemporary political economy, considering in particular the separation of economics from politics and the reduction of political economy to instrumental rationality and maximising choice. Section 5.3 critically engages with the foundations of contractualism in political economy, with a focus on some elements in the writings of Machiavelli, Hobbes, Locke, Rousseau, and Hegel. Section 5.4 builds on Chapter 2 and turns to the work of Paolo Mattia Doria and Antonio Genovesi, referring in particular to Genovesi's definition of civil economy as 'the political science of the economy and commerce' (Genovesi, 2013 [1765–1767], p. 11). This section develops Doria's and Genovesi's analysis of the interlocking institutions that channel human dispositions within the body politic. Section 5.5 considers the formation of a non-contractualist view of the evolution of civil life in the writings of David Hume, Adam Smith, Adam Ferguson, Cesare Beccaria, and Gaetano Filangieri. Section 5.6 draws on elements in the thought of Montesquieu, Burke, and Tocqueville to conceptualise the primacy of intermediate affiliations in the development of the body politic. Section 5.7 concludes the chapter with reflections on the primacy of a general theory of human association encompassing plural levels of aggregation in society.

5.2 Contractualism and Contemporary Political Economy

Political economy differs from both economics and politics. Economics, in the version of it that John Hicks labelled as *catallactics* (Hicks, 1975, 1982 [1976]), primarily denotes decision-making about the allocation of resources between *individuals*, whereas politics concerns collective decision-making about the distribution of power and resources between different *groups* in society (Green and Shapiro, 1994). Both fields are seen as largely self-contained spaces governed by instrumental rationality. They are characterised by the overriding goal of individual utility or collective welfare maximisation and a trade-off between rival interests – a zero-sun game of winners versus losers in which conflict is more fundamental than mutual adjustment and cooperation.

This approach denies political economy an autonomous space of inquiry and leads either to the absorption of politics into economics or its opposite (e.g. respectively, North, Wallis, and Weingast, 2010; Blyth, 2013). Either way, the distinction between economics and politics gives way to a dualism that brackets out of relevance the multilayered structure of social relations in which both the economy and the polity are embedded. However, political economy can in principle straddle the disciplinary divide between economics and politics because it draws attention to the social relations that underpin the state's strategic and administrative activities and the instrumental activities in the economic sphere (Pabst and Scazzieri, 2012; Pabst, 2014).

Contractualism views markets, states, and individuals as foundational categories that constitute the economic-political domain. However, what remains unexplained is, first, why these categories are – or should be – seen as given and, secondly, on what type of social relations they depend, that is, the manifold and complex social linkages that underpin the interdependence of individuals and/or groups. For this reason, the contractualist conception of political economy focuses on the purely contractual arrangements between market agents or political actors at the expense of the social bonds on which both economic and political relationships ultimately rely (Pabst, 2018a). As we argued in Chapter 1, contractualism ends up subsuming the social domain under the logic of exchange or the logic of power, or indeed both at once.

Here we can go further and make the point that contractualist theories ignore the pre-existing social linkages in which individuals are embedded and which are *not* a matter of personal choice at each point in time. These linkages provide opportunities, constraints, and affordances in relation to conflict and cooperation. A focus on pre-existing social ties can overcome a series of dualisms that characterise contemporary conceptions of political economy, including instrumental *versus* the non-instrumental action, vertical *versus* horizontal interaction, intended *versus* non-intended outcomes, and interdependence between homogeneous *versus* interdependence between heterogeneous actors.

These and other dualisms fail to reflect the complex connections between individuals and/or social groups on which the polity and the economy rest.

The above argument points to a divide between alternative conceptions of political economy. The partitioning of social reality into foundational categories such as individuals, markets, and states correlates with the strict separation of academic disciplines that characterises the relationship between modern economics and modern political science. This disciplinary divide has deepened since the 1870s Marginalist revolution in economic theory, insofar as the theory of rational (economic or political) choice moved the agenda away from the classical analysis of system-wise opportunities and constraints and directed it firmly towards the study of the allocation of given resources/capabilities between alternative uses (Collison Black et al., 1973; Dobb, 1973; Blaug, 1997). In this manner, marginalism (and, more generally, the rational choice research programme) shifted the emphasis away from the consideration of different systems with their own specific production and exchange relationships towards the claim that all value depends on preference rankings and deliberate comparisons (as in marginal utility theory). This approach made economic analysis focus on maximising choice within a particular system of opportunities and constraints and turned it away from the structural interdependencies that limit human agency. In reality, system-wide opportunities and constraints are associated with different institutional and organisational patterns that affect division of labour and exchange. Therefore, from a constitutionalist perspective, each system encompasses alternative *political economies* that move beyond the simplified dichotomy of markets versus state and encompass a plurality of economic and political spaces associated with the intermediate associations within the social body (Pabst and Scazzieri, 2012).

The lack of plural spaces and the limits on political agency, which the 'catallactic' approach to economics favoured, highlights a wider problem of contractualist approaches. Since the end of the nineteenth century, the body of social sciences (notably economics, politics, and social theory) has become increasingly fragmented under the pressure of increasing autonomy and ever-greater specialisation, both by fields of inquiry and by analytical tools. However, the respective 'objects of study' (the economy, the polity, and society) are closely intertwined with one another. More fundamentally, purely contractualist arrangements that are abstracted from social linkages bring about a situation wherein individuals and/or groups are at once more interdependent in the market sphere and less embedded in intermediate economic and political bodies. As a matter of fact, these bodies are key in defining the boundaries of the economic system and its different institutional and organisation patterns that affect the division of labour and exchange. In the words of Lorenzo Ornaghi (1990, p. 25 [original italics]),

[t]hrough the permanent interaction between political institutions and structure, individual and collective actions coalesce into a specific 'economic system' that can be historically identified and represented. Again through this interaction, in every historically identified system, the economic structure is founded upon (and perceived as) a *durable* framework of relations providing the basic framework for economic activity. It is precisely the 'surplus value' (*Mehrwert*) of political institutions that permits the existence and durability of correspondences and symmetries between politics and economics.

In consequence, the modern separation of economics from political science is correlated with a split between economic structures and political institutions, which has reduced the scope of political economy and separated the analysis of markets and states from the social interdependencies in which they are both embedded. By contrast, this book develops a conception of political economy that explores the complex links between the economy and the polity with a particular emphasis on the different, and multi-layered, forms of sociability within which interactions between individual or collective actors take place.

5.3 Foundations of Contractualist Political Economy: A Critical Assessment

Contractualism in political economy has roots in a dualistic approach of which there are, broadly speaking, three distinct versions.[1] First, the Machiavellian and Hobbesian heritage of inherently adversarial and

---

[1] In all the three versions one may distinguish two variants, which are related to the distinction between two different types of social contract discussed in the medieval and Renaissance literature: the *pactum subiectionis* (the contract of government establishing the bond between private actors and a sovereign authority) and the *pactum societatis* (the contract stipulated between private actors). Mario Salamonio's *De principatu* (published in 1544) is possibly the first explicit appraisal of that distinction: therein we find 'the statement that the whole constitutional texture of the State, and therefore also of sovereignty, *summa potestas*, [...] must be founded on the social contract [interpreted as *pactum societatis*]' (D'Addio, 1954, p. xiii).

lawless sociability in the 'state of nature' that gives rise to a 'war of all against all' which only the absolute power of the sovereign over the people can regulate (Hobbes, 1998 [1651], part I, chap. XIII, p. 84; part II, chap. XVII–XX, pp. 111–139).

Second, the Rousseauian legacy of viewing humankind as born free but constrained by human association, and the Hegelian legacy of seeing civil society as a mere extension of state structure (*Du contrat social*, Rousseau, 1997 [1762], Book I, 6, 4; Book I, 6, pp. 6–10; Book IV, 1, pp. 1–2, 5, 7; Hegel, 1991 [1821], II, 1, §§102–112, pp. 130–140; III, 2, §§180–256, pp. 220–274). Both these versions of contractualism lead to conceptions of political economy that emphasise the exclusive and undivided nature of state sovereignty beyond that of multi-layered social linkages between individuals or groups. Third, the Lockean emphasis on commercial society as a set of contractually based interactions between private individuals where the self-interest of some is limited by the self-interest of others (Locke, 1988 [1690], II, §6 and §135). This approach shifts the focus of political economy to the role of market exchanges. In different ways, all three theories subordinate association either to individual or collective agency, thereby ignoring the relational opportunities, constraints, and affordances involved in social interdependence. This dualistic logic underpins contemporary conceptions of the relationship between economics and politics that our conception of political economy seeks to overcome.

5.3.1 The Primacy of the State over the Economy and Society

Underpinning the primacy of the state over society and the economy is the notion of an *inherently adversarial sociability* that defines the natural condition of humankind and requires the regulating power of the centrally enforced social contract, as for Hobbes and Rousseau. Niccolò Machiavelli is also an example, up to a point. In Machiavelli's *The Prince*, for example, it is the exercise of violence and the use of fear that regulate civic life (Machiavelli, 1988 [1532], pp. 34–39, 51–53, 76–79). Connected with the primacy of a violent anarchy is the redefinition of virtue: according to the Florentine writer, virtue is the military and political excellence required to achieve and sustain collective independence. In his *Discourses*, however, Machiavelli puts greater emphasis on the balance between rival interests as part of a political or civil order. His conception is based on a hierarchy of different goals or ends – from a minimal constitutional order that provides 'secure living' (*vivere sicuro*) to a maximal constitutional order in which the objective of politics is to achieve 'free living' (*vivere libero*) (Machiavelli, 1996 [1531]). Yet overall, Machiavelli's conception of the body politic is shaped by his understanding of *virtù*, which is not primarily aimed at the formation of personal character linked to citizenship (Hankins, 2019). Rather, according to Machiavelli, *virtù* can be instilled by a certain controlled maintenance of factional struggle within the polity, which serves as a training ground for the combative spirit and prepares the city in the fight against external powers (Skinner, 1983, 1998, pp. 60–62). In short, this conception of the body politic assumes a given ontological *agon* – a conflict more primary than any attempt to create a cooperative politics – which is to be regulated and manipulated but cannot be overcome by alternative arrangements that might favour cooperation over conflict (Milbank and Pabst, 2016).

Crucially, the survival and the security of the city are the primary objectives, which not only precede the pursuit of peace but also trump notions of honour and justice: '[a]ll means are acceptable when the survival of the state is at stake' (Machiavelli, 1996 [1531], pp. 41–42). This is not limited to the internal realm of domestic politics but also applies to relations between different polities because there is an unmediated anarchy between states that only the power of rulers can try to mitigate: in his 1503 treatise *Words to Be Spoken on the Law for Appropriating Money*, Machiavelli writes that 'among private individuals laws, contracts, and agreements make them keep faith, but among sovereigns only force can' (Cesa, 2004, p. 2).

Like Machiavelli, Hobbes rejects the ancient and medieval idea that human beings are inherently political, social beings in favour of the view that humankind does not by nature seek society for its sake but in view of reaping some direct benefit from it:

[b]y nature, then, we are not looking for friends but for honour or advantage [*commodum*] from them. This is what we are primarily after, friends are secondary. Men's purpose in seeking each other's company may be inferred from what they do once they meet. If they meet to do business, everyone is looking for profit not for friendship. If the reason is public affairs, a kind of political relationship develops, which holds more mutual fear than love; *it is sometimes the occasion of faction but never of good-will.* (Hobbes, 1998 [1642], p. 22 [original italics])

Similar to Machiavelli, the world is for Hobbes in a condition of anarchic violence. It is this belief – and undoubtedly his experience of the English civil war – that shaped Hobbes's conception of the 'state of nature', in which life is famously described as being 'solitary, poor, nasty, brutish, and short' (Hobbes, 1998 [1651], part I, chap. XIII, p. 84) because 'man is a wolf to man' (*homo homini lupus*) (Hobbes, 1647a, p. 2) and there is a 'war of all against all' (*bellum omnium contra omnes*) (Hobbes, 1647b, p. 4). For Hobbes, this original threat of violent death does not apply to any specific period in history but instead constitutes a principle that is internal to the state, a condition that becomes only fully visible when the polity faces the threat of its violent dissolution. However, it remains the case that Hobbes's conception of human nature and politics is based on the assumption that self-interest and conflict are more fundamental than sociability and cooperation.

Rather like Machiavelli, Hobbes assumes a natural condition of anarchy that cannot be overcome and he therefore envisions the body politic in terms of the imposition of an artificial order – the commonwealth – that merely regulates the violent 'state of nature'. Even though there is a distinction between a commonwealth by free, contractual institution and a commonwealth by forceful, violent acquisition, in either case the sovereign has supreme power to 'give life' or to withdraw it from his subjects. Obedience to Leviathan – much like obedience to Machiavelli's Prince – is due to fear of violent death, 'the foresight of their own preservation' (Hobbes, 1998 [1651], part II, chap. XVII, p. 111). And since human beings are driven by fear, stability and cooperation can only be enforced through the absolute authority of Leviathan. There is no differentiated body politic in which both persons and groups enjoy sufficient autonomy in mutual relations and pursue shared ends within different and relatively independent spheres of sociability because the commonwealth reduces them to isolated individuals, or bodies who do not stand in relations of reciprocity with other individuals and/or groups independently of the Leviathan's sovereign authority.

Hobbes's treatment of 'subordinate bodies' is to be found principally in Chapter XXII of *Leviathan* ('Of Systems Subject, Political, and Private'). In that chapter, Hobbes defines 'Systems' as 'any numbers of men joined in one interest, or one business' (Hobbes, 1998 [1651], part II, chap. I, p. 148). Such 'Systems' can be '*absolute*, and *independent*' as only sovereign Commonwealths are (Hobbes, 1998 [1651], part II, chap. XXII, p. 148 [author's emphasis]), or they can be 'dependent; that is to say, subordinate to some sovereign power, to which every one, as also their representative is *subject*' (Hobbes, 1998 [1651], part II, chap. XXII, p. 149 [original emphasis]). The distinction between independent and dependent 'Systems' is central to Hobbes's conception of the body politic, as is shown by the different treatment of 'protestation' in the two cases:

[i]t is manifest [...] that in bodies politic subordinate, and subject to a sovereign power, it is sometimes not only lawful, but expedient, for a particular man to make open protestation against the decrees of the representative assembly, and cause their dissent to be registered, or to take witness of it; because otherwise they may be obliged to pay debts contracted, and be responsible for crimes committed by other men. But in a sovereign assembly, that liberty is taken away, both because he that protesteth there, denies their sovereignty; and also because whatsoever is commanded by the sovereign power, is as to the subject [...] justified by the command; for of such command every subject is the author. (Hobbes, 1998 [1651], part II, chap. xxii, p. 152)

As a result, Hobbes tends to define social relations largely independently of civic bonds (Macpherson, 1962, pp. 34–95). Hobbes's redefinition of the state as an artificial order is based on the idea of Leviathan who rules by dividing society and the body politics into its smallest components and thereby subordinates all forms of association to its central sovereignty. Hobbes's view of 'partial societies' is at variance with the view of intermediate bodies maintaining a degree of independence even after entering a more comprehensive political body, as in Johannes Althusius's or Samuel Pufendorf's conceptions of the multiple layers of political association (Althusius, 1932 [1614]; Pufendorf, 1672; see also Bobbio, 1989; Palladini, 1978). The latter type of political organisation was addressed in the discussion between Pufendorf and Leibniz on the constitutional structure of the Holy Roman Empire. Pufendorf was critical of the different degrees of 'esteem' assigned to partial political bodies located at different levels of the constitutional hierarchy, whereas Leibniz defended the overall constitutional structure of the Empire while arguing for the need of a tight normative framework ensuring fairness and 'duties of esteem' across the different components of the overall, composite political body (Pufendorf, 1668; Leibniz, 1677; see also Blank, 2022).

For his part, Jean-Jacques Rousseau 'inverted' Hobbes by arguing that the isolated, natural individual is 'good' and not yet egotistic, because vice arises from rivalry and comparison. However, Rousseau (*Du contrat social*, 1997 [1762]) took the latter to be endemic once the individual is placed in a social context. Accordingly, his optimism about innocent isolation is tampered and ultimately trumped by a pessimism about human association (Milbank and Pabst, 2016). This encourages scepticism about the role of corporate bodies beneath the level of the state: for it is only the state that can lead human beings to sacrifice all their petty rivalries for the sake of the 'general will' (cf. Riley, 1986). Just as the sovereign state seeks to stand above the interests of faction and sectional intrigue, so too the concentration of authority in the centre undermines the civic bonds between people and the social linkages that underpin the intermediary institutions of society, all of which co-constitutes the body politic. In Rousseau's view, the latter rests on social contract and coercion leading to the primacy of the *volonté générale*, rather than free association and the pursuit of shared purposes.

This also applies to G. W. F. Hegel's conception of the body politic. In his *Philosophy of Right* (Hegel, 1991 [1821]), Hegel views society (*Gesellschaft*) in terms of the interplay between 'objective' state authority, on the one hand, and the satisfaction of subjective needs, on the other. By contrast with Machiavelli, Hobbes and Rousseau, Hegel does accord an important role to the principle of reciprocity as a way of blending the universality of a shared ethical outlook with the particularity involved in the pursuit of private and even selfish ends in social and economic activities. Society is both a system of economic interdependence and a realm of social mediation whereby individual wills are directed towards a greater social good through individual efforts and struggles as well as mutual recognition based on the division of labour and the centrality of human work:

[a] man actualises himself only in becoming something definite, i.e. something specifically particularised; this means restricting himself exclusively to one of the particular spheres of need. In this class-system, the ethical frame of mind therefore is rectitude and esprit de corps, i.e., the disposition to make oneself a member of one of the moments of civil society by one's own act [...] [I]n this way giving recognition both in one's own eyes and in the eyes of others. (Hegel, 1991 [1821], §207)

In Hegel, the link between society and the economy is the corporation (*Korporation*), which is a voluntary association of person based
on professional or social interests that can convert apparently selfish
purposes into communities of shared goals, but at the same time finds
itself subject to central state control: 'unless he is a member of an authorised Corporation (and it is only by being authorised that an association
becomes a Corporation), an individual is without rank or dignity, his
isolation reduces his business to mere self-seeking, and his livelihood
and satisfaction become insecure' (Hegel, 1991 [1821], §253). So while
the association as Corporation raises individual self-seeking to a higher
level of common purpose, it is nevertheless the case for Hegel that the
state restricts it to the 'authorized interests' of a sectional group through
central control by a collective body. Accordingly, both the plurality of
spaces and the political agency of different groups are curtailed.

5.3.2 The Primacy of the Economy over Society and the Polity

Another strand in the contractualist tradition posits the primacy of
the economy over society and the polity. A contractually based society
is seen as the outcome of private individuals who are interconnected
primarily through market exchanges and transactions, not social ties
or civic bonds. John Locke, in the social contract tradition of Hobbes,
argues that human beings are born into an asocial state of nature
until they agree to set up a political society in order to protect their
pre-political natural rights (life, liberty, and estate or property) and
their status as free and equal persons. In this manner, Locke established an economically determined sphere of society that could be
envisioned in some sense as an extension of the state of nature – this
sphere is distinguished by the primordial importance to secure private
property, which

makes him [man] willing to quit this Condition [the state of nature], which
however free, is full of fears and continual dangers: And 'tis not without reason, that he seeks out, and is willing to joyn [*sic*] in Society with others who
are already united, or have a mind to unite for the mutual *Preservation* of
their Lives, Liberties and Estates, which I call by the general name, *Property*.
(Locke, 1988 [1690], p. 350 [original italics])

The point for Locke is that both the central authority of the state and
the more diffuse organisation of society are a function of individual

freedom and private choice with view to securing property: 'The great and *chief end* therefore, of Mens [sic] uniting into Common-wealths, and putting themselves under Government, is the *Preservation of their Property*' (Locke, 1988 [1690], p. 351 [original italics]). In other words, Locke views the state and society as a means to balance individual liberty and private property with mutual security and the shared interest of stability under the aegis of the rule of law and minimal government.

Property for Locke includes life, liberty, and estate, and such an expansive sense of property has been interpreted by scholars like C. B. Macpherson (1962) to mean that Locke argues for the accumulation of capital (as property) by individuals. Each of the three restrictions on accumulating property (decay, sufficiency for others, and accumulation based on one's own labour) diminishes and even disappears as Locke's argument progresses in the *Two Treaties* (Locke, 1988 [1690]) – notably when he considers money as a store of value that is not subject to natural decay, growing productivity for capital owners, and the existence of property independently of the proprietor's labour (e.g. slavery). Whatever the merits of this interpretation, Locke does suggest that the coming into being of society does not fundamentally alter property rights in the state of nature. Put differently, he views the economic order as pre-social and as more primary than the political order. And the realm of society is seen as neither more fundamental than the polity and the economy nor as having autonomy but rather as an extension of economic activities, themselves conceived in terms of the satisfaction of individual needs and interests. For Locke human beings need to submit to a common public authority whose power has to be limited in order to allow people to produce, trade, and accumulate more privately owned wealth.

Locke's conception of society as an order founded on individual property and *politically* related but *economically* independent citizens shaped the notion of 'commercial republic' in the writings of America's founding fathers, whose *Federalist Papers* defined the purpose of government to protect private possessions and to create the conditions for economic liberty – besides political freedom (Hamilton, Madison, and Jay, 2003 [1788], No. 10 and No. 51). Central to this vision is a combination of consent, contract, and competition to turn the diversity of interests into an economic order governed by individual security and commerce: 'the prosperity of commerce is now perceived and acknowledged by all enlightened statesmen to be the most useful as well as the most productive source of nation wealth, and has accordingly become a primary object of their political cares' (Hamilton, Madison, and Jay, 2003 [1788], No. 12).

5.4 Civil Economy as Political Science: Doria and Genovesi

The priority accorded to 'commerce' clashes with notions of civic virtue that are bound up closely with ideas of trust and cooperation. Linked to this is the tendency of powerful economic interests to organise politically in the pursuit of passions and not to be constrained by a substantive conception of an encompassing interest that rests on civic institutions in order to shape the polity and the economy (Hirschman, 1977). These limits of the social contract tradition open up a space to reconsider two other modern traditions that gave rise to a rather different conception of political economy and the constitution of the body politic, on which the remainder of this chapter focuses. One is the Neapolitan Enlightenment tradition of Paolo Mattia Doria and Antonio Genovesi (with roots in the work of Giambattista Vico) and the other is the tradition of anti-absolutist thinking associated with figures such as Montesquieu, Edmund Burke, and Alexis de Tocqueville. Linking together both traditions is a renewal of older notions of civic virtue and an emphasis on the intermediary spheres of association that mediate between the person, on the one hand, and the institutions of states and markets, on the other hand. An important forerunner of these traditions was Ralph Cudworth, one of the Cambridge Platonists. In his *True Intellectual System of the Universe*, Cudworth outlines his conception of civil life in explicit opposition to Hobbes: '[i]t is manifest, how vain the attempts of these politicians are to make justice artificially, when there is no such thing naturally; (which is indeed no less than to make something out of nothing) and by art to consociate into bodies politick those, whom nature had dissociated from one another; a thing as impossible, as to tie knots in the wind or water; or to build a stately palace or castle out of sand' (Cudworth, 1743 [1678], p. 895).

Much like Vico (Robertson, 2005, pp. 185–200), Doria developed a conception of the body politic that is in sharp contrast with the contractualist tradition. Faced with the entrenched privileges of the nobility and the poverty of the peasantry, Doria looked for leadership among the magistracy of the city, the *ceto civile*. In his book *Vita Civile* (Doria, 1729 [1709]), he contrasts a politics of virtue with a politics driven entirely by self-love (*amore proprio*), which had given rise to a reductive view of politics as 'reason of state' rather than the public and common good. Echoing strands in the Greco-Roman legacy, he suggests that the flourishing of human capabilities is the ultimate end of humankind and that this underpins our natural human disposition towards union with one another (Doria, 1729 [1709]), p. 1). Alongside a mixed constitution, Doria's conception of civil life rests on the division of labour as the coordination of different 'virtues', conceptualised as capabilities. Crucially, he views the proper governance of the economy in terms of the just distribution of natural resources and the fruits of human work. For this reason, he warns about the potential domination of the *economia naturale* (agriculture and human ingenuity) by the *economia astratta* (the accumulation of abstract wealth as money; see Scazzieri, 2012a). Central to a balance of rival interests was interpersonal cooperation and trust (*fede*) as the indispensable prerequisite for agreements upon which both production and trade are based – a commitment to the common good above and beyond particular interests (Doria, 1981 [1740]).

Doria's view of economic and political life is characterised by the role of reason in harnessing passions and making them conducive to a proper balancing of dispositions ('virtues'). Rational images of perfection are indeed essential in driving human practice in view of both individual and social improvement: 'I do not lay any hope in perfection [...] but I cannot withdraw from aiming at it; if I do not strive for it, corrupted nature would certainly lead me to its opposite: and by attempting to attain perfection, I would at least cast a good human being, if not the best; similarly, by altogether forgetting about perfection, I would end up with the worse' (Doria, 1729 [1709], p. 399). Doria's notion of perfectibility suggests that rational arrangements can enable human beings and societies partially to overcome drawbacks and imperfections and thereby approximate their natural potential for mutual wellbeing:

[t]he invention of civil life aims at providing a remedy to this almost moral impossibility, which is in human beings, of possessing all virtues, and to the human property that each human being possesses only some of them [...]

[Civil life] aims at providing this remedy by assigning every particular virtue to its own place in the company of others, so that it may be an advantage to them, and also so that individual vices are not harmful to others [...]. This shows the true essence of civil life as that mutual exchange of virtues, and of natural faculties, which human beings make with one another, so as to achieve human happiness; or else an harmony brought about by all particular virtues mutually supporting each other in order to constitute a perfect political body. (Doria, 1729 [1709], pp. 82–83)

Important themes of Doria's *Vita civile* resurface in Antonio Genovesi's *Lezioni di economia civile* (Genovesi, 2013 [1765–1767]). The starting point is Genovesi's core analytical argument that the economy is fundamentally *political* and accordingly that the interdependence between social units (individuals or groups) takes precedence over the specific dispositions and actions of particular actors within the social domain (Pii, 1973; Di Battista, 2007; Pabst and Scazzieri, 2019). For Genovesi, this interdependence highlights the prevalence of '*forza concentriva*' (concentrating force) over '*forza diffusiva*' (dispersing force) and is conducive to the analysis of the conditions allowing the mutual fitting of heterogeneous socio-economic groups in a political economy capable of maintaining itself in a state of balance between those two forces (Genovesi, 1973 [1766]; Guasti, 2006). Our argument is that this attention to the structural conditions permitting a polity to survive and to make progress constitutes a key characteristic feature of Genovesi's contribution to political-economic thinking.

In the preface ('*Proemio*') to his *Lezioni di economia civile,* Genovesi discusses the position of his discipline relative to political studies, and outlines a distinction of the latter between 'civil economy' (*economia civile*), considered as that part of political science 'that encompasses the rules to make one's nation populous, rich, powerful, wise, and polite' and 'political tactics' (*tattica politica*), considered as the 'art of making laws and preserve State and Empire' (*Proemio* to the *Lezioni*, in Genovesi, 2013 [1765–1767], p. 9). This point of view also distances Genovesi's '*economia civile*' from 'economia' strictly speaking, which he clearly describes in terms of classical *oikonomia*: 'economics looks at the human being as head and prince of his family and instructs him how to well preside over it, and to bestow it with virtue, riches and glory' (*Proemio* to the *Lezioni*, in Genovesi, 2013 [1765–1767], p. 9). The political character of *economia civile* is also shown by the three references given in the *Proemio*: Montesquieu's *Esprit des Lois* (Montesquieu, 1989 [1748], Bielefeld's *Institutions politiques* (Bielefeld, 1760), and Melon's *Essai politique sur le commerce* (Melon, 1736).

Simultaneously, Genovesi makes clear that political science (which includes *economia civile*) cannot be addressed without a prior investigation into the inner structure of human beings (their *'impasto'*); the nature of their 'instincts, affections and motives'; and the ultimate grounds for the good life (*'ben vivere'*) (*Proemio* to the *Lezioni*, in Genovesi, 2013 [1765–1767], p. 9). This conception is central to Genovesi's economic thought because it raises fundamental questions about the connection between human nature, sociability, and commerce.

Genovesi's philosophical anthropology is remarkably consistent with Doria's analysis of the relationship between passions and reason, and the role of rational images in governing the acquisition of knowledge and the determination of practice in view of both individual and social improvement (see above). Doria's 'mutual exchange of virtues and of natural faculties' is also at the heart of Genovesi's approach to social differentiation and division of labour. This makes Genovesi's view noticeably different from Smith's grounding of the division of labour in 'the propensity to truck, barter, and exchange one thing for another' (Smith, 1976 [1776], Book 1, chap. 2; see, however, Smith, 1976 [1759] for an explanation of that propensity in the relational framework of social mirroring).[2] The emphasis on the congruence of dispositions as the ultimate foundation of civil life is common to Doria and Genovesi, and leads Genovesi to approach civil economy through a preliminary investigation into the nature of 'political bodies' (*corpi politici*), and into the human dispositions on which political bodies are founded. In this connection, Genovesi maintains that political science should avoid a narrow concentration of attention upon certain human dispositions instead of others (see Pabst and Scazzieri 2019). As already indicated in Chapter 2, this

---

[2] The principal difference between Doria and Smith is that Doria roots division of labour in the 'mutual exchange of [different] virtues, and natural faculties' (see above), whereas Smith *presupposes* a single 'propensity' (the 'propensity to truck, barter, and exchange one thing for another') and makes it the foundation of civil life.

is especially true in the case of 'interest', whose meaning Genovesi carefully examines:

[i]f we call *interest* to lessen pain and worry [...] it is clear that the human being only acts after this motive. However, I believe it is a delusion to say that the actions of human beings are only motivated by interest, as it is a delusion to deny it [...]. There are people who by interest only mean a *reflective self-love*, and it is untrue that every human being always acts out of this interest, since nothing is clearer in experience than the fact that human beings are *electrical beings*, and that the sympathetic principle is the spring of most human actions. But if by interest we mean indulging in, and assuaging, those pains, troubles and discomforts in which the *restlessness of the soul* consists, we would find we do not act under any other principle, independently of whether our action is motivated by a good or a bad passion. (*Lezioni*, I.2.vi, in Genovesi, 2013 [1765–1767], p. 34 [author's emphasis])

The distinction between 'reflexive self-love' and 'interest' leads Genovesi to address the question of 'virtue' as central to human dispositions and an ordering principle of human actions towards a viable polity (cf. Marcialis, 1994, 1999). In line with Shaftesbury and Doria, Genovesi views virtue as 'the harmonic consilience between passions and reason, both with regard to ourselves and our care for the public good' (Shaftesbury, *Inquiry Concerning Virtue and Merit*, Book II, as quoted in Genovesi's *Lezioni*, I.2.xii, footnote 1; in Genovesi, 2013 [1765–1767], p. 38*n*). In this manner, 'virtue' is conceptualised as a means to assess the consilience between passion and reason in the actions of human beings, as well as to gauge the proper balance of different passions that is compatible with a well-ordered polity (building on the idea of a proportionality requirement for the harnessing of passions as discussed in Chapter 2).[3] Crucially, Genovesi defines virtue not as 'an invention of philosophers' but instead 'a consequence of the nature of the world' (*Lezioni*, II.10.xiii, in Genovesi 2013 [1765–1767], p. 349).

---

[3] As Aristotle argued, virtue is a mediating middle between extreme dispositions, just as courage is halfway between recklessness and cowardice. Contrary to Machiavelli's contrast between virtue and vice, Genovesi draws on the classical tradition of viewing virtue as a 'middle' between vices (see Pabst, 2011). The ideas of Vico and Doria shaped Genovesi's conception of reason and judgement as key faculties in achieving a balance between extreme dispositions rather than pure rationality or abstract speculation. That is why Genovesi rejects rationalism and instead argues that 'reason is not useful unless it has become practice and reality' (Genovesi, 1962 [1753], p. 245).

This conception of the polity has important implications for our understanding of political economy. Doria's work is a critical source for Genovesi's view of the political economy as a multi-layered system of social and economic relationships (Costabile, 2012, 2015; Perna, 1999). In Doria, the 'mutual exchange of virtues, and of natural faculties, which human beings make with one another' (Doria, 1729 [1709], pp. 82–83) is constitutive of 'civil life' and underpins his distinction between 'natural economy' and 'abstract economy' (see Scazzieri, 2012a). The former concerns 'the appropriate arrangement and distribution, and the increase of real wealth' (Doria, 1729 [1709], p. 318) whereas the latter is about 'the maintenance and increase of money, which is imaginary' (Doria, 1729 [1709], p. 318). By extension, the embeddedness of economic life within the body politic informs Doria's other distinction between 'real trade' and 'ideal trade'. 'Real trade' follows the principle of *mutuo soccorso* and provides mutual benefit for trading parties. By contrast, 'ideal trade' is based on the logic of zero-sum games applied to the role of price differentials in the transactions between economic actors (Doria, 1981 [1740], p. 148; cf. Poni, 1997).

According to Doria, what distinguishes a 'natural economy' are the right proportions between activities that enable a viable *vita civile* (civil life).[4] This conception also shapes Genovesi's view of 'civil economy' and his position on internal commerce as well as international trade. Reciprocal needs (*bisogni reciproci*) and the reciprocal obligation to assist one another (*reciproca obbligazione di soccorrerci*; Genovesi, 2013 [1765–1767], p. 22) are the fundamental links between trade and civil life. Genovesi's argument is that a properly embedded economy pursues mutual benefit based on the exercise of virtue, which is both intrinsically good by forming character and fostering human flourishing, and engenders a more prosperous economy by favouring trust and promoting cooperation. For Genovesi, the economy is no exception to the rule that true happiness – in Doria's sense of mutual flourishing – involves sympathetic ties, which tend to influence economic transactions: 'for contracts are bonds and civil laws are [...] also compacts and public contracts' (Genovesi, 2013 [1765–1767], p. 341). This statement

---

[4] Doria's conception of the natural economy foreshadows contemporary contributions to economic theory that emphasise proportionality conditions to achieve 'natural' dynamic paths ensuring full employment and full utilisation of productive capacity (Pasinetti, 1981, 1993; Scazzieri, 2012b).

suggests that for Genovesi, there is no strict distinction between formal laws and informal commitments, since both are engendered by Doria's conception of public faith, which Genovesi defines as follows: 'Public trust is therefore a bond that ties together and binds persons and families of one State to one another, with the sovereign or other nations with which they trade' (Genovesi, 2013 [1765–67], p. 341, n121). Put differently, public faith is not so much the aggregation of private attitudes to trust as a kind of universal 'sympathy' that includes a commitment to a shared good (Pabst, 2018b).

Public trust can thus be seen as connecting civil economy to the wider sphere of civil life: 'public faith is to civic bodies what to natural bodies is the force of cohesion and of reciprocal attraction; without which there can be no solid and lasting mass, and all is but fine sand and dust' (Genovesi, 2013 [1765–1767], p. 342).[5] For him, public trust is so central because it promotes the social bonds and civic ties that are indispensable for successful economic interdependence. Criminal activity that undermines public trust leads to a situation where 'society will either dissolve itself, or it will convert in its entirety into a band of brigands' (Genovesi, 2013 [1765–1767], p. 343, here echoing St Augustine's dictum that 'without justice what else is the state but a band of brigands', *De Civitate Dei*, Book IV, 4). Without reciprocity, individual rights and commercial contracts cannot ultimately work.

5.5 Civil Life as an Evolutionary Process: Hume, Smith, Beccaria, and Filangieri

In the latter part of the eighteenth century several writers addressed the development of civil life as an evolutionary process taking place through history independently of any actual or virtual process of deliberation involving the shift 'from a set of known individual tastes to a pattern of

---

[5] This view of public trust is akin to Shaftesbury's conception that 'a thing discovers its real nature only through its participation in a system, so that a concern for the "good of the system" is not artificially constructed out of natural egoism, but is itself perfectly natural to the individual' (Passmore, 1990 [1951], p. 99). Passmore also notes in the above passage the close acquaintance Shaftesbury had with Ralph Cudworth's criticism of Hobbes's contractualism (see the quote at the beginning of Section 5.4). The relationship between Shaftesbury and key figures of the Neapolitan Enlightenment, such as Doria and Vico, during Shaftesbury's stay in Naples (1711–1713) is discussed in Croce (1925).

social decision-making' (Arrow, 1972 [1951], p. 2). In this line of thinking, David Hume's and Adam Smith's non-constructivist appraisals of the development of morals are of central importance. Hume started with the distinction between rational understanding and passions and argued that '[w]hen we leave our closet, and engage in the common affairs of life, [the conclusions of reasoning] seem to vanish, like the phantoms of the night on the appearance of the morning; and 'tis difficult for us to retain even that conviction, which we had attain'd with difficulty' (Hume, 1978 [1739–1740], p. 455). This point of view leads Hume to maintain that '[t]he rules of morality [...] are not conclusions of our reason' (Hume, 1978 [1739–1740], p. 457) and that they are instead the outcome of the gradual establishment of a convention that 'is not of the nature of a *promise*' (Hume, 1978 [1739–1740], p. 490):

I observe, that it will be for my interest to leave another in the possession of his goods, *provided* he will act in the same manner with regard to me. He is sensible of a like interest in the regulation of his conduct. When this common sense of interest is mutually express'd, and is known to both, it produces a suitable resolution and behaviour. And this may properly enough be call'd a convention or agreement betwixt us, tho' without the interposition of a promise; since the actions of each of us have a reference to those of the other, and are perform'd upon the supposition, that something is to be perform'd on the other part. (Hume, 1978 [1739–1740], p. 490)

The evolutionary (rather than contractualist) character of morals, and of the associated ideas of justice, injustice, and property, is further developed in Smith's *Theory of Moral Sentiments* (Smith, 1976 [1759]). However, Smith's analysis is distinguished by the attention given to the influence of particular circumstances and historical conditions in determining moral customs:

[t]he different situations of different ages and countries are apt, in the same manner, to give different characters to the generality of those who live in them, and their sentiments concerning the particular degree of each quality, that is either blamable or praise-worthy, vary, according to that degree which is usual in their own country, and in their own times. (Smith, 1976 [1759], p. 204)

At the same time, and differently from Hume, Smith acknowledges that the variety of morals arising from different customs may in fact be explained by the working of a general criterion determining the propriety of human conduct under specific conditions: '[i]n general, the style of manners which takes place in any nation, may commonly upon the whole be said to be that which is most suitable to its situation' (Smith, 1976 [1759], p. 209). As a result, Smith maintains that 'we cannot complain that the moral sentiments of men are very grossly perverted' by the influence of custom on morals (Smith, 1976 [1759], p. 209).

The non-contractualist character of Hume's and Smith's views on the development of human dispositions in a social setting provide the conceptual background to Adam Ferguson's *Essay on the History of Civil Society*, in which we find an explicit reference to the 'blindness' of unintended outcomes in giving shape to human dispositions and institutions:

[l]ike the winds, that come we know not whence, and blow whithersoever they list, the forms of society are derived from an obscure and distant origin; they arise, long before the date of philosophy, from the instincts, not from the speculations, of men. The croud of manking, are directed in their establishments and measures, by the circumstances in which they are placed; and seldom are turned from their way, to follow the plan of any single projector. Every step and every movement of the multitude, even in what are termed enlightened ages, are made with equal blindness to the future; and nations stumble upon establishments, which are indeed the result of human action, but not the execution of any human design. (Ferguson, 1966 [1767], p. 122)

Cesare Beccaria, writing a few years before Ferguson's *Essay*, maintained a similar evolutionary view concerning the introduction of money in economic transactions: 'the introduction of money was not born from an explicit convention (*which never preceded any human institution*), but from what people call *chance* [azzardo], which is an arrangement of circumstances that human beings could not foresee' (Beccaria, 1986 [1762], p. 196 [added emphasis]). In a later writing Beccaria also hinted at an evolutionary explanation of social differentiation, which he considered a result of the discovery that 'everyone could live so much more commodiously and pleasantly if everyone could induce a great number of others to provide such advantages and pleasures, and that such an occurrence would take place more easily and frequently if they could make themselves more clearly visible and distinct from others' (Beccaria, 1971b [ms. 1769], p. 615; see also Scazzieri, 2014b). In other writings on the evolutionary process leading to changes in human dispositions and institutions, Beccaria emphasised that the matching or mismatching between awareness of needs and knowledge of the means to meet those needs is the central criterion for judging, respectively, of the degree of civility (*coltura*) or barbarism (*barbarie*) of a nation (Beccaria, 1971c [ms. 1768], p. 802), adding that one should not confuse 'barbarism' with the primitive condition of a society (Beccaria, 1971c [ms. 1768], pp. 802–805). In this connection, Beccaria also introduced a distinction between 'objective' practices, which he calls '*usanze*' (uses) and 'subjective' attitudes, which he calls '*costumi*' (customs, or *mores*) (Beccaria, 1971d [ms. 1768], p. 810). He emphasises that

need has greater influence on customs than on uses since customs reflect the succession of needs and uses the succession of opinions. Needs give command, while opinions give advice [...] [T]he influence of uses and opinions on human passions and customs is such that need itself does not generate that change that it would produce if it were the sole influence on human beings'. (Beccaria, 1971d [ms. 1768], pp. 810–818)

Indeed, the strength of established uses may be so strong that human beings 'adjust old uses to new customs [generated by need] even if the old practices are useless and often contrary to the need' (Beccaria, 1971d [ms. 1768], p. 811).

Beccaria's writings call attention to the open ended character of sociability, which may evolve from barbarism to civility, *and vice versa*, depending on contingent and often unpredictable factors (*azzardo*). The evolutionary character of civil life is also central to Gaetano Filangieri's reconstruction of the emergence of legal structures from a background of fundamental sociability in which the civilization process develops mutual dependencies linked with differentiation between positions and influence across human beings. Filangieri shares Rousseau's conception of sociability as a natural condition but maintains that primitive society 'coeval with man, is not [...] to be confounded with civil society, for they differ widely from each other' (Filangieri, 1806 [1780], p. 5). As a matter of fact, '[p]rimitive society [...] was strictly a natural union, where the distinctions of the noble, the plebeian, the master, and [the servant], and the names of the magistrate, the laws, civil offices, impositions and punishments, were equally unknown' (Filangieri, 1806 [1780], p. 6). In Filangieri, inequality and relationships of dependence are unavoidably associated with the civilization process but, differently from Rousseau, he views civil society and social hierarchies as arising from an *evolutionary process* generated by the expansion and differentiation of needs rather than from the deliberate surrender of independence to a sovereign authority (see also Giarrizzo, 1981). In short, Filangieri acknowledges the intrinsically dual role of sociability in promoting natural unions but also in triggering distinctions and asymmetric power relationships. In his view, evolution replaces the social contract as the mainspring of civil life, but the uncertain outcome of evolutionary processes makes it necessary for legislation to reduce the corrosive effect of destitution for the well-being of the political body:

[e]xorbitant riches in particular individuals, and luxurious idleness in others, are symptoms of national infelicity, and suppose the misery of the bulk of the people. They are civil partialities prejudicial to the public interest; for a state can only be rich and happy in the single instance, where every individual by the moderate labour of a few hours can easily supply his own wants and those of his family. (Filangieri, 1806 [1780], p. 10)

5.6 The Primacy of Association: Montesquieu, Burke, and Tocqueville

From a distinct yet related perspective, the tradition of anti-absolutist thinking associated with figures like Montesquieu, Burke, and Tocqueville focuses on the crucial role of mixed constitution to uphold a body politic constituted by autonomous intermediary institutions, which can embed state and market activities in a complex, multi-layered web of social relations. Montesquieu contrasted the autarchy of despotism with the reciprocity of a balanced constitution in which the sovereign, the public, and intermediate associations interact based on civil laws (Callanan, 2018): '[d]espotism is self-sufficient; everything around it is empty. Thus when travellers describe countries to us where despotism reigns, they rarely speak of civil laws' (Montesquieu, 1989 [1748], p. 74). In addition to civil law, Montesquieu argued that intermediary institutions require a strong civic culture – a substratum of 'mores, manners and received examples' that complement a body of law to protect the integrity of the 'intermediate, subordinate and dependent bodies' that compose political and civil life (Montesquieu, 1989 [1748], p. 187).

These intermediate bodies play a key role in relation to a political economy, as they help to ensure a balance of power and wealth

between the sovereign and individual actors, as well as among the
three branches of government (executive, legislative, and judiciary).
Montesquieu wrote that in balanced constitutional orders, such as
the one he saw in eighteenth-century England, there are 'intermediate channels through which the power flows' (Montesquieu, 1989
[1748], p. 188), channels which for Montesquieu are 'established' and
'acknowledged' because they reflect in part the prevailing mores and
manner. In addition, 'the most natural, intermediate and subordinate
power is that of the nobility [...] no monarch, no nobility; no nobility,
no monarch; there can be but a despot' (Montesquieu, 1989 [1748], p.
188). However, these intermediate bodies have to be counter-balanced
by what he calls a 'depositary of the laws': 'it is not enough to have
intermediate powers in a monarchy, there must also be a depositary of
the laws. This depositary can only be the judges of the supreme courts
of justice, [i.e., *The Parlements*] who promulgate the new laws, and
revive the obsolete' (Montesquieu, 1989 [1748], p. 189).

Key to the plurality of political spaces and the exercise of agency is
for Montesquieu the practice of 'virtue', which he defines as follows:
'virtue is a feeling, and not a consequence of knowledge, a feeling
that may inspire the lowliest as well as the highest person in the state'
(Montesquieu, 1989 [1748]), V, 2). Not unlike Genovesi, he views virtue as an ordering device for the polity, the economy, and even society
as a whole, which mediates between different unsocial dispositions –
notably avarice, ambition, and idleness. Without 'virtue', man's base
nature ends up enslaving and dominating societies:

[w]hen virtue is banished, ambition invades the hearts of those who are
capable of receiving it, and avarice possesses the whole community. Desires
then change their objects; what they were fond of before, becomes now
indifferent; they were free with laws, and now they want to be free without
them; every citizen is a slave who has escaped from his master's house; what
was maxim is now called rigor; to rule they give the name of constraint [...].
Frugality, then, and not the thirst for gain, passes for avarice. (Montesquieu,
1989 [1748], III, 3)

A polity without virtue means a lack of plural spaces of political
agency, since power and wealth would flow upwards, creating the
conditions for an oligarchic and ultimately a despotic system.

Both Edmund Burke and Alexis de Tocqueville went further in their
defence of intermediate bodies and the practice of virtue. They viewed

intermediate bodies not only as autonomous and self-governing but also as bulwarks against the excessive power of *both* states and markets. Burke's rejection of state absolutism (whether the *ancien régime* or the revolutionary republic) is well known, but what is perhaps less documented is the set of themes that are shared with the thinkers of the Neapolitan Enlightenment:

[t]he constituent parts of a state are obliged to hold their public faith with each other and with all those who derive any serious interest under their engagements, as much as the whole state is bound to keep its faith with separate communities. Otherwise competence and power would soon be confounded and no law be left but the will of a prevailing force. (Burke, 2014 [1790], p. 22)

The emphasis on intermediate bodies leads Burke to emphasise that enforced equality can strengthen the power of the central state over intermediary institutions. Therefore, as Ehrenberg (1999, p. 160) writes, for Burke,

legislation must 'furnish to each description such force as might protect it in the conflict caused by the diversity of interests that must exist and must contend in all complex society' [Burke] because any attempt to impose a politically derived uniformity on a differentiated civil society is a prescription for disaster. Only a frank recognition that inequality stabilizes social relations could enable France's intermediate institutions to protect civil society from the Crown and the mob.

Of equal importance is his critique of the political economy underpinning the French Revolution, which put in place a new settlement revolving around central state power and debt-funded commerce – in which the autonomy and property of intermediary associations were sacrificed to provide the stable guarantee for a new flood of paper money. The creation of public debt reached a *new* acme with the French Revolution because the revolutionaries brought about, according to Burke, a new settlement in which

everything human and divine [is] sacrificed to the idol of public credit, and national bankruptcy the consequence; and to crown all, the paper securities of new, precarious, tottering power, the discredited paper securities of impoverished fraud and beggared rapine, held out as a currency for the support of an empire, in lieu of the two great recognised species that represent the lasting conventional credit of mankind, which disappeared and hid themselves in the earth from whence they came, when the principle of property, whose creatures and representatives they are, was systemically subverted (Burke, 2014 [1790], p. 126).

Burke's critique anticipated not only looming Terror, and political totalitarianism but also the 'paper-money despotism' that consists in increasing state indebtedness as a result of corruption and expensive wars. First the revolutionaries converted the confiscated property of the Crown and the Church into money. Then public debt was contracted to wage war. This created a new class of 'monied interest' that charged usurious interest rates, making money out of money and generating speculative profits. Then the state taxed the people and robbed them of their assets to service the growing mountain of public debt financed by private creditors. This produced an 'ignoble oligarchy' composed of state agents and private speculators who colluded against society, as Burke observed:

if this monster of a constitution can continue, France will be wholly governed by the agitators in corporations, by societies in the towns formed of directors of *assignats* and trustees for the sale of church lands, attorneys, agents, money-jobbers, speculators and adventurers, composing an ignoble oligarchy founded on the destruction of the crown, the church, the nobility and the people. Here end all deceitful dreams and visions of the equality and rights of men. (Burke, 2014 [1790], p. 199)

Burke also rejects the Hobbesian idea of a violent and anarchic state of nature, which can be merely regulated by the central state and an international system of sovereign states. Nor does he agree with the Rousseauian notion that in the state of nature human beings do not depend on each other – pre-social liberty as self-sufficiency. On the contrary, for him the natural condition of humankind is social and relational, and human nature is intrinsically creative and self-transforming:

[t]he state of civil society is a state of nature; and much more truly so than a savage and incoherent mode of life. For man is by nature reasonable; and he is never perfectly in his natural state, but when he is placed where reason may be best cultivated, and most predominates. Art is man's nature. (Burke, 1791, p. 108)

In line with this thinking, Burke views rights as social and relational too, such as the right to property by descent, the right to due process (including trial by jury) and the right to education. In the *Reflections*, he contrasts these '*real* rights of men' (Burke 2014 [1790], p. 59 [original italics]) with purely individual rights either in the state of nature, as for Rousseau, or in the artifice of political society, as for Hobbes.

Central to Burke's account of the body politic is his conception of human beings as naturally linked to one another by bonds of sympathy, which prevent fellow human beings from being 'indifferent spectators of almost anything which men can do or suffer' (Burke, 1993 [1759], p. 68). Coupled with the passions of imitation and ambition, sympathy helps to produce an order that is not imposed upon some pre-existing chaos but rather emerges from nature. It does so by fusing a concern for others (sympathy) with following the example (imitation) of those who excel and can offer virtuous leadership (ambition). Even though they are 'of a complicated kind', these three passions 'branch out into a variety of forms agreeable to that variety of ends they are to serve in the great chain of society' (Burke, 1993 [1759], p. 68). Therefore, the key difference between the social contract tradition based on an anarchic state of nature and Burke's emphasis on 'natural sociability' is that the latter evolves with the grain of humanity, starting with the innate desire of human beings to associate with one another. The primacy of association underpins Burke's conception of community as expressed by his famous invocation of the 'little platoons': 'To be attached to the subdivision, to love the little platoon we belong to in society, is the first principle (the germ as it were) of public affections. It is the first link in the series by which we proceed towards a love to our country and to mankind' (Burke, 2014 [1790], p. 47). Here, as before, we find the polity embedded in a complex web of multi-layered social relations (see also Collins, 2020).

It was Tocqueville who outlined a more fully developed conception of political sociability in which civil society is the fundamental locus in which individual liberty could be balanced with mutual awareness and respect by preventing the monopoly positions of vested interest and guarding against either majority will or mob rule. Tocqueville considers humans as primarily social beings with a unique propensity to associate in manifold ways beyond Smith's propensity to 'truck, barter and exchange'. In his view, the complex web of civil associations is indispensable for the purpose of a democratic polity, economy and civil society:

[a] government can no more be competent to keep alive and to renew the circulation of opinions and feelings among a great people than to manage all the speculations of productive industry. No sooner does a government

attempt to go beyond its political sphere and enter upon this new track than it exercises, even unintentionally, an insupportable tyranny [...] Governments therefore should not be the only active powers; associations ought, in democratic nations, to stand in lieu of those powerful private individuals whom the equality of conditions has swept away. (Tocqueville, 1969 [1835–1840], I, p. 109)

In Tocqueville's view, the responsibility of the state, which is in principle limited to the political sphere, should however be suitably expanded to protect the 'inferior classes' from the inequality and uncertainty of economic conditions associated with industrialization, also in order to 'make public life the most varied and effective, and of making the inferior classes interested in public affairs in a regular and peaceful way' (Tocqueville, 2005 [1847–1848], p. 188). This approach, which Tocqueville develops in view of the destitution he discovered in conjunction with economic progress in England, highlights the need of a social polity contrasting the unrestrained working of markets and taking advantage of the complex web of associations constituting the domain of civil society. From this perspective, neither economics nor politics as disciplines can provide first principles or final ends for humankind. Rather, 'in democratic countries, the *science of association* is the mother of sciences; the progress of all the rest depends on the progress it has made' (Tocqueville, 1969 [1835–1840], I, p. 110 [added emphasis]).

5.7 Association and the Body Politic

This chapter has explored rival conceptions of the body politic in political economy. Our argument seeks to highlight the fundamental difference between contractualist approaches in political economy, which view relations between individuals and/or groups predominantly in terms of formal arrangements under the aegis of a social contract, and alternative conceptions, which emphasise social interdependence and diverse forms of associations. The former emphasises legal and contractual interactions between the macro and the micro level, whereas the latter shift the focus to intermediate bodies and spaces of decision and action that are plural and hybrid (see also Galli, 2010; Manent, 2013). We argue that contemporary political economy can build on thinkers such as Doria, Montesquieu, Genovesi, Burke, and Tocqueville who in different ways conceptualised the interdependence between the material and the political dimensions of sociability. In this view, both the fulfilment of human abilities and the meeting of human needs presuppose patterns of interdependence that are inherently political, in the sense that they require the systemic fitting of differentiated activities and interests. At the same time, this view highlights the structural grounding of political life in the web of relations that provides material support to the economy.

Our focus has been on modes of association and the intermediate associations that constitute the body politic. The reason for this is that, first of all, they reflect the relational nature of human beings and their embeddedness in social structures more fully than formal interactions at the level of the market or the state; secondly, intermediate bodies are indispensable to the proper functioning of the polity and the economy, which are itself embedded in multi-layered social relations underpinning both conflict and cooperation. Such bonds *pre-exist* the emergence of conflict and cooperation and are characterised by more hybrid relationships than the more homogeneous links associated with state sovereignty and commercial society. These bonds are grounded in different types of sociability and point to the existence of a more fundamental domain that can be conceptualised as a 'primary constitution of connectivity [which] *embeds* the causal structures determining the relationship between intended and unintended outcomes in any given social domain' (Pabst and Scazzieri, 2012, pp. 338–339). This means that the differentiated social linkages that constitute the political-economic domain are not a given fact that economics and political science either ignore or subsume under the logic of exchange or the logic of state power but rather a dynamic reality that gives rise to plural spheres of political agency. Instead of reducing economics to politics or vice versa, our approach shows that these ties also point to partially realised connections that could embed the economy and the polity in a wider social sphere. As the following chapters will argue, this conception of the body politic has far-reaching implications for the structuring of interests, the emergence of institutional architectures, and the design and implementation of policies.

6 | *Constellations of Interests and Institutional Architecture*

6.1 Positions, Interests, and Structures of Interdependence

As we have argued in the previous chapter, the body politic can be conceptualised as an organised plurality of actors who are bound together by a proper ordering of different levels of agency that ensures its viability over time. We have also shown in Chapters 3 and 4 that the constitution of any given economy involves features of invariance in the constellations of interests arising from the existing pattern of division of labour. This means that constellations of interests are inherently associated with a pattern of interdependence between actors, and that they are central to the political economy conceived as a political body organised in view of economic conditions and objectives.

In particular, the positions of individual or collective objectives relative to one another turn a mere collection of actors into a *structured body* that is already political and economic prior to its formal establishment through a visible constitutional settlement.[1] Constellations of interests differ from one another depending on the relative positions of individual or collective actors. For example, certain constellations of interests introduce a partition of the economic-political domain into distinct *nuclei* with little or no overlap. Other constellations of interests introduce a partition consisting of partially overlapping *nuclei*, so that certain actors share certain interests with other actors while allowing for divergence and conflict when other interests are considered.

The structure of any given constellation of interests is captured by the analytical mapping Nicholas Georgescu-Roegen introduced in his analysis of peasant communities in South East Europe:

---

[1] The political and ultimately social source of economic organisation is an idea that we owe to ancient Greco-Roman thought – including Plato, Aristotle, and Cicero – and that is developed in the writings of modern thinkers such as Antonio Genovesi and Edmund Burke, as discussed in Chapter 5.

[a] study of peasant institutions must focus its first of all on that social entity which is certain to display their entire spectrum. Villages within a geographical region may have identical institutions and, moreover, be connected with each other in different ways so as to form a social entity, some *terra*, as its name goes in medieval tradition (for which, see [Stahl, 1939]). Its study is of no little value. But if one would decide to exclude the village altogether from the picture, the analysis of this higher social organization will bring the village back in full force. A simple formalization of the structure will show this without difficulty. Lat A_1, A_2, ... be the individuals belonging to such a *terra* and R_1, R_2 ... be all institutional relations that may exist between an A_i and an A_j. The analytical map of the true relations $A_i R_k A_j$ will immediately separate the whole structure into several distinct nuclei, each corresponding to one of the villages. The analytical separation results from the fact that the number of relations true for any pair A_i, A_j of the same nucleus exceeds by a significant magnitude the number of relations applicable to internuclear pairs. Of course, a whole group of villages may be related so as to form a tribe; or the families of the same village may be associated in clans which in turn may cut across a number of villages. Yet the relations applicable to families belonging to the same village outnumber by far those between the families of the same clan but of different villages. (Georgescu-Roegen, 1976 [1965], pp. 205–206)

In Georgescu-Roegen's analytical framework, the mapping $x_i R_h y_s$ decomposes a given social domain into subsets (*nuclei*), such that the individual or collective actors x_i ($i = 1, ..., n$) and y_s ($s = 1, ..., m$) are grouped together by the set R_h ($h = 1, ..., m$) of relations, which may express partial objectives (i.e. partial interests) shared by the x_is and y_ss. This formalization shows that constellations of interests with little or no overlap of partial interests are associated with a mapping R_h that includes either a single partial objective or a small number of partial objectives. By contrast, constellations with a significant overlap of partial interests are associated with a mapping R_h that includes many partial interests, if not all of them.

This argument highlights the possibility of classifying constellations of interests by the degree to which different partial interests may or may not coalesce into clusters of overlapping interests that are potentially conducive to a synthesis of interest shared by a significant plurality of actors. Alternative constellations of interests highlight the possibility of establishing connections that may involve different numbers of actors and that may also introduce linkages of different strength between different actors or sets of actors.

The above analytical map brings into focus the possible affiliations and cleavages that may or may not materialize depending on the way in which individual or collective actors map and realise the possibilities open to them in each context. It is also important to note that different mappings of possible affiliations or cleavages have different degrees of relative persistence over time. This provides a heuristic into the dynamics of affiliations that characterise the objective constitution of a political economy at any given stage of its history.

The structure of this chapter is as follows. Section 6.2 examines the constitutional arrangement of a political economy considered as a set of positions of the main actors (both individuals and groups) together with the corresponding mapping of their fundamental interests. This section calls attention to the relationship between the dominant mapping of interests and the institutional architecture of a given political economy. The section also highlights the need of a constitutional heuristic aimed at detecting the matching or mismatching of dominant interests and institutions in a specific context.

Section 6.3 addresses cleavages as an expression of interdependence, which generally results in the formation of separate nuclei of stakeholders. These nuclei determine overlapping or non-overlapping lines of separation between stakeholders and are at the origin of the multiple instances of compromise or conflict that characterise a given political economy. This section emphasises that, in general, any given pattern of interdependence (such as the interdependence between producers through division of labour) is conducive to a plurality of ways in which interests arise and group affiliations are shaped. An example of this is when interests and affiliations follow predominantly horizontal or vertical patterns of interdependence.

Section 6.4 examines conciliation of interests and its prerequisites. This section makes a distinction between two forms of conciliation: first, conciliation as compromise between the partial interests of different actors; second, conciliation as pursuit of partial interests under a condition of 'systemic interest'. The latter condition implies that both compromise and conflict are subject to a primary prerequisite of sustainability for the political economy as a whole. Section 6.5 switches to the consideration of the different routes from partial interests to systemic interest depending on what is the prevailing mapping of interdependence.

Section 6.6 addresses the schemes of interdependence between actors involved in division of labour, and investigates the way in which alternative patterns of division of labour may be associated with different identifications of systemic interest. Sections 6.7 turns to the consideration of 'institutional architectures' seen as the relatively stable constellations of formal and informal rules that determine both which social actions are possible and which ones are to be expected in a given context. This section examines the relationship between path dependence and design as the principal route by which institutional architectures emerge and are transformed in the course of time. In particular, the section calls attention to the possible lack of synchronization between institutions, human dispositions, and systemic interest as the source of mismatch between material interdependencies and their mapping by relevant stakeholders.

Section 6.8 concludes the chapter by discussing the relationship between patterns of interdependence and the dispositions of actors under conditions of institutional change. This section argues that changes in connectivity between stakeholders and in their dispositions bring about important changes in institutional architecture while the latter are a significant influence behind stakeholders' mapping of interests. This affects in an important way the route taken by policy-making in a political economy subject to the transformation of interdependencies that characterises processes of structural change.

6.2 Constellations of Interests and Constitutional Settlements

The constitution of a political economy is a complex arrangement of positions and patterns of interdependence characterised by relative invariance and allowing a plurality of connections and group affiliations. A constitutional heuristic is needed to detect the most significant constellations of interests together with the most salient mappings of relative positions. It therefore provides a cue into the most stable group affiliations in the political economy under consideration.

As we have seen in the previous section, constellations of interest disclose alternative patterns of compromise or conflict depending on which relative positions are mapped as the dominant ones in a given context. For example, a constellation of interests showing the relative positions of interests based on a classification of activities by industry (such as metal-making, textiles, and so on) is likely to be different from a constellation of interests based on a classification of activities by vertically integrated sectors or supply chains, seeing that each supply chain may include activities belonging to a plurality of industries but delivering intermediate inputs to the same consumption or investment good.

Realised affiliations or cleavages depend on which constellation of interests is principally mapped. A constellation of interests based on a classification by industries highlights the possibility of group affiliations reflecting interdependence of activities delivering intermediate inputs to one another (this is a case of 'horizontal' or circular interdependence). In turn, this type of interdependence may disclose different patterns of affiliation depending on the relevant sphere of interdependence, which could be a region, a state, or a multi-state network of activities. Each sphere of interdependence is a possible source of a constitutional settlement that may be adopted as a function of conjunctural factors and/or deeper structural conditions. For example, interdependence at the regional level can engender a political economy whose constitution may or may not be associated with self-government depending on constraints generated at other levels of interdependence. In this connection, a particularly interesting case is that of formal or informal regional affiliations cutting across different states. Examples are multi-state regional affiliations such as the Adriatic and Ionian Region (EUSAIR), the Union of Baltic Cities in Europe, the Pacific Northwest Legislative Leadership, and the Great Lakes 'region state' in North America. Here we have affiliations that are conducive to a constitutional settlement independent of, even if not necessarily opposed to, the objective and/or the formal constitutions of the different states to which the regions belong (Ohmae, 1993).

Other group affiliations may *presuppose* a multi-state domain while being conducive to a constitutional settlement that cuts across national borders. A multi-state polity such as the European Union is a case in point (Moravcsik, 2005; Cardinale, Coffman, and Scazzieri, 2017a, b). Lastly, group affiliations may generate a set of self-standing normative arrangements independent of formal political units, as in the case of the medieval law merchant (*lex mercatoria*) (Hicks, 1969; Grossi, 2007) or of their contemporary emergence in the space of non-state international relationships (Trackman, 2003; Bernstein, 2013; Ferrarese, 2015).

A classification of activities by vertically integrated sectors suggests a different constellation of collective interests and group affiliations. In this case, the activities involved in a given supply chain generate interests different from those associated with a different supply chain. Here the issue arises whether the linkages *within* individual supply chains (vertically integrated sectors) generate mutually compatible constellations of interests *across* several distinct supply chains. Under certain conditions supply chains may generate mutually compatible interests, and can even be compatible with a systemic interest encompassing several or all supply chains under consideration. For example, a number of supply chains can depend on the same material input, or can draw upon the same pool of human capabilities. In this case, connections between activities can give rise to a constellation of interests that brings to light a degree of complementarity between different supply chains.

However, the way in which stakeholders look at possible complementarities is very different as a function of stakeholders' positions within a particular collection of supply chains. For instance, supply chains depending on the availability of the same essential non-produced resource, such as oil or a particular mineral ore, give rise to alternative interests according to whether we take the point of view of the actors supplying that resource (the 'delivery route') or the point of view of its final users (the 'acquisition route').[2] Examples of shared interest from the 'delivery' point of view are the Organization of the Petroleum Exporting Countries (OPEC), and former organisations such as the International Bauxite Association (IBA) and the

---

[2] The distinction between 'delivery route' and 'acquisition route' draws attention to a dual perspective in the formation of shared interest when activities are lumped together by vertically integrated sectors. The 'pyramid-like' arrangement of activities associated with vertically integrated sectors identified by final consumption or investment goods ('acquisition route') is different from the 'inverted-pyramid' arrangement of activities associated with vertically integrated sectors identified by utilisation of the same non-produced resource (see Landesmann and Scazzieri, 1993, pp. 211–217, 234–239). The 'pyramid' metaphor for representing the hierarchical connectivity of production activities was already used by Cesare Beccaria (1971 [ms 1769]) when he argued that industrial policy should stimulate production by arranging activities not according to disorganised groupings ('*disuguali ammucchiamenti*') but 'in the manner of a pyramid' ('*a guisa di piramide*') (Beccaria, 1971 [ms 1769], vol. I, p. 395).

Association of Iron Ore Exporting Countries (APEF). An example of shared interest from the 'acquisition' point of view could be, at least partly, the International Energy Agency (IEA).

From the suppliers' position, shared interest is more likely to be visible when substitute resources do not exist or are irrelevant within a significant time horizon (as has been the case with the oil industry), so that differences between qualities of the same resource (e.g. between different oil fields) can be overlooked. From the users' position, identifying shared interest is more likely in the case of a resource whose users all belong to the same industry (as the steel industry with respect to iron ore).[3]

However, the same conditions may also pinpoint strong potential or actual conflicts of interests between supply chains if supply chains have to compete for the provision of the same material inputs or capabilities. This situation calls attention to the relative openness of constellations of interests with respect to the configuration of connections. For the same pattern of interdependence may alternatively engender complementarity or opposition depending on the historical context and on how stakeholders identify their respective positions and interests in that context. In the case of supply chains based on the same material input, or on the same pool of capabilities, stakeholders may realise that a better provision of that material input or of the relevant capabilities can be secured through collective action across supply chains. This may generate a constellation of mutually compatible interests, in which a type of shared interest can arise across different supply chains.

---

[3] The role of aggregation criteria in generating economic phenomena depending on human action is addressed by Piero Sraffa in his analysis of how differences in the classification of activities using the same non-produced resource (in his case, land) may or may not generate a diminishing returns trajectory. In particular, Sraffa maintains that to generate diminishing returns when a certain resource is fixed for the industry as a whole but not for individual producers, 'it is necessary to have recourse to a stratagem that moves the cause of the increase in cost from the conditions of the industry to the conditions of the single producer. This is achieved by supposing that the number of producers is fixed, and that each of them, with the increase in his production, cannot increase the quantity used by him of the factor of which there exist a fixed quantity for industry as a whole, so that the individual cost of production has to increase. In these conditions, the individuality of the "enterprise" is no longer characterised solely by the unit of management, that is, by the entrepreneur, but also by the presence of a unit of the "constant factor"'(Sraffa 1998 [1925], p. 343).

On the other hand, a different configuration of relative positions (and advantages), and a different mapping of them, may lead stakeholders away from identifying a shared interest making them more inclined to highlight opposition and possibly conflict.

6.3 Cleavages, Associations, and the Economic Constitution

As we have seen, the economic constitution of society arises from the existence of multiple patterns of interdependence between economic stakeholders (Chapter 4). By distinguishing between horizontal and vertical interdependence in production networks, different classification schemes allow us to identify different and mutually compatible patterns of interdependence (Pasinetti, 1980 [1973]; Baranzini and Scazzieri, 1990; Scazzieri, 2022). Horizontal interdependence means that a production network is a collection of activities delivering intermediate inputs to one another (this network is a 'circular flow' of system-wide relationships).[4] By contrast, vertical interdependence means that a production system is a collection of activities coordinated with one another along sequences of fabrication stages leading from work-in-process materials to finished products. This production system would be a collection of vertically integrated sectors in which each supply chain is held together by 'one-way' connections from one fabrication stage to the next. The switch from one configuration of interdependencies to another presupposes a change in the way activities are grouped together (Stone, 1962). However, each classification scheme is also a focal point for the convergence or divergence of interests between social groups (Cardinale, 2017; Cardinale and Landesmann, 2022). Each configuration of interdependence highlights a specific way of connecting activities with one another so that the focus of actors' interests is likely to shift as their consideration moves from one type of configuration to another (Cardinale, 2018a).

---

[4] The concept of the economic system as a circular flow of production and consumption activities goes back at least to François Quesnay's *Tableau économique* (Quesnay, 1972 [1759]). Wassily Leontief explored the analytical premises of the circular-flow approach in Leontief (1991 [1928]) and later used the circular-flow viewpoint in the empirical analysis of his *Structure of the American Economy* (Leontief, 1941). Subsequent contributions to the analytics of circular-flow theory are, among others, Sraffa, 1960; Pasinetti, 1980 (1973), 1977; Quadrio Curzio, 1986, 1996; Seton, 1992.

The possibility of alternative focal points triggering alternative patterns of economic group affiliation has far-reaching consequences. In particular, this possibility suggests that any given focal point is necessarily *selective* in the sense of inducing identification of a subset of similarity features from among the wider set of characteristics describing the socioeconomic setting under consideration. Similarity features may be distributed between individual or collective actors in a variety of patterns.

This point has important implications considering that economic actors are generally associated with a vector of different characteristics (e.g., goods produced, material inputs required, human capabilities needed). As a result, actors can be grouped together according to a variety of criteria, which may lead to different measures of distance between them. For example, actors A_i and A_j may share characteristic s_1 (which therefore becomes a feature of similarity) while *not* sharing any other characteristic s_2, ..., s_k in the relevant social domain. This implies that A_i and A_j can be considered as close to each other in terms of similarity feature s_1 but distant in terms of any other standard of comparison. For example, two industries may provide intermediate inputs to each other but may also contribute work-in-process materials to a plurality of supply chains (vertically integrated sectors). In this case, the association with the same circular network of intermediate inputs provides a feature of similarity, but that similarity feature may or may not provide a focal point for convergence of their respective interests depending on the degree to which the two industries contribute to the same supply chains. More generally, the joint contribution to the same structure of intermediate inputs by the two industries tends to provide an effective focal point for the coordination of interests only if the interdependence arising from the mutual supply of intermediate inputs is strong enough to overcome the potentially divisive effect generated by the plurality of supply chains to which the two industries contribute. On the other hand, the common interest arising from joint contribution to the same circular network of intermediate inputs is reinforced if the two industries also contribute in a significant way to the same supply chains (vertically integrated sectors).

In short, the plurality of characteristics by which similarity features can be identified may or may not contribute to the internal cohesion of the political economy under consideration. For example, the binary classification of productive activities as contributing either to a horizontal network of intermediate inputs or to a collection of vertical supply chains highlights either the strength or the weakness of the set of inter-dependencies under consideration. By the same token, the above binary classification shows that activities can be distant from one another by one criterion (say, their contribution to different supply chains) but also close to one another if we consider a different criterion (say, their contribution to the same structure of intermediate inputs). In general, the plurality of relevant characteristics tends to increase the likelihood of similarity features and the potential cohesion of any given collection of activities provided the cleavages arising from the distribution of characteristics across individual or collective actors are *non-overlapping* (or overlapping only to a limited degree) (Rae and Taylor, 1970).

Under certain conditions, cleavages between stakeholders leave room for compromise generating convergence towards a common synthetic objective. Multiple, and not fully overlapping, cleavages may be conducive to a situation in which compromise is more likely than destructive conflict (Rae and Taylor, 1970; Lijphart, 1968, 1969, 1975 [1968], 1977; see also van Schendelen, 1984). In consequence, '[t]he fact that individual or group *A* may be opposed to individual or group *B* on issue *x*, but also closely allied to group *B* on issue *y*, may provide an important condition for congruence in a fragmented, heterogeneous social domain' (Pabst and Scazzieri, 2016, p. 346). However, 'fragmentation of interests may also lead to the opposite outcome. Cleavages, even if not coinciding, may still make congruence more difficult rather than easier. This may happen when the social domain is so completely fractured that spheres of shared interest become very difficult, if not altogether impossible, to detect' (Pabst and Scazzieri, 2016, p. 347). In a setting like this, identification of a synthetic and shared objective may critically depend on the ability to envision a 'constitutional' systemic interest beyond the fragmentation of partial interests in society. Arend Lijphart discusses this way of overcoming divisive cleavages both in democracies of the 'consociational type' (Lijphart, 1969) and in pre-democratic polities, like the Dutch United Provinces in the early modern age (Lijphart, 1969, 1975 [1968]).[5] This type of constitutional settlement requires:

---

[5] In his discussion of the conditions for political stability in a fragmented society Lijphart makes reference to 'Johannes Althusius' concept of *consociatio* in his *Politica Methodice Digesta*' (Lijphart, 1969, p. 211; see also Daalder, 1966; Lijphart, 1975 [1968]).

(1) [t]hat the elites have the ability to accommodate the divergent interests and demands of the subcultures. (2) This requires that they have the ability to transcend cleavages and to join in a common effort with the elites of rival subcultures. (3) This in turn depends on their commitment to the maintenance of the system and to the improvement of its cohesion and stability. (4) Finally, all of the above requirements are based on the assumption that the elites understand the perils of political fragmentation. (Lijphart, 1969, p. 216)

A specific feature of the consociational overcoming of divisive partial interests is that several issues take a 'constitutional' character and cannot be solved by simple majority rule: '[c]onsociational democracy violates the principle of majority rule, but it does not deviate very much from normative democratic theory. Most democratic constitutions prescribe majority rule for the normal transaction of business when the stakes are not too high, but extraordinary majorities or several successive majorities for the most important decisions, such as changes in the constitution. In fragmented systems, many other decisions in addition to constituent ones are perceived as involving high stakes, and therefore require more than simple majority rule' (Lijphart, 1969, p. 214). Convergence to a common synthetic objective is more likely when stakeholders share the same 'list' of partial objectives (which may involve conflict under limited resource constraints) but attach different weights to different objectives (Pabst and Scazzieri, 2016). This situation arises 'when the number of divisive issues is not too great and provided individuals or groups weigh social outcomes in a sufficiently differentiated way across possible social situations' (Pabst and Scazzieri, 2016, p. 348).

For example, division of labour may generate multiple cleavages between productive activities, but this plurality of cleavages *may or may not* reduce system cohesion depending on whether cleavages reinforce one another and therefore enhance the mutual independence of separate tasks (overlapping cleavages), or else increase selective connectivity between tasks by generating *mutually offsetting* cleavages (and therefore making explicit or *de facto* coordination more likely). For instance, certain stages of production can contribute to several *distinct* productive networks that supply intermediate inputs to one another, and at the same time they can contribute to the supply chain for the same finished product. In this case, the potential cleavage due to separation between networks of intermediate products may be offset by the fact that the production stages under consideration contribute to the same supply chain. Alternatively, the shared interest provided by the common supply chain could be too weak relative to the shared interest associated with membership of different intermediate-product networks.

In the latter case, it is likely that *for each production stage*, the prevailing interest would be the one generated by the corresponding (dominant) intermediate-product network, even if the joint contribution of all production stages to the supply chain for a particular finished product may act as a 'compensating interest' reducing the likelihood of conflict between production stages that may arise from membership of distinct intermediate-product networks. (The implications of this complex overlap of production linkages for industrial policy are discussed in Chapter 7; see also Best, 2018; Di Tommaso et al., 2020).

Cleavages are an important factor determining the economic constitution of society. As we have seen, the economic constitution rests upon the constellation of interests associated with the existing network structure of the economy. Division of labour and connections through the mutual transfer of goods and services are central to the configuration and working of economic networks. They are compatible with multiple classifications of activities, which may in turn generate several distinct nuclei of shared interest. The *economic constitution* of any given society will be defined by what is its dominant shared interest, and such dominant shared interest will provide the focal point of economic coordination between individual or collective actors.

The above conception of the economic constitution provides a heuristic for analysing the relationship between the economic constitution and the political constitution. For economic linkages and lines of separation do not necessarily coincide with the linkages and separations between different political units. A given activity (say, a production process carried out in a particular establishment) may formally belong to a certain political unit (say, a particular nation state) and yet be part of the economic constitution of another political unit (say, another nation state), or of a supranational constellation of activities. There may be a cleavage between the economic and the political constitution, and this cleavage can be an important factor in determining the character of economic policy in each political unit, as well as the dynamics of the economic and political constitutions over time.

6.4 Conciliation of Interests

To conceptualise the political constitution in relation to the economic constitution, it is useful to draw on the work of the English political theorist Bernard Crick and his notion of conciliation of rival interests in a polity using compromise rather than force. Crick's conception of politics shifts the focus away from pure ideology towards the praxis of 'preserving a community' that has 'grown too complicated for either tradition alone or pure arbitrary rule to preserve it without the undue use of coercion' (Crick, 1992, p. 24). As with the thinkers discussed in Chapter 5, Crick focuses on the material constitution rather than the formal constitution. His argument is that material interests are the foundation of both political and economic order and that a conciliation of material interests is both desirable and feasible.

Two conditions are necessary for a practice of political conciliation. First, the existence of pluralistic societies that are culturally complex and in which values divide people, which captures our contemporary condition of heterogenous cultures. Second, a commitment to rule out the use of force in settling conflicts, which applies to functioning democracies. In the words of Crick, to conceptualise politics in this manner 'is to assert, historically, that there are some societies at least which contain a variety of different interests and different moral viewpoints and [also] to assert, ethically, that conciliation is at least to be preferred to coercion among normal people' (Crick, 1992, p. 141).

Key to Crick's conception of politics is the recognition that diversity of interests and ethical values are themselves goods and that therefore politics cannot be about the imposition of a single truth or set of absolute truths, for that would amount to absolutist rule or even tyranny. Nor can politics deny any sense of truth altogether, for that would lead to anarchy and violent conflict between rival groups. In between those extremes that fuel each other, the goal of politics is to represent 'at least some tolerance of different truths, some recognition that government is possible, indeed best conducted, amid the open canvassing of rival interests [...] that type of government where politics proves successful in ensuring reasonable stability and order' (Crick, 1992, pp. 18, 21). Survival and security are the common interests holding disparate actors or groups together, not 'some allegedly objective "general will" or "public interest"' (Crick, 1992, p. 24).

It is here that Crick makes the decisive argument about the nature of politics – that there are no absolutely rational or scientific ways of resolving conflicts between incommensurable values or even rival interests. The reverse side of a rational objective order that has supposedly universal validity is the other contemporary tendency of reducing moral judgements to expression of personal preferences based on subjective emotions, which Alasdair MacIntyre calls emotivism (MacIntyre, 2000 [1981]). As rationalism and emotivism dominate contemporary political discourse, the conception of politics as the pursuit of shared ends is subordinate to purely rational or emotive standards. In reality, politics goes beyond both rational ordering and human emotions in the direction of what Aristotle calls *phronêsis* or practical wisdom, by which he means linking our dispositions to the "right" (in the sense of reasonable) course of action.

Such a conception of politics can be found in the works of Edmund Burke, notably his notion of 'principled practice', which means striving for a middle path between mere facts without ideas and pure abstraction without practical meaning. Burke's characterisation of what distinguishes a statesman from a politician illustrates this well: '[a] statesman, never losing sight of principles, is to be guided by circumstances' (Burke, 1792, p. 317, quoted in Boucher, 1991, p. 140) and '[a] statesman forms the best judgement of all moral disquisitions who has the greatest number and variety of considerations in one before him, and can take them in with the best possible consideration of the middle result of them' (Burke, 1991 [1782], p. 304, quoted in Fidler and Welsh, 1999, p. 39).

Drawing on both Burke and Crick, it is possible to suggest that the continued existence of a polity depends on the conciliation of rival interests, which are central to the emergence of *shared objectives* and/ or to the acknowledgement of *shared conditions* for the pursuit of objectives specific to particular actors of groups. The idea of shared conditions is akin to Michael Oakeshott's notion of 'civil condition', which he describes as a setting in which actors are 'acknowledging themselves to be *cives* in virtue of being related to one another in the recognition of a practice composed of rules' so that they are 'related solely in terms of their common recognition of the rules which constitute a practice of civility' (Oakeshott, 1975, pp. 127–128). Oakeshott contrasts this view with the approach that considers the polity as a '"community of wills", with a "common good" and with the specification of this common interest' (Oakeshott, 1975, p. 118). This raises questions about the nature of interest and arrangements of different categories of interest, which the next section explores.

6.5 From Partial Interests to Systemic Interest

Interests can be individual, collective or 'systemic'. Individual interests reflect the conditions and partial objectives of actors as distinct expressions of agency. Collective interests reflect the conditions and partial objectives of individual actors joined together by a criterion of group affiliation. Systemic interest reflects the condition of different socioeconomic groups joined together by a common set of constraints and opportunities, which may or may not induce a shared or 'synthetic' objective deliberately pursued. The concept of 'synthetic objective' is introduced in de Finetti (1979). The potential mismatch between 'systemic interest' and more traditional concepts such as 'public interest', 'national interest', and the like is highlighted in Cardinale, 2015: '[s]ystemic interest derives from interdependencies and is a generalization of the traditional category of national interest [...] It is worth reiterating that sectors may well constitute potential rather than manifest interest groups: whilst interests are grounded in the structure of the economic system, not every sector may be aware of them and act accordingly at the political level. As a consequence, it is possible that a system of interdependencies affords a systemic interest but the groups involved do not consider it as such in the construction of their own interest' (Cardinale, 2015, p. 203; see also Cardinale, 2017, 2018a; Cardinale and Coffman, 2014).

The shift from collective (group) interests to systemic interest is not straightforward, since it presupposes common constraints and opportunities, and these may lead to different ways of 'synthesizing' the interests of different socioeconomic groups. An example is the distinction in the previous section between the horizontal aggregation of production processes within a single 'circular flow' of intermediate products, and the vertical aggregation of processes within distinct supply chains leading to distinct finished products. Synthetic interest in a horizontal pattern of interdependence will be different from synthetic interest in a vertical pattern of interdependence between different supply chains.

Horizontal interdependence will bind the relevant stakeholders together by means of a 'connectivity loop' such that all processes require one another's products as essential inputs. On the other hand, vertical connections bind relevant actors together along a 'one-way' route from means of production to finished products that is in principle open-ended, seeing that different layers of means of production may be delivered by socioeconomic systems different from the systems of destination of finished products. Vertical connections per se are no guarantee that a systemic interest covering *different* supply chains will arise. For this reason, the mapping of systemic interest across different vertically integrated sectors requires the identification of a covering condition external to the links within individual supply chains, and yet capable of joining *different* supply chains in view of a systemic condition. An example of a covering condition of that type is the full employment condition that can be introduced in a pure labour economy (with no intermediate product requirements) to ensure the mutual consistency of different supply chains (or fractions of them) from the point of view of a particular collection of activities, such as the activities carried out in a particular region or country.[6]

The distinction between horizontal versus vertical patterns of interdependence highlights two different routes along which it may be possible to identify the systemic interest consistent with a particular collection of activities. This means that dominance of horizontal or, respectively, vertical interdependence suggests a distinction between two different types of economic constitution. Horizontal interdependence means that systemic interest reflects the *mutual interdependence* of the activities carried out within the relevant economic unit, as in the prototypical case of an economic systems in which all finished products are also intermediate products for one another. Here, systemic interest may coincide with the condition making it possible for the collection of mutually related processes to be self-sustainable, and the corresponding economic constitution may support socioeconomic and institutional arrangements characterised by a criterion of 'connectivity

---

[6] A pure labour economy, such as the model economy studied by Luigi Pasinetti (1993, 2007), consists of processes delivering final consumption goods by means of labour only, with the exclusion of non-produced resources and intermediate inputs. This model economy can be considered as a prototype for an economy consisting of a collection of supply chains not significantly dependent on one another and brought into mutual relationship by an external policy objective such as the full employment of the active labour force living on a given territory.

closure'. This means that the economic constitution is primarily oriented to achieving sustainability of the circular flow of intermediate productions into one another. Other objectives – such as achievement of a satisfactory growth rate in the aggregate or for specific activities, full employment, net export growth, and so on – can only be considered after the principal objective is achieved.

Dominance of vertical interdependence leads to a different mapping of systemic interest. For a systemic condition cannot be extracted from mutual dependencies between production processes, and should be introduced from the outside. One example is when the outside systemic condition coincides with the full employment (or even 'full nourishment') condition for the population living on a given territory. Another example may be when the systemic condition is determined by one particular supply chain to the detriment of other supply chains. Economic constitutions would be very different in the two cases. In the former case, the synthetic condition (say, full employment) will constrain the relationship between the different supply chains (and in particular their relative proportions). In the latter case, the whole system will have to adjust its structure to the objective of one particular line of production, and the objectives of the other supply chains will have to adapt accordingly.

6.6 Patterns of Interdependence and Systemic Interest

The approach to systemic interest in terms of consistence of linked activities in a *horizontal pattern of interdependence* highlights systemic interest as *condition* for the attainment of a variety of collective objectives reflecting different distributions of weights between actors. In this case, compromise or conflict leads from one distribution of weights to another, and leads the polity from one collective (political) objective to another. However, the systemic consistency condition constrains the distribution of weights between actors' partial interests (and therefore also the political objective derived from them) within the boundaries of what is compatible with the continued existence of the overall system of interdependencies (its 'viability condition').

The situation is different if we switch to a *vertical pattern of interdependence*. In this case, as we have seen, connections may link activities belonging to different horizontal schemes of interdependence. This means that the partial interests associated with the different vertically integrated sectors (or supply chains) are not directly constrained by a condition arising from within the system of interdependencies. In this case, partial interests are constrained by a condition external to productive interdependencies as such, as is the case if the activities carried out within the different vertical sectors have to meet a systemic full employment constraint. Here we have a situation in which there are structural links between activities carried out *within* each vertical sector (supply chain) but no significant structural links *across* different vertical sectors. The coherence of the overall system (considered as a collection of relatively independent supply chains) is to be achieved by an external macroeconomic condition, such as the full employment condition. However, full employment could in general be achieved by a *variety of proportions* between the different supply chains. This means that in this case too we may think of a variety of solutions (achieved through agreement or conflict) to the problem of identifying a synthetic objective associated with a plurality of partial interests. However, as with the horizontal pattern of interdependence, the variety of possible syntheses is constrained by a systemic condition (in this example, the full employment condition). This variety of solutions highlights that a plurality of political objectives (i.e. objectives *de facto* pursued by the collection of vertical sectors as a comprehensive system) would be compatible with the condition of full employment.

Of course, the two above cases are a highly simplified picture of what is likely to be a much more varied constellation of positions and linkages. We may have a horizontal pattern of interdependence such that activities (and the corresponding actors) are connected with one another in the sense of being mutually necessary and also sufficient to provide the work-in-process materials and semi-finished products needed to deliver all quantities of goods produced in the system. However, we may also have a horizontal pattern of interdependence that is 'incomplete' in the sense that a semi-independent horizontal subsystem exists side by side with inputs flows coming from outside that subsystem and output flows leaving the subsystem and connecting it with external sources of utilisation.

In the latter case, we meet a problem different from the one we have just examined. The issue is no longer how to determine a synthesis of partial interests compatible with the systemic viability condition. For the viability condition would realistically constrain only the activities belonging to the inner core subsystem (the subsystem of mutually necessary activities). The 'peripheral' activities would only be interested in the supply chains to which they contribute, not in the viability of the overall system. In this case, the convergence of different stakeholders to a synthetic objective consistent with systemic interest (as expressed, for example, by the viability of the inner core of interdependent activities) is more likely if there are sufficiently strong links connecting peripheral to core activities. Similarly, a vertical pattern of interdependence may also be 'incomplete' in the sense that the collection of vertical sectors forming the system includes inputs and outputs external to the system. In this case, finding a synthetic objective consistent with a systemic condition (such as full employment) is, respectively, less or more difficult depending on the degree to which the different supply chains are also connected to one another through links that are internal to the system. We can even think of a collection of vertical sectors such that each sector is a supply chain completely detached from the other sectors in the economy. In this case, finding convergence to a synthetic objective consistent with a systemic condition may be more difficult and may require a criterion different from economic interdependence.

In either the horizontal or the vertical case, convergence to a synthetic objective by a variety of stakeholders does not imply that the systemic interest will be met. For example, in a horizontal pattern of interdependence, stakeholders expressing the partial interests of different industries may converge to a set of industrial proportions incompatible with the viability condition for the whole system of interdependent industries. In a vertical pattern of connectivity between activities, actors expressing the partial interests of different supply chains may converge to a shared objective that may or may not be compatible with whatever systemic condition is considered for the polity under consideration (such as full employment). In other words, structural conditions or circumstances conducive to compromise make the pursue of a shared objective more likely but are *no* guarantee that the shared objective would be consistent with a systemic interest condition. We may have situations in which stakeholders agree on a set of proportions between industries that is not compatible with viability, or stakeholders may agree on a set of proportions between supply chains that is not compatible with full employment.

Both with horizontal and vertical connections, achievement of systemic interest leaves room for a plurality of political arrangements (a plurality of routes by which different partial interests may lead to a shared objective consistent with systemic interest). However, this plurality of arrangements should not be confused, *and indeed does not necessarily coincide*, with the arrangements capable of translating partial objectives into a shared synthetic objective compatible with systemic interest, be it viability or full employment.[7]

In short, alternative mappings of connectivity between activities call stakeholders' attention to different features of material structure, which may in turn induce dispositions to act in a certain way rather than others. This means that, depending on which features are highlighted, stakeholders will be inclined to map specific constraints and opportunities and will have a propensity to follow certain courses of action rather than others. As we have seen, there is no guarantee that collective actions resulting from political compromise or conflict would be consistent with a systemic interest condition either of the horizontal or vertical type. However, dispositions triggered by a given mapping of structure make stakeholders open to actions that are *potentially* compatible with a condition of systemic interest corresponding to that mapping. A significant consequence is that policy actions too are likely to be more or less effective depending on their degree of matching with the prevailing mappings and dispositions of stakeholders.

The world of systemic interest highlights a variety of conditions constraining the possible outcomes of political conflict and compromise within the boundaries of certain structural conditions. These conditions determine to what extent stakeholders' partial interests are conducive to a solution (attained by conflict or compromise) that is compatible with the objective properties of the prevailing pattern of connectivity between actors. In particular, we have seen that a horizontal scheme of interdependence *across* industries highlights viability conditions that may be met by the industrial proportions arising from political compromise or conflict between stakeholders in the polity under consideration. We have also seen that a vertical scheme of connectivity *within* supply chains highlights a systemic condition (say, full employment, or maximum expansion, for the polity under consideration) that may or may not be met by the proportions between supply chains arising from political compromise or conflict.

---

[7] The open-endedness of political solutions relative to systemic interest is highlighted in Cardinale and Coffman, 2014; Cardinale, 2015.

Mixed cases bring into focus the possibility of *alternative mappings of connectivity* within the same polity. For example, stakeholders in the same polity may alternatively map a horizontal or a vertical scheme of connectivity depending on their position relative to other stakeholders internal or external to the system under consideration. We have seen that actors who belong to the core of mutually necessary activities (what we may call the 'structural apparatus' of the economic constitution in place; Quadrio Curzio and Scazzieri, 1986, 2022) are more likely to map a systemic condition such as viability (a condition constraining the range of industrial proportions compatible with the sustainability of the horizontal pattern of interdependence under consideration). On the other hand, actors belonging to 'peripheral' activities (i.e. activities external to the system's inner core of interdependent activities) are more likely to identify links with stakeholders belonging to their own supply chains independently of whether those stakeholders are internal or external to the polity under consideration (these supply chains identify what we may call the 'transformation apparatus' characterising the economic constitution; Quadrio Curzio and Scazzieri, 1986, 2022). 'Peripheral' stakeholders are less inclined to map a systemic condition such as viability and more inclined (if at all) to map a macroeconomic systemic condition such as full employment or maximum growth rate for the collection of supply chains coexisting in a given polity.

6.7 Patterns of Systemic Interest and Institutional Architectures

As we have seen in the previous section, different mappings of the relative positions of stakeholders and the corresponding modes of connectivity lead to different ways of approaching the identification and possible pursuit of a systemic interest for the economic constitution under consideration. This has far-reaching implications for what concerns the relationship between systemic interest and institutional architecture. This is because the pattern of relative positions and connections generating a particular economic constitution may or may not be compatible with the institutional arrangements in place at any given time. But what do we mean by 'institutional arrangements' in the context of the present discussion? It seems reasonable to take a broad definition of this concept encompassing the formal and informal channels that determine which actions are likely, both in the sense of *being possible* and in the sense of *being expected*, in a given context. The distinction between 'to be possible' and 'to be expected' goes back to the distinction between *probability* and *possibility*. On this distinction Lotfi A. Zadeh noted that '[t]here is a basic difference between the concepts of probability and possibility. The concept of probability is rooted in perception of likelihood, while the concept of possibility is rooted in perception of possibility. What is the possibility of squeezing six passengers in a five-passenger car?' (Zadeh, 2011, p. 104). The concept of possibility entails a consideration of *objective feasibility* that is distinct from, even if not incompatible with, the concept of probability.

This view of institutional arrangements involves seeing those arrangements both as constraints and opportunities for actions to take place, as well as activation mechanisms for *dispositions to action* to arise. In this connection, Ivano Cardinale has noted that 'structure not only constrains and enables but also actively orients actors toward some courses of action over others. *Structure orients: it makes a given actor more likely to settle on some possibilities out of those it enables*' (Cardinale, 2018b, p. 136 [author's emphasis]). The relationship between the view of institutions outlined above, Cardinale's discussion of the relationship between actions and structures, and Doria's conception of dispositions as principal triggers of human action is worth noting (Doria, 1729; Scazzieri, 2012a, see also Chapter 2 above).

Institutional arrangements in the above sense may give rise to relatively persistent configurations of actions and structures that make certain actions possible or impossible and more likely or less likely in particular contexts and under particular circumstances. By the concept of 'institutional architecture' we mean any such relatively persistent configuration of actions and structures. The *constitution* of a political economy arises from a given structure of possible positions, connections, and dispositions to action, and provides a degree of persistence to the range of interdependencies feasible in that structure.[8] Within the domain of a given political economy, the

---

[8] Any given structure of relative positions and connections in turn arises from the resource and technology basis of society and from the web of possible social bonds associated with it (Pabst and Scazzieri, 2012; Pabst, 2018a).

institutional architecture identifies the relatively persistent range of
actions that are possible and to be expected in a given context. The
economic constitution provides a first condition for the persistence
of potential patterns of connectivity. Within any given economic
constitution, modes of social action and active connections 'mark
the partial actualisation of the existing potential for cooperation or
conflict' (Pabst, 2017, p. 195). Institutional architecture provides
a further condition for the relative persistence of modes of social
action and connectivity within the range of possibilities associated
with the economic constitution. Institutional architectures derive
from habit and history at least as much as from the deliberate
actions of individuals or collective bodies. In many cases they have
the character of unintended outcomes, as Adam Ferguson noted in
his *Essay on the History of Civil Society* (Ferguson, 1966 [1767];
see also Chapter 5, Section 5.5).

In several important circumstances, however, deliberate reflection and
design also play a role in determining the introduction and development
of institutional architectures. The intertwining of unintended path dependence (which is implicit in Ferguson's argument) and deliberate institution building is emphasised in Masahiko Aoki's view that '[a]lthough
the institution is socially constructed as an equilibrium phenomenon, it
becomes objectified to the agents in the domain as if it were independent
of, and beyond the control of, individual agents' (Aoki, 2001, p. 200).[9]
In a similar vein Vernon Smith argues that deliberate institution building
(what he calls 'constructivism') 'uses reason deliberately to create rules
of action, and to design human socioeconomic institutions that yield outcomes deemed preferable, given particular circumstances, to those produced by alternative arrangements' (Smith, 2008, p. 31).

However, Vernon Smith also points out that '[a]ltough constructivism is one of the crowning achievements of the human intellect, it is
important to remain sensitive to the fact that the human institutions
and most decision making are not guided only or primarily by constructivism. Emergent arrangements, even if initially constructivist in
form, must have fitness properties that take account of opportunity

---

[9] Aoki considers institutions as 'compressed perceptions about others' action-
choice rules' and argues that only when such perceptions 'become stabilized
and reproduced', actors' action-choice correspondences 'also become stabilized
and serve as useful guides' to actors' behaviour (Aoki, 2001, p. 11).

costs and environmental challenges invisible to our modelling efforts: What *is* depends vitally on what is *not*' (Smith, V., 2008, pp. 31–32).

The historical development of certain legal arrangements is an interesting case of the way in which institutional architectures may derive from combining path dependence and design, even if design itself arises within contexts shaped by history and unintended circumstances. The formation of two alternative Common Law traditions in England and Continental Europe is a case in point. Continental Europe saw the emergence of a Common Law corpus from habits and customs introduced as a response to changing historical conditions (in particular, the growth of trade and monetary transactions since the eleventh century). But those habits and customs were interpreted by legal scholars in terms of a formal benchmark provided by Justinian's *Corpus Iuris*, and those scholarly interpretations in turn became the foundation of a body of jurisprudence influential across many countries for several centuries (Grossi, 2007, 2010 [2007]).

By contrast, English Common Law took a different course. It started from the legal decisions of the king sent to ordinary courts. Then it developed through the formation of a body of jurisprudence based on those commands and it ended up in a body of law itself subject to interpretation in the courts (Stein, 1999; Ibbetson, 2001, 2006). There had indeed been an historical juncture at which the two traditions crossed each other, when Franciscus Accursius, from the legal school of Bologna, lectured at Oxford University and acted as secretary to King Edward I of England, presumably introducing elements of Continental *ius commune* into the king's legal practice and therefore into English Common Law (Ibbetson, 2016). The development of English common law and of Continental European *ius commune* are both instances of the combination of deliberate action and (unintended) path dependence, even if they both highlight that the relationship between intended and unintended outcomes can follow a sequential causation going from unintended to intended outcomes or vice versa depending on circumstances.

In Continental *ius commune,* interpretive practice is based on a formal normative structure (the *Corpus iuris*). However, it stemmed, many centuries before, from the systematisation of a pre-existing body of legal practice (Grossi, 2007, 2010 [2007]). In English Common Law, royal writs preceded legal practice but were eventually merged in a body of legal traditions that in turn became the basis of further

interpretations and decisions (Ibbetson, 2001).[10] In a nutshell, the
relationship between deliberation and path dependence in institution
building highlights the mutual influence of actions and structures in
determining the trajectory of institutional practices. As shown by the
twists and turns of English Common Law and Continental *ius commune* between tradition and deliberation, institutional architectures
appear to be the result of deliberation when they are in fact the outcome of actions made possible and guided by existing structures of
practice, or they may appear as the materialisation of traditions when
they are in fact the result of deliberations lost in a distant past (see, for
instance, Pocock, 1987). From this point of view, the emergence and
functioning of institutional architectures over time shows an interplay
of constraining, enabling and 'orienting' that underscores the central
role of dispositions and their embeddedness in historical contexts.[11]

The above view of institutional architectures suggests that the constitution of a given political economy is subject to both material and
cognitive influences. Material conditions and interdependencies introduce constraints and opportunities while also triggering dispositions
to act in a certain way, or even to turn one's eye away from certain
courses of action that would have otherwise been feasible. On the
other hand, dispositions, while rooted in pre-existing structures, may
give rise to changes in structures themselves. For example, actors mapping constraints that arise from a limited availability of resources may
be inclined to generate a sequence of technological changes along a
decreasing returns trajectory, while actors visualizing opportunities
that arise from indivisibilities and bottlenecks internal to production
technology may be inclined to generate an increasing returns trajectory

---

[10] The legal historian William Holdsworth noted that '[t]he common law
had [...] grown up round the royal writs. They formed the ground plan upon
which its builders worked; and it is for this reason that the learning of writs
was the first thing taught to students of the law' (Holdsworth, 1903–1972
[1909], p. 431; see also Ibbetson, 1986, for developments during the reign of
Edward I).

[11] This view has been forcefully argued by Ivano Cardinale, who maintains that
institutionally embedded action 'derives from how actors draw on structure
at different levels: individual-level structure (habitus) and social structure
(positions). While the former is shaped by experience in the latter, and the
latter can be modified by the former, this mutual influence occurs over time;
at any given moment, habitus and positions are different structures and are
autonomous from one another' (Cardinale, 2019, p. 468).

characterised by greater division of labour and specialisation of processes (Scazzieri, 1993; Cardinale and Scazzieri, 2019).

The interplay of material conditions and dispositions is also important for what concerns actors' mapping of partial interests, and of a possible systemic interest. This is because any particular mapping of material interdependencies draws the actors' attention to certain partial interests while inducing them to disregard partial interests that may be associated with alternative mappings of interdependence in the material sphere. This would mean disregarding mappings of interdependence that may give rise to alternative conditions for the cohesion of the body politic, and therefore to alternative constraints to the pursuit of partial interests in the polity.

The above argument has several important implications concerning the relationship between systemic interest, institutional architecture, and political compromise or conflict. As we have seen at the beginning of this section, institutional architecture can be seen as the relatively invariant set of arrangements (such as material, customary, and statutory conditions) that constrain, enable, and drive human actions by triggering dispositions. Mapping is central to the driving function of institutional architecture while being firmly rooted in the material structures of connectivity. This means that mapping arises from existing patterns of connectivity even if a given pattern of connectivity may lead to a *variety of mappings* depending on contingent factors such as actors' position in the web of interdependencies, and their exposure to certain impulses rather than others.

At the same time, any given mapping of interests is open to a *variety of solutions* for what concerns the outcome of political compromise or conflict, and therefore the possible identification of a synthetic (or 'collective') objective out of the manifold partial interests at play in a given context. The institutional architecture of a political economy reflects the material structure of connectivity as well as the pattern of mapping which prevails at given times. It also drives stakeholders' dispositions along certain trajectories rather than others, and makes certain policy actions more likely than others. This Janus-faced character of institutional architecture makes it subject to a *tension* between structural determination and open-endedness: institutional architecture reflects the material structure and mapping of interests from which it arises, but remains open to the manifold avenues along which dispositions may further develop.

As a consequence, a given institutional architecture is subject to a dual influence. On the one hand, the structures of interdependence between actors may follow a trajectory that is not synchronized (at least in the short and medium period) with actors' mapping patterns; on the other hand, actors' mapping of their position and prospects (which is itself a fundamental component of the way in which a given institutional architecture works over time) may show features of persistence that are at variance with changes of interdependence, or it may even follow a dynamic path fully disconnected from that. This view of the relationship between the structures of interdependence between stakeholders and the working of institutional architectures within which stakeholders are acting is closely related to Ivano Cardinale's discussion of the relationship between the positions of actors and their dispositions to act:

while the habitus is shaped by the positions occupied over time, the shaping is not an automatic imprinting of dispositions attuned to positions; rather, it results from how the actor engages with individual and social structure over time, both reflectively and prereflectively. In fact, at time t the actor makes a decision by engaging reflectively and prereflectively with positions and habitus, as described by the constrain, enable, and orient model. This decision leads to occupying new positions, which results in an updated habitus at time $t + 1$. Hence, the new habitus is not the result of an automatic imprinting but of the actor's engagement with structure at time t. (Cardinale, 2018b, p. 142)

Lack of synchronisation between connectivity structure and the mapping of interests is not uncommon. This has important implications for the constitution of political economy seeing that stakeholders' positions may change over time while their mapping remains stuck in a representation of linkages more in tune with a past pattern of interdependence, or the change of mapping may be out of tune with a more persistent structure of connectivity. The mismatch between connectivity and visualization highlights the importance of time horizons in assessing the relationship between actions and structures, and ultimately the character of the inherent tension within institutional architectures.[12] The likely mismatch between time horizons of *different*

---

[12] As Ivano Cardinale argues, '[o]n the one hand, an exclusive or prevalent focus on actors, unless properly qualified, might suggest a view of the system as being recreated, almost arbitrarily ("freely" within constraints) at every interaction [...] On the other hand, an exclusive or prevalent focus on systemic

objective processes of the social or natural type adds further complexity to the dynamic relationship between connectivity and visualization. Lorenzo Ornaghi highlights the problems due to the mismatch between the time horizon of political decision-making and the time horizon required for transformative action in the economic sphere (Ornaghi, 1990, pp. 36–37). In any case there would be a mismatch between connectivity and mapping, which makes the overcoming of partial interests by conflict or compromise often disconnected from the actual dynamics of interdependence.

For example, actors' positions may have shifted from a horizontal to a vertical pattern of interdependence while their mapping is still of the horizontal type, or actors' mapping may have prematurely shifted to a horizontal pattern when their positions are still arranged in a vertical pattern. A polity may think of itself as largely self-contained while in fact many of its actors are strongly connected to supply chains largely external to it; or actors' mapping may have 'prematurely' shifted to a horizontal pattern of interdependence even if still connected to supply chains that are far from forming a pattern of mutually connected activities. The mismatch between interdependence and its mapping has far reaching implications for actions in a political economy. We may expect that mapping of interdependence would be the primary influence in inducing actors to shift from partial interests to a synthetic interest by political compromise or conflict. However, the possible mismatch of actors' mapping from actual interdependence means that the identification of a synthetic, or 'shared', interest may be incompatible with the systemic condition appropriate to the prevailing pattern of interdependence (be it of the horizontal or of the vertical type).

The relative stickiness of either interdependence or its mapping makes it likely that, at any given time, interdependence and mapping will match only to a limited extent, or not at all. Clearly the extent of mismatch is likely to be larger the more dynamic is the political economy in view. In other words, actors are likely to search and try

conditions can obscure from view the choices that translate *possible* dynamics into *actual* dynamics [...] [I]n the analysis of time, the subjective and objective views are both necessary. Yet if we try to bring them together into a general framework for the definition of time horizons of the kind we are concerned with here, this dualism can have important consequences, which originate from the interaction between individual activities and social and natural processes' (Cardinale, 2018c, pp. 238–239).

political and policy solutions they are able to conceive, but these solutions are not necessarily compatible with the systemic interest condition corresponding to the prevailing scheme of connectivity and its pattern of transformation. As we shall see in the following section, this mismatch has important consequences for the formation of policies and their effectiveness.

6.8 Institutional Dynamics, Interdependence, and the Formation of Policies

Institutional architectures provide a degree of persistence to actions undertaken in the political economy domain. However, institutions are not a black box. In particular, they are subject to inherent tension between the material structures supporting interdependence between socioeconomic groups, the dispositions arising from that interdependence, and eventually the feedback from dispositions to interdependence itself. This means that any given institutional architecture is in principle subject to an internal dynamic reflecting the relative speeds of change of material structures and dispositions, where the trajectory of transformation followed by institutional architecture will depend on whether changes in material connectivity or dispositions set the trend.

The inherent dynamism of institutional architecture allows institutional persistence only if connectivity structures and dispositions fully match each other, which may only be the case in a stationary or semi-stationary political economy characterised by unchanging or moderately changing but substantially stable connectivity structures and dispositions. A political economy subject to changes in the division of labour is likely to trigger changes in connectivity patterns, which may in turn set off changes in actors' positions and dispositions. We can also think of a political economy in which changes in cultural beliefs set off changes of dispositions that may in turn induce the introduction of new patterns of connectivity. In either case, the relationship between connectivity and dispositions is the guiding principle of institutional dynamics. In turn, institutional transformation is a fundamental circumstance behind the twists and turns of stakeholders' mappings, which are an important influence on compromise and conflict taking place in a political economy subject to structural change.

The way actors map patterns of interdependence draws attention to the different routes by which different and often diverging partial interests are addressed. In turn, the 'collective interest' identified by compromise or conflict is the central influence on the formation of policy. This makes policy formation dependent on the *distribution of dispositions* across relevant actors, which means that policies reflect actors' positions within changing patterns of interdependence and their mapping of those positions. This process of policy formation has far-reaching implications for policy effectiveness. Indeed, effectiveness itself is a contested field, seeing that it may be evaluated in different ways depending on whether we take the point of view of individual actors, of coalitions of actors, or of the political economy as a whole. Individual actors may consider a policy to be successful if of advantage to themselves and nobody else. The same is true for coalitions of actors, when coalitions only include certain actors excluding others.

Coalitions of powerful stakeholders may twist collective decisions towards their partial objectives (often a compromise between different actors' objectives within the coalition) through their influence on the formal decision-making procedures of parliamentary democracy in what has been described as 'democratic despotism' (Pabst, 2016). Interest groups' influence on the electoral processes by financial intervention in party politics is an important example of the latter situation (see the analysis of this issue in Thomas Ferguson's investment theory of party competition, as outlined in Ferguson, 1983, 1995, and further updated and discussed in Ferguson, Jorgensen, and Chen, 2018, 2019).

The issue of a 'universal coalition' is more complex. We may have a universal coalition in which compromise or conflict attain a policy consensus that approximates 'collective interest', considered as consensus reached by synthesis of actors' partial interests (see above). And yet, consensus policy attained by synthesis of actors' partial interests at a given time may or may not be attuned to the evolving patterns of interdependence in the political economy due to the existence of lags between changes in interdependence and changes in the corresponding patterns of visualization. Johannes Althusius' *Politica methodice digesta* (Althusius, 1932 [1614]) is an early attempt to address the problem of a 'perverse' universal coalition (a coalition attaining political consensus incompatible with systemic interest) by decomposition of a universal political-economic domain into a multi-layered system of circumscribed political spaces (see also Duso, 1996; Elazar, 1998). Amartya Sen's theory of 'spheres of justice' addresses the related issue of the mismatch between universal and particular normative frameworks (Sen, 2006, 2009; see also Malloy, 2022). A heuristic aimed at detecting by successive stages of circumscription a hierarchy between spheres of interest of different generality is suggested in Scazzieri (2006).

As a consequence, we may expect that collective interest (as defined above and has attained by compromise or conflict between actors' partial interests) would often be unable to map in a sufficiently transparent way the prevailing condition of systemic interest arising from existing structures of interdependence.[13] This means that the process of policy formation may lead to actions that may look effective from a strictly political point of view (i.e. from the point of view of actors' partial interests) but that may be out of tune with conditions of systemic interest. For example, actors' visualizations may allow a political compromise based on a horizontal pattern of interdependence when interdependence has muted into a prevailing vertical pattern, or vice versa. The possibility of mismatch between interdependence and visualization highlights by opposition what would be the status and prospects of policy formation attuned to the evolving patterns of interdependence (embedded policy formation). This issue will be the focus of the following chapter.

---

[13] One reason behind this difficulty may be that 'our understanding of natural time horizons is influenced by the fact that time delays do not allow us to see the likely effects of current actions, and actions based on such understanding in turn affect natural time horizons in ways that are often undesirable' (Cardinale, 2018c, p. 240; see also Hanski, 2018).

7 | *Policy Actions in an Embedded Polity*

7.1 Constitution and Policy-Making

In the previous chapters of this book, we have taken the view that both the economy and the polity are embedded in a relational field. This field generates the range of relative positions that individuals and groups may take within it, while also making other positions impossible. From this point of view, both the constitution of the economy and the constitution of the polity reflect objective arrangements of positions that provide constraints and opportunities for human agency. They may also *orient* actors to follow certain courses of action rather than others.[1]

As we have seen, objective arrangements of relative positions provide the interpersonal foundations of the economic and political constitution. The economic constitution is the relatively invariant set of relative positions corresponding to the prevailing modes of association in the material sphere. Certain changes of relative positions are compatible with a given economic constitution while other changes require switching to a different constitution of the economy (see Chapter 4). In a similar way, the political constitution is the relatively invariant set of relative positions reflecting the prevailing modes of interdependence between spheres of interest in each social set-up (see Chapter 6). As with the economic constitution, certain changes in the relative positions of group interests are compatible with a given political constitution while other changes are incompatible with it and may require switching to a political constitution of a different type.

In a political economy, policy actions are located at the interface between the economic and the political sphere. Certain policy actions may be compatible with the existing economic constitution but not with the existing political constitution, and vice versa. Only policy

---

[1] See Cardinale, 2018b, 2019 for a discussion of relational structures as the orienting framework with respect to actions in the social domain.

actions compatible with both the economic and the political constitution can be carried out without changes in either. A *constitutional heuristic* is needed to assess whether a certain policy is feasible under a given constitutional settlement or not.

This chapter is organised as follows. Section 7.2 addresses the policy principles consistent with the constitutional point of view developed in the previous chapters. This section focuses on the multidimensional and multi-level architecture that policy design should follow in the light of the above discussion of the economic and political constitution. In particular, the section will consider policy actions as triggered and developed across manifold modes of association in the material sphere and manifold modes of collective action in the political sphere. This section provides the groundwork for the following analysis of policy measures in the industrial, credit, and international trade fields, which will be outlined in Sections 7.3, 7.4, and 7.5, respectively. Section 7.6 suggests a heuristic for assessing the role of embedded policy-making in a political economy facing systemic challenges that may require a new mapping and rethinking of the constitutional principles ordering its economic and political spheres.

7.2 Embedded Policy-Making: Framework and Heuristics

We shall consider policy making as the pursuit of any given objective or set of objectives whose attainment would change the condition of the polity, and whose pursuit requires collective actions instrumental to the achievement of that objective or set of objectives. It therefore presupposes: (i) identifying objectives, that is, of the state (or states) of the world to be achieved; (ii) identifying actions conducive to that state of the world; (iii) implementing the actions identified under (ii); (iv) assessing whether the actions identified under (ii) and implemented under (iii) have been successful in achieving the state of the world (or states of the world) identified under (i).

In the political economy sphere, policy-making involves identifying objectives at the systemic level (be it the local, the regional, the national, or the supranational level), and the implementation of actions deemed to be instrumental to the achievement of those objectives. Policy-making, as defined above, can be embedded or disembedded. Embedded policy-making requires the following conditions: (i) objectives must be identified consistently with the arrangements defining the relative positions of individual or collective actors in the polity under consideration; (ii) policy actions must be identified consistently with the arrangements under (i) (see also Amable, 2018; Bourdieu, 2005; Cardinale and Coffman, 2014; Dubois, 2018). The two conditions imply that not all actions potentially effective in making the political economy to move, say, from state s to state s^* may actually be implemented. Embedded policy-making means that it is only possible to implement policy actions compatible with the relatively invariant constellation of relative positions, and permissible shifts of positions, that are compatible with the polity under consideration. It is also important to emphasise that in embedded policy-making, the success or failure of any given policy action cannot be assessed independently of the unintended consequences of that action regarding the relative positions of relevant stakeholders in the polity. In embedded policy-making, the evaluation of unintended consequences of policy actions is as important as the assessment of whether policy has successfully shifted the political economy from state s to state s^*. Collateral damage or collateral benefit must also be considered in policy assessment. Each condition for embeddedness of policy-making reflects the existence of multiple layers of interdependence between individual or collective actors in the polity under consideration.

The identification of embedded policy objectives is a complex exercise requiring consideration of multiple levels of aggregation and identification of different partial objectives as we move from one level of aggregation to another (Cardinale, Coffman, and Scazzieri, 2017a; Fligstein and McAdam, 2012; McCormick, 2007; Martin, 2003; Pabst, 2014; Pabst and Scazzieri, 2012). This process involves the assignment of weights to different partial objectives at any given level of aggregation (i.e. to the objectives of the different groupings relevant at that level of aggregation), as well as the assignment of weights to the 'synthetic' objectives associated with each level of aggregation (as we move from one level of aggregation to another). The assignment of weights to objectives is a hierarchical process in which the plurality of objectives at a given level of aggregation is 'mapped' to a synthetic objective that, in turn, must be assessed against other synthetic objectives as we move to a higher level of aggregation. For example, the partial objectives associated with towns in a region must be assigned specific weights in order to identify a synthetic objective for the whole region. Then the partial objectives of different regions may be assigned specific weights in order to shift to the level of aggregation of, say, the state that includes those regions. Then the objectives of different states may be assigned specific weights in order to shift to a larger polity, such as a federation or another type of supranational unit. This hierarchical mapping of objectives in a multi-layered polity has a historical precedent in Johannes Althusius's analysis of the legal and political organisation of a multi-centred polity (Althusius, 1932 [1614]). A formal scheme for a hierarchical setting of objectives is presented in de Finetti (1979): '[the scheme] means introducing first of all different functions $f_1(P)$, $f_2(P)$, ..., $f_n(P)$, and only subsequently introducing, after assessing the pros and cons of each partial objective, a final function $f(P)$, which will obviously be an increasing function of all the $f_h(P)$' (de Finetti, 1979, p. 645).

The embedded identification of policy objectives involves a plurality of weighing criteria since different interests at any given level must be weighed against one another and eventually synthesized in the objective relevant at a higher level of aggregation. The process by which partial objectives (partial interests) at a given level of aggregation are associated with identification of a synthetic objective at a higher level of aggregation may be repeated several times, and each time the aggregation of interests moves one step forward till we reach the aggregation level corresponding to the polity whose objective we want to identify.

This hierarchical process is a route by which partial interests may find a synthesis in a 'collective interest' identified stepwise across different levels of aggregation of social groupings (Cardinale, 2017; Pabst, 2017). However, this approach is inherently open-ended and context-dependent. In certain cases, as in the example above, the territorial criterion may be relevant. In other cases, the hierarchical composition of partial interests may be based on the industrial classification of productive activities (Leontief, 1941; Stone, 1962), so that shifts from lower to higher levels of aggregation are based on the assumption of common interests between actors involved in similar activities.[2]

---

[2] An interesting case showing the relevance of aggregation level for the distinction between divided versus shared interest is that of a non-produced resource, which highlights a conflict of interest at lower levels of aggregation (allowing for shifts of resource between different users) and a shared interest at higher levels of aggregation (at which shifts of that resource are increasingly difficult or impossible) (see Sraffa, 1998 [1925]; Sraffa, 1960, chap. x; Quadrio Curzio, 1996).

In yet other cases, there may be a composition of interests across activities belonging to different supply chains (vertically integrated sectors) provided all supply chains share the utilisation of the same essential input – for example, the same non-produced resource, or the same infrastructure (Quadrio Curzio, 1986) – and/or depend on the same macroeconomic source of effective demand (Pasinetti, 1981, 1993). As we have already seen, there is no guarantee that the 'collective interest' identified by the above stepwise aggregation of partial interests would be consistent with the 'systemic interest' of the economic body and the body politic under consideration (see Section 6.6).

We cannot exclude cases in which different approaches to the composition of partial interests apply. For instance, supply chains cutting across territorial border lines mean that there may be regions, or even states, in which productive activities are split between supply chains internal to their territory and supply chains spread across different territories or states. In this mixed configuration of supply chains, the synthesis of partial interests requires coordination between different levels of governance. For example, a systemic objective expressing the synthesis between internally and externally oriented supply chains may require coordination between a regional level, a state level, and also a number of supra-state levels, which could include a supranational polity (such as the European Union) or international organisations, such as the World Trade Organization, the World Bank, and the International Monetary Fund.

A formal outline of this multi-stage identification of objectives can be given as follows. Let us denote by $\{C\}$ the classification scheme of individual or collective actors c_is relevant to the policy issue under consideration. Actors $c_i s$, $i = 1, ..., k$ are the individual or collective interested parties identified by means of classification scheme $\{C\}$. Following de Finetti's formalization introduced above (de Finetti, 1979), we assign a different objective $f_i(c_i)$ to each actor c_i, so that the collection of actors $\{C\} \equiv \{c_1, c_2, ..., c_k\}$ corresponds to the collection of actors' objectives $\{F\} \equiv \{f_1(c_1), f_2(c_2), ..., f_k(c_k)\}$. For any classification scheme $\{C\}$, a 'collective objective', which we may denote by $S\{C\}$, can be associated with the collection of actors' partial objectives $\{F\}$ by assigning weights λ_i's to the partial objectives: $S\{C\} = \lambda_1(f_1) + \lambda_2(f_2) + ... + \lambda_k(f_k)$. This formal argument implies that any classification scheme $\{C\}^j$, $j = 1, ..., s$ generates a *different* collection of partial objectives $f_1(c_1), f_2(c_2), ..., f_k(c_k)$. Switching, say, from classification scheme $\{C\}^1$

to classification scheme $\{C\}^2$ involves switching from one set of objectives $\{F\}^1$ to another set $\{F\}^2$. This argument highlights the central role of classification schemes in determining both the formulation of actors' objectives and the way in which those objectives *are* weighed against one another in determining a collective objective.

This stepwise procedure refers to the derivation of actors' 'collective' or 'synthetic' objectives from actors' partial objectives, and should be distinguished from 'systemic interest', which is a structural property. As we have seen in the previous discussion, different classification schemes are often associated with different policy domains, so that the embedding of policy objectives is bound to change depending on which collection of actors is considered and which set of weights is attached to them.

In spite of the open-endedness of policy objectives derived from a synthesis of the partial objectives of different individual or collective actors, embedded policy-making suggests a way by which those partial objectives can be made mutually consistent, not so much through a synthesis reflecting actors' differential assignments of *weights* to objectives as through the explicit constraining of partial interests by a *common systemic condition* (see Chapters 4 and 6). In this context it is important to distinguish between the different levels at which actors' partial interests may be expressed. Actors' relative positions and interdependencies suggest a first-level synthesis based on actors' relative weight and influence. This type of synthesis is often thought as stemming from political compromise or conflict, and it is likely to suggest a trade-off between the partial objectives of different actors. It is a synthesis conducive to the 'realist' investigation of collective choice solutions in terms of the relative influence of different socioeconomic groups (de Finetti, 1979) or to the collective choice paradoxes stemming from the discovery of lack of congruence between different normative goals (Arrow, 1951, 2008; Arrow, Sen, and Suzumura,1996; Sen, 1977, 1999b, 2017 [1970]).

The synthesis between actors' objectives takes a different character if we switch from the weighing of actors' partial objectives to the issue of whether *any synthesis* of those objectives meets systemic conditions for the sustainability (survival) of the political economy under consideration. In this light, the distinction introduced in the previous chapters between the 'material constitution' of a polity (in the sense of the relatively persistent ordering of social forces allowing that polity to survive as a political and legal body), and its economic constitution (in the sense of the relatively persistent structuring of activities allowing that polity to meet the fundamental economic needs of its members) is key.[3]

The material constitution provides a relatively stable framework allowing actors to reach a synthesis of partial objectives compatible with the existing economic order of society. Several different syntheses of partial objectives are compatible with a given material constitution, but there may be other syntheses (whether attained by compromise or conflict) that are not. This suggests interpreting the material constitution as a *condition* for the existence of a certain political body (*body politic*). The material constitution may act as a constraint on policy-making, in the sense that it excludes policies whose implementation would endanger the very existence of the fundamental (and often implicit) covenant on which the political body is based.

The economic constitution provides a relatively stable framework for the interdependence between economic activities. It covers the institutional and organisational arrangements allowing division of labour and transactions between actors as well as the resulting network of material flows sustaining the functioning of the economic body. In this case too, several different syntheses of actors' partial interests are compatible with a given economic constitution. However, it also possible that actors are inclined to attain, by compromise or conflict, political-economic syntheses that are not compatible with the existing economic constitution. This may happen when a political synthesis clashes with institutional or organisational arrangements governing the division of labour and established modes of coordination, but it may also happen, at a more fundamental level, when actors reach a political-economic synthesis incompatible with the *viability condition* ensuring the maintenance of essential material flows over time (Hawkins and Simon, 1949; Pasinetti, 1977).

An economic constitution is a multi-layered arrangement of institutional and/or organisational linkages and material interdependencies that are often subject to different modes of connectivity. As a result, there may be political-economic syntheses that are wholly or partially

---

[3] See Chapters 4 and 6 above; see also, in particular, Grossi, 2007, 2010 [2007], and Mortati, 1998 [1940], for the concept of 'material constitution'; and Cardinale, Coffman, and Scazzieri, 2017b; Pabst, 2017, 2018a; and Pabst and Scazzieri, 2016, for the concept of 'economic constitution'.

incompatible with the existing economic constitution. For example, a given political-economic synthesis may be compatible with the existing institutional/organisational arrangements but not with the viability condition associated with existing technology, capabilities, and resources. Alternatively, a certain political synthesis may be within the range of the material networks compatible with existing technology, capabilities, and resources but could be incompatible with the existing institutional and organisational framework of society. The multi-layered character of an economic constitution suggests the existence of a *hierarchy of conditions* that constrain the attainment of a synthesis between different actors' partial interests. Political (and policy) syntheses falling within the range of existing institutional and organisational arrangements may appear to be consistent with the systemic interest of the economic body. However, those syntheses may be incompatible with the viability condition allowing maintenance over time of the material foundation of that body. This potential source of tension within the economic constitution requires central attention when assessing the extent to which a policy derived from the synthesis of partial interests is compatible with the existing constitutional set-up of society.

Policy embeddedness involves not only the setting of objectives but also the identification of actions taken to implement those objectives. This means that actions instrumentally taken to achieve objectives must be feasible under higher-order constraints expressing the constitution of both the economic body and the body politic. These constraints are directly relevant for what concerns the *relative motions* required from different actors along the transitional path associated with the implementation of any given policy. Identification of the latter constraints is a necessary condition of embedded policy-making. For certain policy actions required on a particular implementation trajectory may induce changes in actors' relative positions that are not compatible with the existing pattern of structural invariances and the associated pattern of feasible relative motions. The feasibility stage of policy assessment presupposes the ability to follow the sequence of economic and social transformations resulting from policy implementation through the web of interdependencies that characterises the policy domain. As we have seen, interdependencies may be mapped differently depending on which classification scheme is adopted. For example, the relationships between production processes highlight different transitional paths depending on whether, in the context under consideration, horizontal interdependence between industries or vertical interdependence between vertically integrated sectors (supply chains) is more prominent. Different constraints are relevant depending on the prevailing pattern of interdependence. This means that policy actions theoretically effective in achieving a certain policy objective may or may not be actually feasible depending on which pattern of interdependence is dominant in the given context.

A similar argument applies to the assessment of policy outcomes. As we have seen, embedded policy-making requires that the success or failure of a given policy action be assessed not only in view of the declared policy objective but also considering whether policy implementation generates unintended benefits or damages in other spheres of the economic-political system. Policy embeddedness requires that the state of the economic-political system after policy implementation be compatible with the range of constraints that expresses in its full complexity the objective constitution of the relevant social domain.

To conclude: policy embeddedness requires a *structural heuristic*, by which what constitutes a given polity at any given time must be evaluated considering both which relationships between actors are relatively invariant and which ones are subject to flexibility in the relevant context. In the following sections we shall explore the consequences of embedded policy principles in the fields of industrial policy, liquidity policy, and international trade policy.

7.3 Industrial Policy: Structural Interdependencies and the Governance of Production

Supply chains are the backbone of a production system based on advanced division of labour (see Chapter 3). This means that division of labour, once it has moved to the stage of coordination between activities supplying and/or receiving intermediate products from other activities, involves a complex network of interdependent stages of production. These interdependencies provide the structural framework for policy measures aimed at facilitating the working of the existing pattern of division of labour, or to induce a shift to a different pattern of interdependence. Embedded industrial policy is a means of intervening in the network of production interdependencies by triggering certain patterns of connectivity in the light of systemic objectives, such as full or satisfactory employment, manufacturing growth and whole-economy expansion, environmental sustainability, or resilience to systemic shocks.

This view of industrial policy makes it necessary to evaluate the objectives, implementation strategy, and results of industrial policy by considering the constitution of political economy. The determination of policy objectives is a contentious issue in the industrial policy literature. It has been argued that targeting specific activities or supply chains can make industrial policy vulnerable to particular sectoral or group interests, or to informational gaps, thus turning it into a channel for misallocating resources (Baldwin, 1969; Bhagwati, 1982; Morris and Stout, 1985; Ades and Di Tella, 1997; Pack and Saggi, 2006; see also, on the political influence of industrial interests, Ferguson 1995; Ferguson, Jorgensen, and Chen 2018, 2019). On the other hand, it has also been maintained that industrial policy can be an effective instrument for achieving objectives that require a sustained concentration of resources in specific production activities, as is often the case at critical stages of the industrialization process (Hamilton, Madison, and Jay, 2003 [1788]; Gioja, 1819; List, 1904 [1841]; Rosenstein Rodan, 1943; see also Hirschman, 1958; Ames and Rosenberg, 1963; Amsden, 1997; Perez and Soete, 1988; Chang, 1993; Arora, Landau, and Rosenberg, 1999; Mazzucato, 2018; Chang and Andreoni, 2020).

Embedded industrial policy shows a way to overcome the above duality by calling attention to the *different* policy actions that are required depending on the classification of productive activities, their level of aggregation, and the timing of the corresponding policy objectives (Ames and Rosenberg, 1963; Reinert, 1995, 1999; Chang, 2003; Andreoni, 2016). As we have seen in Section 7.2, switching from one classification to another can trigger a shift from one collection of actors' objectives to another. This has important consequences for identifying the systemic condition relevant to any given collection of partial objectives. For instance, a classification by industry suggests a systemic interest coinciding with the 'viability' of the set of interdependent industries, that is, with the capacity of interdependent industries to reproduce itself by supplying one another's intermediate inputs (Hawkins and Simon, 1949; Pasinetti, 1977; Bellino, 2018) (see Chapter 4).

In this case, a collection of industries such as I_1, I_2, ..., I_k may generate a collection of partial objectives such as $\{F\} \equiv \{f_1(I_1), f_2(I_2), ..., f_k(I_k)\}$, which may be weighed against one another by assigning weights to industries that correspond to industries' shares in gross domestic product or total employment. As we have seen, the viability condition allows certain proportions between industries while excluding others (Sraffa, 1960). This means that a given collection of industrial interests may be compatible with the viability of the system of interdependent industries provided the weights λ_i's attached to industrial interests $f_1(I_1)$, $f_2(I_2)$, ..., $f_k(I_k)$ are subject to the proportionality condition $\{\lambda_1, \lambda_2, ..., \lambda_k\} \in \{\Lambda\}$, where Λ is the set of industrial proportions $\{\Lambda_1, \Lambda_2, ..., \Lambda_k\}$ compatible with the viability of the industrial system under consideration.

If we switch to a classification of production activities based on supply chains (vertically integrated sectors delivering a particular consumption or investment good, or a particular collection of such goods), we may 'generate' a completely different industrial policy objective. In this case, the relevant classification scheme is a collection of vertically integrated sectors such as $V = \{V_1, V_2, ..., V_s\}$, which may give rise to a collection of partial objectives such as $\{f_1(V_1), f_2(V_2), ..., f_k(V_k)\}$. The switch from these partial objectives to a collective objective corresponding to a systemic condition requires attaching weights to these objectives, which may express the employment shares of the different supply chains, or their shares in the gross production of the collection of supply chains under consideration. In this light, a systemic interest identified with full employment can be expressed by a macroeconomic consistency condition such as $\sum^k_{i=1} \lambda_i = 1$ (by this condition the employment shares of all supply chains add up to 1) (see Pasinetti, 1993, pp. 20–22). However, there is no a priori guarantee that the vertically integrated sectors generating supply chains only include activities belonging to the same economic-political system. Indeed, it is often the case that supply chains consist of components belonging to different economies. As a consequence, the condition for full employment may be satisfied for the whole collection of supply chains as it encompasses a plurality of polities, but *not* at the level of each economic-political system contributing to one or more supply chains.

There is no a priori reason why the means to achieve a policy objective under a certain classification of activities would also be compatible with the policy objective identified under a different classification of the same activities. For example, the employment shares compatible with systemic viability under a classification by industry are unlikely to coincide with the employment shares that allow full employment under a classification by vertically integrated sectors. This argument leads to the conclusion that industrial policy may follow a plurality of routes depending on the way in which productive activities are grouped together. Switching from one classification to another indicates different ways in which a systemic objective may be identified on the basis of different arrangements of actors' interests.

A classification by industry highlights a condition (systemic viability) that is embedded in the mutual dependence of activities delivering intermediate inputs to one another. On the other hand, a classification by vertically integrated sectors highlights a systemic interest associated with total employment and its splitting between sectoral employment shares independently of the viability of interindustry product flows in the economic system under consideration. Changing from one classification of activities (and partial interests) to another entails switching from one route to another in the identification of systemic interest. This conceptual framework brings into focus a policy heuristic aimed at identifying the systemic interest that arises from the prevailing pattern of actors' interdependence in each context.

It is worth noting that the dynamic pattern followed by stakeholders' interdependence may be central to determining the outcome of policy actions: a policy designed on the basis of a given constellation of stakeholders' objectives may be thwarted along its implementation trajectory due to a change in the prevailing constellation of interests:

[w]e may assume that the innovation becomes an individual action divergent from the past and therefore different from what society expects; this behavioural change tends in practice to change the relationships existing within the set of interacting subjects; this change however is evolutionary in character seeing that remaining actors at the following stage are themselves capable of adopting the same behaviour and to make it general, or they can terminate that behaviour by means of sanctions that can also become general'. (Bianchi, 1992, p. 213)

The above situation gives rise to the distinction between 'progressive coalitions', that is, a coalition of stakeholders supporting transformation, and 'regressive coalitions', that is, a coalition of stakeholders opposing change (Bianchi and Miller, 1996; see also Olson, 1971 [1965], 1982).

Embeddedness is central in the implementation of industrial policy and in the assessment of its outcomes. As argued in the previous section, policy implementation can be a protracted process, in which a policy action intended to uniformly address a plurality of industrial activities ('horizontal' industrial policy) may bring about significant asymmetries between industries, territories, social groups, and so on. On the other hand, policy actions targeting specific activities considered to be of strategic importance may trigger a diffusion process affecting a much larger range of activities, which may eventually encompass the whole economic system (Chang, 2003; Best, 2019). One example could be the possible application of anti-trust legislation to the case of technology platforms (Coyle, 2018, 2019; Pabst, 2019).

The interplay of intended and unintended outcomes is central to assessing policy embeddedness (Bianchi, 1992; Sainsbury, 2020; Cai and Harrison, 2021). Horizontal industrial policy may be deeply asymmetrical in its implementation and final outcome (Bianchi, 1992; Bianchi and Labory, 2018; Aiginger and Rodrick, 2020), while targeted industrial policy may generate either a lifting up of the whole industrial system (Rosenstein Rodan, 1943; Lee and Lim, 2001; Best, 2018, 2019; Di Tommaso and Tassinari, 2017; Di Tommaso et al., 2020) or a systemic decline of the economy as a whole (Bauer, 1971; Krueger, 1990; Williamson, 2000), depending on the nature of backward and forward linkages within economic structure as a network of production flows (Hirschman,1958; Antràs et al., 2012; Andreoni, Chang, and Scazzieri, 2019; Liu, 2019). As a result, the duality between horizontal and vertical policies gives way to a more nuanced picture, which requires considering complex patterns of interdependence and criss-crossing transitional paths as a necessary condition for the design and implementation of embedded policy actions (Andreoni and Chang, 2019). The embedded policy framework highlights the context-dependence of industrial policy in its formative and implementation stages, as well as the context-dependence of its outcomes.

7.4 Structural Liquidity and Embedded Credit Policy

Asymmetrical needs for intermediate inputs or final consumption goods characterise the division of labour in a system of interdependent activities. Division of labour, in its simplest form, consists of specialised processes delivering final consumption goods to actors who may or may not be producers themselves, but who are the source of a generic (i.e. non-specialised) demand for goods.[4] In this case, not all consumers make use of their purchasing power at the same time and/or to the same degree at any given time. As a result, debt-credit relationships may arise between individual or collective actors, for some purchasing power may be shifted from actors holding it at a given time, but not needing it at that time, to actors needing it but not having it at the same time. A more advanced division of labour includes specialisation in production processes delivering goods that may enter one another's production as intermediate inputs. In this case, an *additional* time asymmetry may arise. For production processes would generally be of different time lengths, so that long-lasting processes may need extended sequences of intermediate inputs without delivering finished products for a significant time interval (Strigl, 2012 [1934]). Here, 'material' debt-credit relationships also arise, but they would be different from those characterising the simplest pattern of division of labour considered above. For we may think of the relationship between long and short processes as a type of borrowing and lending situation, in which the short processes lend liquidity to long processes allowing these processes to reach completion in spite of the longer time they take to reach the finishing stage. Advanced division of labour reveals debt-credit relationships embedded in the interdependencies between specialised processes delivering inputs to one another.

The lack of synchronization between production and consumption activities, as well as between interdependent production processes, generates a type of liquidity (*structural liquidity*) that arises from within the relational structure associated with division of labour itself (Cardinale and Scazzieri, 2016; see also Kyotaki and Moore, 1997; Costabile and Scazzieri, 2008; Costabile and Nappi, 2018). In this case, the central mechanism is the *lack of synchronization* between specialised activities. This lack of synchronization highlights an important, yet generally neglected, advantage of division of labour. The splitting of complex processes into specialised processes allows the simultaneous activation of specialised processes that are not directly synchronized with one another. Lack of synchronization is already manifest in the simplest pattern of division of labour (pure labour economy) and takes increasing momentum as we move to increasingly

[4] The 'pure labour economy' discussed in Pasinetti (1993) illustrates the fundamental features of this pattern of division of labour.

advanced forms of division of labour. This lack of synchronization makes division of labour a source of flexibility and leverage for a production economy.

Structural liquidity highlights the potential for liquidity policy as an instrument to enhance coordination over time while also removing bottlenecks and increasing the intertemporal flexibility of the economy. However, the embeddedness of liquidity policy also reveals the conditions that need to be satisfied for its potential to be fulfilled.

In a pure labour economy, with division of labour but no transfer of intermediate goods between production processes, interdependence is reduced to the matching between the composition and timing of different consumer demands. In this case, policy determination is simplified by the pure labour assumption, as this assumption excludes the relevance of levels of aggregation and hierarchies for production processes: all specialised processes are, by assumption, self-contained. In this scenario, the shift from partial objectives associated with individual processes to a systemic objective associated with the polity as a whole may take place in a single step by assigning specific weights to the objectives (interests) associated with different specialised activities. On the other hand, *policy implementation* is subject to a more complex set of conditions depending on whether we consider a short or long time-horizon.

In a short time-horizon, short processes deliver finished goods, while long processes may only 'release' semi-finished products that are not yet ready for consumption. The short-run matching between producers' specialisation and demand composition requires debt-credit relationships allowing the long processes to be carried out in spite of the extended turnover time of the working activities invested in them. In this case, a full employment objective is likely to require a *selective credit policy* shifting liquidity from short processes to long processes, so that a sufficient number of the latter processes can be carried out in spite of their longer duration. A necessary condition for successful liquidity policy is therefore that credit conditions be attractive to both categories of actors (namely the actors associated with short and long processes respectively). This means that lending conditions open to short processes should be attractive enough to trigger sufficient flows of funds from short to long processes, while borrowing conditions available to long processes should induce these processes to take sufficient loans from short processes (Cardinale and Scazzieri, 2013, 2016; Scazzieri, 2017).

A successful liquidity policy must strike a balance between seemingly opposed lenders' and borrowers' interests.[5] The balancing between lenders' and borrowers' interests, which may look difficult to achieve if we think of homogeneous credit arrangements across the macroeconomy, looks more realistic if we think of differentiated debt-credit arrangements between groups of producers connected with one another by the division of labour. This may happen if, say, workers specialised in short process A are prepared to lend liquidity to workers specialised in long process B at favourable lending conditions in so far as workers specialised in process B are prepared to deliver goods to workers specialised in process A at favourable selling conditions. In this case the effectiveness of monetary policy depends on the existence of differentiated credit facilities available to different groups of borrowers and lenders.[6]

More advanced forms of division of labour involve the utilisation of intermediate products specialised in a particular task or narrow set of tasks. This is likely to increase the asymmetries between the time profiles of production and/or utilisation of different products. For greater task-specialisation is likely to increase the differences between delivery and utilisation times of different intermediate products. As Charles Babbage noted in his *Economy of Manufactures* (Babbage, 1835), division of labour in manufacturing allows greater precision in the assignment of tasks to workers (as well as to tools and machines) within the productive establishment (Babbage, 1835, pp. 175–176; see also Scazzieri, 1993, 2014a). Nicholas Georgescu-Roegen emphasised a different yet complementary line of investigation identifying conditions for the continuous utilisation in the individual establishment of a specific category of productive inputs (what he called *fund factors*).

In Georgescu-Roegen's terminology, fund factors are productive inputs that are permanently available in the establishment without being necessarily in use (Georgescu-Roegen, 1969, 1970; see also

---

[5] The lack of symmetry between lenders' and borrowers' interests triggered by disproportionality between short and long processes is a classical source of liquidity crises in the theory of industrial fluctuations. See Aftalion, 1913, 1927, 1929; Robertson, 1915; Bouniatian, 1922, 1933; Scazzieri, 2014c, 2015; Cardinale and Scazzieri, 2017; see also Kyotaki and Moore, 1997; Ozdagli and Weber, 2017; Pasten, Schoenle, and Weber, 2020.

[6] Albert Aftalion based on this view his criticism of inflation (price level) targeting as a principal objective of central banking (Aftalion, 1929).

Landesmann, 1986; Scazzieri, 1993). Georgescu-Roegen identified a sufficient condition for continuous fund-factor utilisation in the 'staggering' of elementary production processes within the establishment, which would allow reduction/elimination of idle times of fund factors by switching them from one productive task to another. This condition, which may be implemented in factory forms of production organisation, is different from the condition that allows continuous fund-factor utilisation in forms of production organisation of the 'job shop' type, such as craft production or other forms of product customisation. In this latter case, a necessary condition for continuous fund-factor utilisation is a sufficient degree of variety *and* proportionality between the different processes carried out in the workshop (Scazzieri, 1993, pp. 115–116). This condition makes 'job shop' production suitable to conditions of volatile demand but unsuitable to conditions of large-scale production for specific goods (see also Chapter 3).

Greater precision in the assignment of tasks has far-reaching consequences when associated with the introduction of processes specialised in making task-specific tools or machines. In this case, proportionality requirements extend from the individual establishment to the whole economy, or at least to the productive sub-system involved in manufacturing production. This generates a set of trade-offs between: (i) the proportionality requirements ensuring *full-capacity utilisation* of capital goods specialised in executing specific tasks (or sets of tasks) (by the Babbage law of multiples, which we discussed in Chapter 3); (ii) the proportionality requirements ensuring the *continuous utilisation* of those capital goods over time (by Georgescu-Roegen's condition for the continuous utilisation of fund inputs); and (iii) the proportionality condition ensuring the synchronization between different time profiles for the production and utilisation of different specialised capital goods.

Debt-credit relationships are primarily associated with proportionality condition (iii), and their effectiveness may depend on what is the dominant pattern of interdependence between production processes in the economy under consideration. Dominance of a 'horizontal' pattern of interdependence may require industry-specific, or even process-specific, liquidity provision, while dominance of a 'vertical' pattern of interdependence may require liquidity provision designed and implemented at the macroeconomic level (Scazzieri, 2017). On the other hand, liquidity policies aimed at coordination over time (synchronization) of specialised *and* interdependent processes may be incompatible with the Babbage condition for the full employment of workers and/or capital goods at any given time, or with Georgescu-Roegen's condition for the continuous utilisation of workers and/or capital goods over time (Cardinale and Scazzieri, 2016).

The conditions for embedded liquidity policy are likely to change in the presence of structural dynamics involving changes in production and consumption structures. In this case, the design of liquidity policy needs to identify expected or desired patterns of division of labour and demand composition as prerequisite for the effective synchronization of economic activities. This requirement is especially stringent when technical changes involve shifts in the hierarchy of processes within the production system, and the formation of new hubs of connectivity between processes. For example, interdependence between *individual* specialised processes may be different from interdependence between *sets of processes* performing the same function in different production networks, which may in turn be different from interdependence between different *production networks*.[7] As we have seen, determination of a policy objective involves the assignment of weights to the partial interests of actors' or actors' groups (see Section 7.2). This implies that the conditions of embedded credit policy under technical change are likely to vary depending on which pattern of interdependence is expected (or desired) for the political economy under consideration.

Policy is also likely to vary depending on changes in the time horizon of policy makers: a longer time horizon is more likely associated within increasingly complex and multi-layered patterns of interdependence. In the medium and long-term interdependence in a complex network of debt-credit relationships is likely to increase the likelihood of feedback loops that may lead to undesired outcomes. For example, 'increasing capital/liquidity and other requirements [for banking firms] during a prolonged recessionary phase implies that all banks try to simultaneously tighten the lending standards. But this may lead to a negative perverse loop: economic activity falls with a further

---

[7] These patterns of interdependence are of primary importance in the case of structural change trajectories, in which shifts from one debt-credit network to another may be required. There are cases in which 'targeted' liquidity policy may be a means to achieve a transition that may otherwise be impossible (Amendola and Gaffard, 1998; Quadrio Curzio, 2017).

deterioration in the credit quality of banks' portfolios, and hence with higher capital requirements' (Masera, 2018, p. 495; see also Crockett, 2000; Masera, 2015).

The above argument brings into focus the complexity of embedded liquidity policy. In particular, it highlights the need to overcome the conventional dichotomy between 'austerity' and 'expansion', which constrains liquidity policy within the straitjacket of a black box view of the economy. What is needed is switching to a structural, embedded view of liquidity needs identifying which credit provisions are compatible with the economic and political constitution of society and with the dominant pattern of division of labour in it (Cardinale and Scazzieri, 2013, 2016, 2017; Cardinale, Coffman, and Scazzieri, 2017a, b; Scazzieri, 2017).

7.5 International Trade: Multi-Level Arrangements and Relation-Specific Policy

International trade highlights multiple levels of interdependence between economic units, such as countries trading finished goods between themselves, or industrial sectors trading intermediate goods between countries. International trade policy of the embedded type requires a heuristic capable of disentangling the different domains of collective action in which policy objectives are determined as well as the multiple levels of interdependence involved in the implementation of policies. This approach highlights the context-dependent character of the free trade versus protection duality, as it calls attention to the existence of multiple possible cleavages and alliances between actors, who may alternatively support free trade or protection (or any combination therefrom) depending on their position in the local and international environment (Cardinale and Landesmann, 2017, 2022; see also, for two opposed classical viewpoints on free trade versus protectionism, Haberler, 1964, and Prebisch, 1951, respectively).

International trade indicates different policy domains depending on which classification of economic units is adopted (see Stone, 1962, for the role of multiple classifications in economic and social analysis). For example, classification of economic units by trading countries or trading blocks (such as China, the European Union, and the United States) shows policy domains that coincide with different 'trading aggregates' independently of the internal plurality of interests (and partial policy objectives) characterising each aggregate. In this case, each policy domain leads to the identification of a synthetic policy objective that only implicitly derives from the assignment of weights to the different interests (partial objectives) of different actors in each trading aggregate.

This weighing process often entails attaching weights to different trade policy options, seeing that different actors in each trading aggregate may have different, and sometimes opposed, attitudes to trade policy options, such as protection versus free trade. This weighing of partial interests may lead to a variety of outcomes as in certain cases the process may lead to a collective objective which may require the adoption of a uniform policy across all actors in the economy, while in other cases the composition of partial interests may lead to a heterogeneous policy mix allowing a different trade regime for different activities or groups of activities belonging to the same trading aggregate.

Classifications of trade activities between units different from trading countries or trading blocks may lead to different compositions of the partial interests of relevant actors. For example, economic units can be industries or vertically integrated sectors, and the synthesis of partial interests (partial objectives) into a collective objective (which may or may not be associated with a systemic condition) would involve the assignment of weights to economic aggregates consisting of elements belonging to different countries or different trading blocks.

Here we meet a completely different type of international trade. For in this case trade gets detached from formal 'political' units (such as trading countries or trading blocks) and highlights domains in which non-state actors may jostle for influence independently of conventional policymaking practices. The role of non-state actors is often key in explaining policy decisions at state level concerning international trade (Mamalakis, 1969, 1992; Baldwin, 1989; Milner, 1999; Daunton, 2010, 2018) and may suggest ways to identify patterns of systemic interest (and possible trade arrangements) under conditions in which exchange between political units such as nation states or trade blocks would not allow clear-cut policy decisions between unfettered free trade and a degree of protection.

Paul Samuelson discusses this situation when acknowledging that 'sometimes free trade globalization can convert a technical change abroad into a benefit for both regions; but sometimes a productivity gain in one country can benefit that country alone, while permanently hurting the other country by reducing the gains from trade that are possible between the two countries' (Samuelson, 2004, p. 142). In this connection Samuelson highlights that '[i]f the past and the future bring both Type A inventions that hurt your country and Type B inventions that help – and when both add to world real net national product welfare – then free trade may turn out pragmatically to be still best for each region in comparison with lobbyist-induced tariffs and quotas which involve both perversion of democracy and non-subtle deadweight distortion losses' (Samuelson, 2004, pp. 142–143). However, he also acknowledges that a situation in which 'worldwide real income per capita does gain net, so that winners' winnings will suffice worldwide to more than compensate losers' losings' may only bring 'some cold comfort in a scenario of many semi-autonomous nations' (Samuelson, 2004, Abstract).

Identification of systemic interest and of a synthetic policy objective reflects a variety of classification schemes depending on which visualization of trading aggregates is adopted. For instance, international aggregates reflecting the classification of activities by industry may be entirely different from aggregates reflecting the classification of activities by vertically integrated sectors (supply chains). Non-state interests based on classification by industry highlights partial objectives associated with aggregates such as the oil industry, the gas industry, or the steel-making industry. In this case, a virtual policy domain may reflect conflict and/or compromise between different industrial interests, and a synthetic objective may or may not involve state action depending on circumstances. A classification by vertically integrated sectors would generally highlight a different constellation of partial interests, which may be associated with the aggregation of partial interests by supply chain (say, the supply chains for cars, electronic devices, textiles, medical equipment, and so on).

Non-state constellations of interests may or may not give rise to an 'active' policy domain depending on whether a significant systemic interest may be visualized across different international actors (say, across actors belonging to the same global industry, or across actors belonging to the same supply chain). Multinational corporations provide a classic instance of unconventional international trade of the 'intra-firm' type. In their case, it has been argued that 'the world as a whole' benefits from their presence, even if 'these gains accrue disproportionately to countries whose factor endowment is such that, in the absence of multinationals, they would have few national firms' (Markusen and Venables, 2000, p. 231). On the other hand, 'there may be welfare loss for a country which, in the absence of multinationals, has a large share of the world industry' (Markusen and Venables, 2000, p. 231).

A policy objective generated by a non-state constellation of interests may or may not require the action of state actors, or other political actors, depending on the character of the non-state policy domain and of the systemic interest associated with it. Policy domains generated by non-state actors are generally virtual fields that may be activated under particular circumstances, as shown by the contrasting cases of OPEC (Organization of the Petroleum Exporting Countries), which is still an important actor in the relevant sphere of international trade, and of IBA (International Bauxite Association) and APEF (Association of Iron Ore Exporting Countries), which are no longer active.

7.6 Systemic Challenges, Resilience, and Policy Actions

Systemic challenges have recently acquired increased relevance due to the need to confront the current and expected consequences of climate change, pandemic crises, energy crises, and geo-political shifts. Policies demanded from nations states, supranational bodies, international organisations are increasingly seen as responses to challenges threatening the way of life, and sometimes even the survival, of societies around the globe. Policy responses to systemic challenges demand a comprehensive approach to policy design and implementation that makes embedded policy-making a necessary route to follow. Responding to systemic challenges requires a heuristic able to identify whether a challenge is truly of a systemic character, to differentiate between types of systemic challenges and corresponding types of systemic responses, and to detect at which level of the political-economic system an effective response can be found and implemented. Embedded policy-making under conditions of systemic crisis should follow the sequence of steps below:

(i) First, determining whether the challenge threatens the whole system, or only parts of it;
(ii) Second, identifying the time horizon of the challenge and the corresponding time horizon of a policy response to it;

(iii) Third, determining at which layer of the system's internal hierarchy policy actions can be designed and implemented;

(iv) Fourth, assessing whether effective policy actions can be designed and implemented as a composition of partial interests under the existing political constitution; whether they can be designed and implemented under the existing economic constitution; whether they presuppose a transformation of the economic body (such as a radical technology shift); whether they presuppose a transformation of the body politic (such as a fundamental change in the rules and procedures for collective decision-making); whether they presuppose a transformation of the social body (such as fundamental change in the dispositions and modes of association in society linked to cultural and demographic developments).

It is important to emphasise that in order to assess the ability of a given political economy to withstand systemic challenges, political economy's vulnerability and resilience have to be addressed. Vulnerability may be defined as a system's 'susceptibility to harm, powerlessness, and marginality' both from the physical and social point of view (Adger, 2006, p. 269). On the other hand, a system's resilience may be defined as 'capacity to self-organise' by adapting 'to emerging circumstances' (Adger, 2006, pp. 268–269), even if we should also take into account the earlier view expressed by Herbert Simon and Albert Ando, according to whom the system's resilience also expresses the system's capacity to withstand shocks by a process of 'diminished propagation' across the different layers of a system's hierarchical structure (Simon, 1962; Simon and Ando, 1961).

Simon and Ando outlined the above view of resilience when discussing the dynamic properties of near-decomposable systems:

[W]e have analyzed the structure of dynamic systems represented by nearly-decomposable matrices. We have seen that such systems may be viewed as composite systems, constructed by the superposition of: (1) terms representing interactions of the variables within each subsystem; and (2) terms representing interactions among the subsystems. We concluded, that, over a relatively short period, the first group of terms dominates the behaviour of the system, and hence each subsystem can be studied (approximately) independently of other subsystems. Over a relatively long period of time, on the other hand, the second group of terms dominates the behaviour of the system, and the whole system moves, keeping the state of equilibrium within

each subsystem – i.e. the variables within each subsystem move roughly pro-
portionately. Hence, the variables within each subsystem can be aggregated
into indexes representing the subsystem. Thus, the system of variables in
the case just described can by represented as a two-level hierarchy, with the
aggregative variables at the higher level. Now, there is no reason why we
need to restrict ourselves to a two-level hierarchy. For, to such a hierarchy,
each of the subsystem variables at the lower level might be an aggregate
of variables at a still lower level of aggregation. (Simon and Ando, 1961,
p. 132)

Simon and Ando's view entails that, due to the dominance of stronger
ties *within* subsystems and of weaker ties *between* subsystems, shocks
impacting specific subsystems may take a significant length of time
to influence the whole system's behaviour. This pattern of interdependence may provide some 'buffering time' for the system to absorb
the shock, as a result either of the gradually diminishing strength
of perturbation, or of the system's restructuring to enhance its own
resilience. However, the relationship between the timing of structural
transformation needed to meet systemic challenges and the timing
of feasible policy responses is a problematic one, due to the specific
timing constraints within the political sphere.[8]

A heuristic of systemic challenges is a necessary condition for the
effective design and implementation of policy responses. The first task
of such heuristic is to identify the system level that is most directly
affected by the challenge. Is it the contingent political synthesis of
actors' partial interests, or the 'material constitution' ensuring the long-
term continuity of the political body, or the viability condition allowing the long-term continuity of the economic body? The constraints,

---

[8] In this connection, Lorenzo Ornaghi notes that '"time" most forcefully emerges
as a fundamental element in the analysis not just of all political phenomena,
but specifically of the role of political institutions with respect to the economic
structure (Morgenstern, 1934, pp. 63–67). Time, being the protagonist of that
"state of choice" that is normally "a state of uncertainty about how a future
self will evaluate the situation in which the choice made now is placing it"
(Pizzorno, 1986, p. 366) plays a fundamental role in the system of symmetries
and compatibilities between the rules of institutions and the goals of human
action [...]. [T]he analysis of time appears decisive in assessing whether the
strongest interdependence between "order" and "transformation" is indeed
given by creative action. It is precisely in the analysis of what makes such
action feasible that political institutions fully display the *Mehrwert* mentioned
earlier: the power to directly affect the temporal horizon of economic action as
creative action' (Ornaghi, 1990, pp. 35–36).

opportunities, and requirements for effective policy-making will be different depending on the type of challenge that the system is facing. It is also important to emphasise that challenges may impact on a political economy in different ways depending on the time horizon in which the challenge makes itself felt. For example, the most evident impact of a pandemic crisis involves the short-term and demands an immediate response; energy crises and geo-political shifts may affect systems across short- and medium time horizons and are therefore likely to require a mix of short- and medium-term policy responses; climate change is likely to have short-, medium- and long-term effects, which may require policy responses across a wide range of different time horizons.

A policy response to systemic challenges may be more, or less, effective depending on: (i) the time horizon in which the challenge impacts the system; (ii) the level of the system's internal hierarchy that is most directly affected by the challenge; and (iii) the congruence, or lack of congruence, between the time horizon of the challenge, the system level directly affected, and the system's capacity to design and implement a resilience-enhancing response.

Effective policy responses to systemic challenges often requires the system's capacity to undertake a transformation of its previous structure and mode of operation. However, the feasibility and likelihood of that transformation depends on the type of challenge and on the system level at which the transformation is required. There are cases in which a resilience-enhancing transformation may be achieved by mere restructuring of the political synthesis of different partial interests. These are relatively mild situations, which can normally be solved by compensation policies between socioeconomic groups. However, there are also crises that can only be addressed by transformation requiring a more fundamental change in the constitution of the political body, or in the viability condition ensuring the material sustainability of the economic body. In the latter two cases, it cannot be taken for granted that the economic-political system will have the capacity to visualize and implement the transformation needed to withstand the challenge.

Changes in a political economy's structure and mode of operation are often a necessary condition for effective policy response to a systemic challenge. However, policy actions can affect system structure differently depending on how fundamental is the required resilience-enhancing transformation. There are cases in which an effective response can be found by modifying the weights (relative influence) between socioeconomic groups while leaving the 'material' constitution of the political body unchanged. However, there are also cases in which that constitution must be altered to allow for a more radical shift in the relative influence of actors in the political body. Finally, there are situations in which the viability condition associated with a given technological and organisational configuration of material flows is compatible with the reproportioning of economic activities required by resilience-enhancing measures, while in other situations effective resilience policies cannot be implemented unless the system switches to a different viability condition, which entails a more fundamental transformation in the material organisation of society.[9]

To sum up: the effective response to a systemic challenge often requires from policy makers the capacity to move beyond the sphere in which different partial interests may found a synthesis by compromise or conflict. This is the sphere in which 'normal' political activity takes place, but systemic crises often require policy makers to directly address conditions of 'systemic interest' relative to the material constitution of the political body and/or to the viability of the nexus of material flows supporting the economic body.[10] The capacity to identify the fundamental conditions for sustainability of the political body and of the economic body is a prerequisite for policy makers to move beyond contingency and to avoid the 'parametric myopia' that could make them blind to the manifold alternative arrangements of partial interests and economic activities compatible with a given material constitution and viability condition. At the same time, the capacity to separate what is essential from what is not essential in the constitutions of the political body and of the economic body is a necessary condition for distinguishing ordinary transformations from fundamental structural changes. Implementing a response to systemic challenge compatible with the existing constitutions of the economic and the political body may be feasible but needs to be visualized as such by policy makers,

---

[9] The latter case is one in which strategically oriented policy intervention may be necessary to trigger and sustain the investment in technology and infrastructure needed for restructuring the resource and product network that provides the material support of societies facing systemic challenges (Cerniglia and Saraceno, 2019; Ferrannini et al., 2021; Quadrio Curzio and Silvani, 2020).

[10] The concept of 'systemic interest' is introduced in Cardinale, 2017, 2022. See also Chapters 4 and 6 of this study.

who may otherwise be inclined to identify the fundamental structure of the economy and of the economic body, respectively, with a contingent synthesis of partial interests and/or a particular arrangement of economic activities. However, there may also be cases in which an effective response to systemic challenge cannot be found within the range of policy actions compatible with the existing constitutions of the economic and political body. These are cases in which a political economy faces a challenge that cannot be met except by shifting to a different constitution of the political body and/or to a fundamentally different organisation of material flows in the economic body.

To conclude this chapter: we have outlined a theoretical framework for embedded policy-making. At the core of policy embeddedness is the view of policy objectives as the result of a multi-layered arrangement of partial objectives and systemic conditions. At any level of aggregation of the actors who are relevant to policy determination, partial objectives may find a political synthesis that identifies the policy objective relevant for economic-political units at that level of aggregation (be it the local community, the region, the state, a multi-state polity). That synthesis may or may not be consistent with the systemic condition for the sustainability ('systemic interest') of the group of actors on behalf of whom the policy objective is determined. In a similar way, policy implementation takes place along a trajectory (*policy traverse*) in which policy outcomes at each stage and level of aggregation may or may not be consistent with the systemic interest of economic-political units at that level of aggregation, or with the objectives of particular actors at those levels of aggregation. Also, at any level of aggregation and stage of policy implementation, it is likely that some policy outcomes will be compatible with systemic interest while other outcomes will not. For a policy action thought to be sustainable to all involved actors at different levels of aggregation may end up delivering results inconsistent with the fundamental interests of some actors at a certain level of aggregation, and/or inconsistent with the systemic interest of the political economy as a whole.

Policy embeddedness brings attention to the constitutional features of policy-making, since both the determination of policy objectives and policy implementation are intertwined with the distribution of interests at the different layers of the polity under consideration. In particular, policy embeddedness requires consideration of the way in which the 'political' synthesis of partial interests is achieved at different levels of aggregation and stages of implementation, as well as assessment of the consistency (or lack of consistency) of 'political' syntheses with the systemic conditions for group viability ('systemic interest') and each level of aggregation and stage of implementation.

The embeddedness of policy-making brings actors' interdependence to the fore and requires considering three distinct spheres of interdependence: (i) the identification of policy objectives within the hierarchy of partial and systemic interests as one moves across different levels of aggregation, and between different schemes for actors' classification (say, by territorial membership, by industry, or by vertically integrated sector); (ii) the consideration of which alternative sequences of constraints may arise during policy implementation (different constraints may arise depending on which aggregation criterion is followed); and (iii) the assessment of which policy outcomes are compatible with the systemic conditions expressing the constitution of the economic and the political body.

8 | Conclusion
The Constitution of Political Economy

8.1 Constitutional Principles and Transformation Maps

This book stands back from present and past divides in political economy in order to explore it as a sphere of intertwining economic and political relations. A distinctive feature of current debates in political economy is the duality between the contributions addressing the economy and the polity as instances of means-ends rationality belonging to the larger domain of allocation reasoning, and the contributions considering both domains as largely homogenous aggregates dependent on the actions taken by a sovereign decision maker. In contrast to both these conceptions, we theorise political economy as a multi-layered arrangement of ordering relationships that provide a degree of stability to the economic and the political sphere in the social domain. Accordingly, the *constitution* of a political economy coincides with the ordering principles behind the economic arrangements in each domain of political relevance and with the range of transformations compatible with maintenance of each domain's fundamental identity. The constitution of a political economy is not a fixed constellation of relationships but a set of principles governing which conditions and transformations are feasible under the existing constitutional arrangements. This view of constitutional principles means that persistence and change are closely intertwined: a degree of persistence is required to ensure the identity and stability of a political economy, while openness to transformation is necessary to allow resilience to shocks and the introduction of improvements. We call this condition *relative structural invariance*.

The criterion of relative structural invariance emphasises a condition in which not all elements of a political economy can move together and/or at the same speed under the ordering principles defining the given constitution (see Chapter 5). As we have seen, relative structural invariance implies that magnitudes responding to a dynamic impulse tend to move by following a particular sequence of changes (or a particular range of such sequences), while excluding other sequences (see our reference, also in Chapter 5, to the conception of 'order of sequence' in Myrdal, 1939). In a nutshell, certain final states of the economy and of the polity can only be envisaged for certain constitutions, and intermediate stages of transformation that are feasible under some constitutions may not be feasible under alternative constitutional arrangements. Our conception of the economic and the political constitution is inherently dynamic, but any given set of ordering principles only allows transformation in view of a certain range of final states, and according to a structurally constrained range of feasible sequences of change.[1] There can be movements that are compatible with the 'constitutional' order of sequence and other movements that do not. This duality brings to light an important feature of dynamic processes in a political economy. On the one hand, ordering principles make certain responses to dynamic impulses possible while excluding others; on the other hand, the ordering principles themselves may change, driving the political economy to a different constitutional arrangement.

8.2 Dispositions, Interests, and Sequences of Change

Human dispositions are of central importance in inducing the way in which the constitution of a political economy responds to dynamic processes, both within the range of transformations compatible with the given constitution and outside it. We have explored the embeddedness of dispositions within existing social and economic interdependencies, pointing out that interdependencies draw actors towards certain actions while excluding others (see, in particular, Chapter 2). For example, the interdependencies associated with division of labour are of central importance in inducing individual and collective dispositions; at the same time, dispositions develop from the intertwining of rational awareness, imagination, and 'protention'.[2] This makes dispositions responsive to the social structures in which individuals

---

[1] These sequences are close in conception to John Hicks's 'traverses', which he describes as trajectories characterised by a given precedence order of the intermediate stages taking the economy from a given initial position to a final target position (Hicks, 1973).

[2] *Protention* is the disposition towards some courses of action that 'present themselves as self-evident', which actors pursue without explicitly choosing them 'among alternatives posited as such' (Cardinale, 2018b, p. 142).

and groups are embedded, but at the same time allows them to move beyond existing structures bringing about new patterns of interdependence and new forms of division of labour.

Chapter 2 examined dispositions as structuring elements of political economies. In that chapter we emphasised the multi-dimensional character of dispositions, seeing that reflexive and un-reflexive modes of thinking and acting interact with each other leading to a social body that is 'split' between the rational awareness of situations, and patterns of responsiveness driven by immediate sense experience and 'phantasy' (Doria, 1724, 1729; Vico, 1709). The heterogeneous dispositions coexisting in the social body make the body politic (and to a certain extent also the economic body) potentially volatile and hardly conducive to a stable political and economic synthesis.

Our argument called attention to the dual route that is open to the body politic and the economic body in the search of a relatively persistent structuring of the interests arising within either domain. On the one hand, we have the route (which Doria and Vico suggested) of developing rational arguments compatible with the dispositions prevailing in the social body. This approach leads to the pursuit of a rational objective (a balance between the different interests and passions in the social body) by an appeal to *sensus communis* (common sense), which is often more responsive to verisimilitude and 'phantasy' rather than to fully argumentative reasoning. On the other hand, there is the route of rational imagination, which is driven by positional inversion and relies upon actors' ability to fully understand and use counterfactual reasoning in the assessment of virtual situations. Adam Smith's theory of social mirroring and the moral sense outlines a route to the governance of passions, both in individual actors and in the social body, which is based on rationally driven imagination. In Smith's analysis, imagination can exert a moderating influence on passions by lowering the pitch of any passion to the level acceptable to an informed, and internalized, 'impartial spectator') (Smith, 1976 [1759]; see also Raphael, 2007).[3]

---

[3] The following passage of Smith's *Theory of Moral Sentiments* is evidence of Smith's rational use of imagination as means to counter unsocial human passions and to sustain the relational structure of the social body: '[i]t is not the soft power of humanity, it is not that feeble spark of benevolence which Nature has lighted up in the human heart, that is thus capable of counteracting the strongest impulses of self-love. It is a stronger power, a more forcible motive, which exerts itself upon such occasions. It is reason, principle, conscience, the

The view of dispositions adopted in this study makes them central to the constitution of a political economy and highlights the embeddedness of dispositions in the relational make-up of society. This embeddedness reflects the positions of individual and collective actors in the division of labour and material interdependencies but, at the same time, highlights that dispositions are open-ended due to the multiple possible images compatible with any given pattern of interdependence, and to the combined influence of un-reflexive and reflexive thinking in the formation of those images. The open-endedness of the process from which dispositions arise brings to light that the constitution of a political economy, while rooted in objective ('material') interdependencies resulting from its history, is conducive to a variety of dynamic trajectories. A political economy will follow one or another trajectory depending on the interplay between structures and dispositions, and on which interests are identified on that basis. The identification of interests in the social body induces coalitions and cleavages in the political and the economic body and drives a political economy along a trajectory compatible with the ordering principles of its constitution, or makes that political economy to shift to a different constitutional arrangement.

Dispositions induce images of interdependence in the social body, and shape the interests that are likely to arise on that basis. In turn, interests are inherently relational, as the concept of 'interest' always denotes a *distinction* between certain objectives and other objectives. Such a distinction allows the identification of what is 'the something peculiar' ('*quid peculiare*') specific to individuals or groups (Althusius, 1614). This is a necessary condition for the emergence of social cooperation or conflict (see also our discussion in Chapter 2). As we have seen, a given pattern of interdependence (say, a given division of labour) may be compatible with multiple images of interdependence, and with alternative ways of identifying the interests of individuals or socioeconomic groups. Each economy as a 'constituted body' presupposes a particular way of representing the interdependencies arising from division of labour, which in turn leads to a representation of the way in which economic interests give rise to coalitions and cleavages in society. At the same time, each economic constitution may or may

inhabitant of the breast, the man within, the great arbiter and judge of our conduct' (Smith, 1976 [1776], III.3.4, p. 137; see also Scazzieri, 2006).

not be sustainable over time depending on whether there is a range of proportions between economic activities that allows the replication of the pattern of socioeconomic interdependencies associated with it. This range of proportions identifies the viability condition for the economic constitution under consideration (see Chapters 3 and 4). Our analysis emphasises that each viability condition may be compatible with *different* patterns of division of labour within a range of variation. Outside that range, the viability condition is not satisfied, and the political economy has to shift to a different constitutional arrangement. A similar argument applies to the body politic. Partial similarities and distinctions between individuals and groups give rise to a complex pattern of affiliations that is compatible with alternative ways of identifying the 'collective interests' of groups and with multiple images of interdependence between those groups. Each polity as a 'constituted body' presupposes a particular way of representing the interdependencies arising from group affiliations, which in turn leads to a representation of the way in which political interests give rise to coalitions and cleavages in society (see Chapters 5 and 6).

As we have seen, interests provide both bridges and cleavages between human beings embedded in structures of interdependence. The distinctions implicit when identifying the interests of individuals or groups bring to light what 'lies between' individuals or groups. At the same time, they also pinpoint that what makes individuals different from some other individuals may also be shared with yet other individuals. The same applies to social groups. In this way, a principle of division (and potentially of conflict) may also become a principle of association (and potentially of cooperation). Indeed, any given individual or group, may express different, and sometimes conflicting, interests. For this reason, group affiliations can be cross-cutting, so that cleavages may coexist with interpersonal bridges within the same social aggregate. In this light, we called attention to the distinction between partial interests and systemic interest, where systemic interest is the *quid peculiare* that makes the joint (and not necessarily cooperative) pursuit of partial interests in the economic and the political body possible. Our discussion in Chapters 6 and 7 emphasises systemic interest as necessary condition for the continued existence (viability) of the political body, which is conceived as a multi-layered arrangement of partial interests based on intermediate forms of association and agency. In this view, actors pursue their partial interests by weighing them against one another in view of a synthesis (a 'collective interest') that may be attained by compromise or conflict, and which may or may not be compatible with the viability condition for the economic body and the body politic.

8.3 Towards a Dynamic Theory of Political Economy

Our approach leads to a constitutionalist view of the political economy in which the relationship between the political body and the economic body is one of mutual dependence. Each economic body, conceived as a constituted body, is identified by a particular division of labour, by a specific representation of interdependencies between economic activities and socioeconomic groups, and by the corresponding dispositions and interests of individuals and groups in the economy. Dispositions and interests are also central in the constitution of the political body, seeing that each political body is identified by a particular definition of systemic interest and by the range of variation within which a given systemic interest can accommodate different ways of satisfying partial interests.

In short, each political economy presupposes an economic body in which relational structures associated with the existing division of labour generate dispositions and interests whose 'synthesis' in the political body may or may not be compatible with the existing economic constitution. There may be cases in which the political synthesis of partial interests is compatible with the viability condition for the economic body, but there can also be cases in which partial interests find a political synthesis that does not allow the persistence of the given economic body, or cases in which changes in the division of labour (e.g. changes resulting from a radical transformation of production technology) are no longer compatible with the received composition of interests in the political body. In either case of mismatch, the constitution of the political economy is likely to change by adjusting the economic body to the political body, or vice versa. For example, a national political body may give way to a supra-national level of governance to avoid mismatch with a supra-national economic body (as in the case of economically induced political integration), or a supra-national economic body may give way to a national one to avoid mismatch with a nationally defined political body (as in the case of politically induced autarchy).

The dominant mapping of interests in the political body arises from compromise or conflict between the principal actors and is in turn at the origin of its institutional architecture. The latter results from a conciliation of partial interests, which may be invariant with respect to changes in the weights of the different actors provided such changes take place within certain limits. In this case, the institutional architecture is likely to expresses a mapping of partial interests compatible with the viability of the political body as a whole. In turn, the constitution of the political body may or may not be compatible with the mapping of interests arising from the division of labour in the economic body. In any case, changes in socio-economic interdependencies (such as changes in the dominant pattern of division of labour) are likely to bring about a reconfiguration of partial interests and/or a change in the identification of a systemic interest for the economic body and the political body alike (see Chapter 6).

Under these conditions, a mismatch is possible between human dispositions, systemic viability conditions for the economic and the political body, and institutional architecture. For example: (i) division of labour may introduce a (systemic) viability requirement that is not compatible with the received constitution of the economic body and of the corresponding political body; (ii) the dominant constellation of interests in the political body may shift away from the dispositions and interests associated with the dominant pattern of division of labour, which in turn makes a mismatch possible between the institutional architecture and material viability requirements; and (iii) changes in the constitution of the economic body and of the political body may take place at different relative speeds, so that the coexistence of the two bodies within the same social domain may become difficult to sustain.

Policy-making is a privileged interface between the economic body and the political body. This study has developed the conception of embedded policy-making, which considers economic policy actions as actions designed and implemented at the interface between the economic and the political sphere (see Chapter 7). Interdependencies are a distinctive feature of both spheres but arise from two different sets of conditions. In the economic sphere, linkages primarily reflect the division of labour and the modes of association engendered by it. In the political sphere, linkages reflect the constellations of partial interests and their organisation (through compromise or conflict) into a

'synthesis' that makes certain partial interests to be mutually compatible. Division of labour and its modes of association generate a constraint on policy actions due to the complementarity requirements of
mutually dependent activities. On the other hand, political synthesis
and its modes of compromise and conflict resolution generate a constraint on policy actions reflecting the balancing of different dispositions and interests in the social body. Under certain circumstances,
the complementarity conditions arising from division of labour in the
economic body are consistent with the balancing of partial interests in
the political body. In this case, policy actions are fully embedded in
the constitution of the political economy. However, there are also circumstances in which the complementarities in the economic body do
not match the affiliations and distinctions in the political body. In this
case, the embedded conception of policy-making suggests a heuristic
aimed at discovering the conditions for the 'constitutional feasibility'
and effectiveness of policy actions in view of the existing *mismatches*
between the economic and the political sphere.

In conclusion, it is time to consider what is the central message of
our analysis and what is the contribution of the theory of political
economy developed in this study to the long-standing discussion about
the relationship between economics and politics. As we have seen, that
relationship is often viewed in terms of economic constraints limiting the possibilities of politics and policy-making or, vice versa, in
terms of political constraints limiting the domain of feasible economic
actions and acceptable outcomes. Several scholars voiced discontent
about the reductionist duality between economics and politics that
the above situation implies, and suggested different solutions for it.
John Dunn called attention to the central role of division of labour in
the economy and to its 'political implications' (Dunn, 1990, p. 12);
Douglass North highlighted the role of human dispositions in shaping
formal and informal constraints on economic choices (North, 2005);
Luigi Pasinetti proposed to cut the Gordian knot of the relationship between economics and politics by a 'separation theorem' that
distinguishes the objective structures of division of labour from the
behavioural and institutional conditions characterising each economic
context (Pasinetti, 2007).

Our view is that the intellectual traditions of political economy suggest a promising, and yet largely unexplored, approach to the relationship between economics and politics in terms of their *mutual*

embedding. In classical antiquity, the dispositional activities included in the notion of household economy ('*oikonomia*') took a distinctly political character once thinkers moved to considering the dispositional activities within the city state ('*oikonomia politikè*') (Migeotte, 2009; Leshem, 2016). In early modern Europe, Antoine de Montchréstien's early use of the notion of '*économie politique*' brought to the fore the objective constraints (both material and social) facing a sovereign authority in the pursue of its goals (Montchréstien, 1889 [1615]; see also Maifreda, 2012).

These early developments, and the ensuing intellectual traditions explored in this study, suggest that a dual track is inherent to the relationship between the economic and the political sphere. Economic considerations take a political dimension when economic arrangements presuppose distinct but mutually dependent centres of agency, while political considerations take an economic dimension when political agency is constrained by ordering principles in the economy and society that are prior to it. In a system of interdependent economic and political activities, the economy has an intrinsic political dimension due to the formation of converging or diverging interests associated with the pattern of division of labour in society. On the other hand, the polity has an intrinsic economic dimension due to the material interdependencies needed to provide means for the pursuit of political objectives. This conception of political economy makes principles of economic ordering essential to the life of the polity, and political alliances or conflicts unavoidable in the division of labour between centres of agency in the economic sphere. In our view, the consideration of the matches and mismatches between the two spheres opens a line of investigation that is central to understanding the trajectory followed by any given political economy in the course of its history.

References

Ades, A. and Di Tella, R. (1997) 'National Champions and Corruption: Some Unpleasant Interventionist Arithmetic', *The Economic Journal*, 107 (443), pp. 1023–1042.

Adger, W. N. (2006) 'Vulnerability', *Global Environmental Change*, 16 (3), pp. 268–281.

Aftalion, A. (1913) *Les crises périodiques de surproduction*, Paris, Rivière.

Aftalion, A. (1927) 'The Theory of Economic Cycles Based on the Capitalistic Technique of Production', *Review of Economic Statistics* (then *Review of Economics and Statistics*), 9 (4), pp. 165–170.

Aftalion, A. (1929) *Monnaie et industrie: les grands problèmes de l'heure présente*, Paris, Librairie du Recueil Sirey.

Aiginger, K. and Rodrik, D. (2020) 'Rebirth of Industrial Policy and an Agenda for the Twenty-First Century', *Journal of Industrial Competition and Trade*, 20, pp. 189–207.

Ainsworth, S. U. (1999) 'Strategic Foundation for the Cooperators' Advantage', *Theory and Decision*, 47 (2), pp. 101–110.

Althusius, J. (1603) *Politica Methodice Digesta et Exemplis Sacris et Profanis Illustrata*, Herborn, Christoff Rab.

Althusius, J. (1932 [1614]) *Politica methodice digesta of Johannes Althusius*, reprinted from the third edition of 1614 and augmented by the preface to the first edition of 1603 and by 21 hitherto unpublished letters of the author, ed. C. J. Friedrich, Cambridge, MA, Harvard University Press.

Amable, B. (2018) 'Economic Policy', in I. Cardinale and R. Scazzieri (eds.), *The Palgrave Handbook of Political Economy*, London, Palgrave Macmillan, pp. 441–461.

Amadae, S. M. (2015) *Prisoners of Reason: Game Theory and Neoliberal Political Economy*, Cambridge, Cambridge University Press.

Amendola, M. and Gaffard, J.-L. (1998) *Out of Equilibrium*, Oxford, Clarendon Press.

Ames, E. and Rosenberg, N. (1963) 'Changing Technological Leadership and Industrial Growth', *The Economic Journal*, 73 (1), pp. 214–236.

Ames, E. and Rosenberg, N. (1965) 'The Progressive Division and Specialization of Industries', *The Journal of Development Studies*, 1 (4), pp. 363–383.

Amsden, A. (1997) 'Bringing Production Back in: Understanding Government's Economic Role in Late Industrialization', *World Development*, 25 (4), pp. 469–480.

Andreoni, A. (2014) 'Structural Learning: Embedding Discoveries and the Dynamics of Production', *Structural Change and Economic Dynamics*, 29 (June), pp. 58–74.

Andreoni, A. (2016) 'Varieties of Industrial Policy: Models, Packages, and Transformation Cycles', in A. Noman and J. E. Stiglitz (eds.), *Efficiency, Finance, and Varieties of Industrial Policy*, New York and Chichester, West Sussex, Columbia University Press, pp. 245–305.

Andreoni, A. and Chang, H.-J. (2019) 'The Political Economy of Industrial Policy: Structural Interdependencies, Policy Alignment and Conflict Management', *Structural Change and Economic Dynamics*, 48 (March), pp. 136–150.

Andreoni, A., Chang, H.-J., and Scazzieri, R. (2019) 'Industrial Policy in Context: Building Blocks for an Integrated and Comparative Political Economy Agenda', *Structural Change and Economic Dynamics*, 48 (March), pp. 1–6.

Andreoni, A. and Scazzieri, R. (2014) 'Triggers of Change: Structural Trajectories and Production Dynamics', *Cambridge Journal of Economics*, 38 (6, November), pp. 1391–1408.

Antràs, P., Davin, C., Thibault, F., and Russell, H. (2012) 'Measuring the Upstreamness of Production and Trade Flows', *American Economic Review*, 102, pp. 412–416.

Aoki, M. (2001) *Toward a Comparative Institutional Analysis*, Cambridge, MA and London, The MIT Press.

Archer, M. (2000) *Being Human: The Problem of Agency*, Cambridge, Cambridge University Press.

Archer, M. (2010) 'Critical Realism and Relational Sociology: Complementarity and Synergy', *Journal of Critical Realism*, 9 (2), pp. 199–207.

Archer, M. (2012) *The Reflexive Imperative in Late Modernity*, Cambridge, Cambridge University Press.

Arendt, H. (1958) *The Human Condition*, Chicago, University of Chicago Press.

Aristotle (1972) *Politics* (ms fourth century BC), with an English translation by H. Rackham, London, Heinemann; Cambridge, MA, Harvard University Press.

Arora, A., Landau, R., and Rosenberg, N. (1999) 'Dynamics of Comparative Advantage in the Chemical Industry', in D. C. Mowery and R. R.

Nelson (eds.), *Sources of Industrial Leadership: Studies of Seven Industries*, Cambridge, Cambridge University Press, pp. 217–266.

Arrow, K. J. (1972 [1951]) *Social Choice and Individual Values*, New Haven and London, Yale University Press.

Arrow, K. J. (2008) 'Arrow's Theorem', in S. Durlauf and L. Blume (eds.), *The New Palgrave: A Dictionary of Economics*, London, Palgrave Macmillan, vol. 1, pp. 124–126.

Arrow, K. J., Sen, A. K., and Suzumura, K. (eds.) (1996) *Social Choice Reexamined*, Proceedings of the IEA Conference Held at Schloss Hernstein, Berndorf, Vienna, Basingstoke, Macmillan; New York, St. Martin's Press.

Audegean, P. (2010) *La philosophie de Beccaria. Savoir punir, savoir écrire, savoir produire*, Paris, Librairie Philosophique Vrin.

Baas, N. A. (1994) 'Emergence, Hierarchies and Hyperstructures', *Artificial Life III, Proceedings,* ed. C. G. Langton, Addison-Wesley/Santa Fe Institute in the Sciences of Complexity, vol. xvii, pp. 515–537.

Babbage, C. (1835) *On the Economy of Machinery and Manufactures*, 4th edition, London, Charles Knight.

Bacharach, M. (2006) *Beyond Individual Choice: Teams and Frames in Game Theory*, Princeton, Princeton University Press.

Baldwin, R. E. (1969) 'The Case against Infant-Industry Tariff Protection', *Journal of Political Economy*, 77 (3), pp. 295–305.

Baldwin, R. E. (1989) 'The Political Economy of Trade Policy', *Journal of Economic Perspectives*, 3 (4, Fall), pp. 119–135.

Barabási, A. L. (2007) 'The Architecture of Complexity', *IEEE Control Systems Magazine*, August, pp. 33–42.

Barabási, A.-L. and Albert, R. (1999) 'Emerging of Scaling in Random Networks', *Science*, 286 (5439), pp. 509–512.

Baranzini, M. (1991) *A Theory of Wealth, Distribution and Accumulation*, Oxford, Clarendon Press.

Baranzini, M. and Scazzieri, R. (1990) 'Economic Structure: Analytical Perspectives', in M. Baranzini and R. Scazzieri (eds.), *The Economic Theory of Structure and Change*, Cambridge, Cambridge University Press, pp. 227–333.

Baranzini, M. and Scazzieri, R. (1997) 'Profit and Rent in a Model of Capital Accumulation and Structural Dynamics', in P. Arestis, G. Palma, M. C. Sawyer, C. Sardoni, and P. Kriesler (eds.), *Essays in Honour of Geoffrey Harcourt*, London and New York, Routledge, vol. I, pp. 121–132.

Bauer, P. (1971) *Dissent on Development: Studies and Debates in Development Economics*, London, Weidenfeld and Nicolson.

Beccaria, C. (1971a [1770]) Ricerche intorno alla natura dello stile, in C. Beccaria, *Opere*, ed. S. Romagnoli, Firenze, Sansoni, vol. I, pp. 197–336.

Beccaria, C. (1971b [ms circa 1769]) 'Elementi di economia pubblica', in C. Beccaria, *Opere*, ed. S. Romagnoli, Firenze, Sansoni, vol. I, pp. 383–649.

Beccaria, C. (1971 c [ms. circa 1768]) 'Pensieri sopra la barbarie e coltura delle nazioni e su lo stato selvaggio dell'uomo', in C. Beccaria, *Opere*, ed. S. Romagnoli, Firenze, Sansoni, vol. II, pp. 802–809.

Beccaria, C. (1971 d [ms. circa 1768]) 'Pensieri sopra le usanze ed i costumi', in C. Beccaria, *Opere*, ed. S. Romagnoli, Firenze, Sansoni, vol. II, pp. 810–822.

Beccaria, C. (1986 [1762]) 'Del disordine e de' rimedj delle monete nello Stato di Milano nell'anno 1762', in *Sul disordine delle monete a Milano nel Settecento, tre saggi di Cesare Beccaria e Pietro Verri*, Introduzione di A. Quadrio Curzio e R. Scazzieri, Quadri storici di M. Bortolotti e B. Cereghini, pp. 49–100.

Bellino, E. (2018) 'Viability, Reproducibility and Returns in Production Price Systems', *Economia Politica: Journal of Analytical and Institutional Economics*, 35(3), pp. 845–861.

Berlin, I. (1969) 'Two Concepts of Liberty', in *Four Essays on Liberty*, Oxford, Oxford University Press, pp. 118–172.

Bernstein, L. (2013) 'Merchant Law in a Modern Economy', The University of Chicago Law School, Coase-Sandor Institute for Law and Economics Working Paper No. 639.

Bessant, J. and Haywood, B. (1986) 'Flexibility in Manufacturing Systems', *Omega: The International Journal of Management Science*, 14(6), pp. 465–473.

Best, M. (2018) *How Growth Really Happens: The Making of Economic Miracles by Production, Governance, and Skills*, Princeton, Princeton University Press.

Best, M. (2019) 'Industrial Innovation and Productive Structures: The Creation of America's "Arsenal of Democracy"', *Structural Change and Economic Dynamics*, 48 (March), pp. 32–41.

Bhagwati, J. (1982) 'Directly Unproductive Profit-Seeking (DUP) Activities', *Journal of Political Economy*, 90 (5), pp. 988–1002.

Bianchi, P. (1992) 'Teoria dell'impresa, dinamiche innovative e mutamento istituzionale', *Economia e banca*, 14 (2), pp. 205–222.

Bianchi, P. and Labory, S. (2018) 'The Political Economy of Industry', in I. Cardinale and R. Scazzieri (eds.), *The Palgrave Handbook of Political Economy*, London, Palgrave Macmillan, pp. 463–488.

Bianchi, P. and Labory, S. (2019) 'Manufacturing Regimes and Transitional Paths: Lessons for Industrial Policy', *Structural Change and Economic Dynamics*, 48 (March), pp. 24–31.

Bianchi, P. and Miller, L. M. (1996) 'Innovation and Collective Action: The Dynamics of Change', *Structural Change and Economic Dynamics*, 7 (June), pp. 193–206.

Bielefeld, J. F. (1760) *Institutions Politiques*, Paris, Chés Samuel et Jean Luchtmans.

Black, A. (1984) *Guilds and Civil Society in European Political Thought from the Twelfth Century to the Present*, London, Methuen.

Blank, A. (2021) 'Pufendorf and Leibniz on Duties of Esteem in Diplomatic Relations', *Journal of International Political Theory*, first published online on 18 March 2021, https://doi.org/10.1177/17550882211002225

Blaug, M. (1997) *Economic Theory in Retrospect*, Cambridge, Cambridge University Press.

Blyth, M. (2013) *Austerity: The History of a Dangerous Idea*, Oxford, Oxford University Press.

Bobbio, N. (1989) *Thomas Hobbes*, Torino, Einaudi.

Böckenförde, E.-W. (1982) *Staat, Gesellschaft, Kirche*, Freiburg, Herder.

Boisguillebert, P. de (1843 [1707a]) 'Dissertation sur la nature des richesses', in E. Daire (ed.), *Economistes financiers du XVIIIe siècle*, Paris, Guillaumin, pp. 394–424.

Boisguillebert, P. de (1843 [1707b]) 'Factum de la France', in E. Daire (ed.), *Economistes financiers du XVIIIe siècle*, Paris, Guillaumin, pp. 267–351.

Bonar, J. (1992 [1893]) *Philosophy and Political Economy*, with a new introduction by Warren J. Samuels, New Brunswick, NJ and London, Transaction Publishers.

Bortis, H. (1996) *Institutions, Behaviour and Economic Theory: A Contribution to Classical-Keynesian Political Economy*, Cambridge, Cambridge University Press.

Boucher, D. (1991) 'The Character of the History of the Philosophy of International Relations and the Case of Edmund Burke', *Review of International Studies*, 17 (1), pp. 127–148.

Bouniatian, M. (1922) *Les crises économiques, Essai de morphologie et théorie des crises économiques périodiques et de théorie de la conjoncture économique*, Paris, Giard.

Bouniatian, M. (1933) *Crédit et conjoncture*, Paris, Giard.

Bourdieu, P. (2005) *The Social Structures of the Economy*, Cambridge and Malden, MA, Polity Press.

Bourdieu, P. (2012) *Sur l'État. Cours au Collège de France 1989–1992*, Paris, Raisons d'Agir/Seuil.

Broome, J. (2009) 'Motivation', *Theoria* 75 (2, May), pp. 79–99.

Bruni, L. and Zamagni, S. (2004) *Economia civile. Efficienza, equità, felicità pubblica*, Bologna, Il Mulino; English Translation: Bruni, L. and Zamagni, S. (2007) *Civil Economy*, Oxford, Peter Lang.

Bruni, L. and Zamagni, S. (2016) *Civil Economy: Another Idea of the Market*, Newcastle upon Tyne and New York, Agenda Publishing/Columbia University Press.

Buchanan, J. M. (1990) 'The Domain of Constitutional Political Economy', *Constitutional Political Economy*, 1 (1), pp. 1–18.

Bücher, C. (1968 [1893]) *Industrial Evolution*, New York, Augustus M. Kelley.

Burke, E. (1791) *An Appeal from the New to the Old Whigs, in Consequence of Some Late Discussions in Parliament, Relative to the Reflections on the French Revolution*, 3rd edition, London, J. Dodsley.

Burke, E. (1792) 'On a Motion for leave to bring in a Bill to repeal and alter certain Acts respecting Religious Opinions' (May 11, 1792)', in E. Burke, *Works*, London, Henry Frowde/ Oxford University Press 1906, The World's Classics series, vol. Ill.

Burke, E. (1991 [1782]) 'Letter to Sir Hercules Langrishe', in *The Writings and Speeches of Edmund Burke*, Vol. 9, ed. R. B. McDowell and W. B. Todd, Oxford, Oxford University Press, pp. 601–628.

Burke, E. (1993 [1759]) *A Philosophical Enquiry into the Origin of our Ideas of the Sublime and Beautiful*, 2nd edition, Part One, Sections VI–XIX, in I. Harris (ed.), *Burke: Pre-Revolutionary Writings*, Cambridge, Cambridge University Press, pp. 63–77.

Burke, E. (2014 [1790]) *Reflections on the Revolution in France*, in Ian Hampsher-Monk, ed., *Burke: Revolutionary Writings*, Cambridge, Cambridge University Press, pp. 1–250.

Butler, J. (1834 [1736]) *The Analogy of Religion, Natural and Revealed, to the Constitution and Course of Nature*, London, J. and P. Knapton, reprint of 2nd corrected edition. [This corrected edition appeared in the same year as the initial imprint and included the two dissertations – "Of Personal Identity" and "Of the Nature of Virtue".]

Buzan, B. and Little, R. (2000) *International Systems in World History: Remaking the Study of International Relations*, Oxford, Oxford University Press.

Cai J. and Harrison A. (2021) 'Industrial Policy in China: Some Intended or Unintended Consequences?' *ILR Review*, 74(1), pp. 163–198.

Callanan, K. (2018) *Montesquieu's Liberalism and the Problem of Universal Politics*. Cambridge, Cambridge University Press.

Caputo, M. (2019) *Memory, Mathematics and Economics*, Roma, Accademia Nazionale dei Lincei, Memorie, series IX, volume XL, n. 1.

Cardinale, I. (2015) 'Towards a Structural Political Economy of Resources', in M. Baranzini, C. Rotondi, and R. Scazzieri (eds.), *Resources, Production and Structural Dynamics*, Cambridge, Cambridge University Press, pp. 198–210.

Cardinale, I. (2017) 'Sectoral Interest and "Systemic Interest": Towards a Structural Political Economy of the Eurozone', in I. Cardinale, D. Coffman, and R. Scazzieri (eds.), *The Political Economy of the Eurozone*, Cambridge, Cambridge University Press, pp. 216–237.

Cardinale, I. (2018a) 'Structural Political Economy', in I. Cardinale and R. Scazzieri (eds.), *The Palgrave Handbook of Political Economy*, London, Palgrave Macmillan, pp. 769–784.

Cardinale, I. (2018b) 'Beyond Constraining and Enabling: Toward New Microfoundations for Institutional Theory', *Academy of Management Review*, 43 (1), pp. 132–155.

Cardinale, I. (2018c) 'A Bridge over Troubled Water: A Structural Political Economy of Vertical Integration', *Structural Change and Economic Dynamics*, 46 (September), pp. 172–179.

Cardinale, I. (2018d) 'Time Horizons and Human Activities: A Position Paper', *Balzan Papers, I*, pp. 235–257.

Cardinale, I. (2019) 'Microfoundations of Institutions and the Theory of Action', *Academy of Management Review*, 44 (2), pp. 467–470.

Cardinale, I. (2020) 'Structural Political Economy: Particular Interests, Systemic Interests and the Structure of Division of Labour', *Rendiconti, Classe di Scienze Morali, Storiche e Filologiche*, Accademia Nazionale dei Lincei, serie ix, vol. xxxi, pp. 257–274.

Cardinale, I. (2022) 'Vulnerability, Resilience and "Systemic Interest": A Connectivity Approach', *Networks and Spatial Economics*, 22 (April), pp. 691–707.

Cardinale, I. and D. Coffman. (2014) 'Economic Interdependencies and Political Conflict: The Political Economy of Taxation in Eighteenth-Century Britain', *Economia Politica: Journal of Analytical and Institutional Economics*, 31 (3), pp. 277–300.

Cardinale, I., Coffman, D., and Scazzieri, R. (2017a) 'Framing the Political Economy of the Eurozone: Structural Heuristics for Analysis and Policy', in I. Cardinale, D. Coffman, and R. Scazzieri (eds.), *The Political Economy of the Eurozone*, Cambridge, Cambridge University Press, pp. 483–551.

Cardinale I., Coffman, D., and Scazzieri, R. (2017b) 'The Eurozone as a Political Economy Field', in I. Cardinale, D. Coffman, and R. Scazzieri (eds.), *The Political Economy of the Eurozone*, Cambridge, Cambridge University Press, pp. 1–33.

Cardinale, I. and Landesmann, M. (2017) 'Exploring Sectoral Conflicts of Interest in the Eurozone. A Structural Political Economy Approach', in I. Cardinale, D. Coffman, and R. Scazzieri (eds.), *The Political Economy of the Eurozone*, Cambridge, Cambridge University Press, pp. 284–336.

Cardinale, I. and Landesmann, M. (2022) 'Generalising the Political Economy of Structural Change: A Structural Political Economy Approach', *Structural Change and Economic Dynamics*, 61 (June), pp. 546–558.

Cardinale, I. and Scazzieri, R. (2013) 'Structural Liquidity: Time Coordination of Economic Activities and Sectoral Interdependence', paper presented at Cambridge Finance Workshop, Newnham College, 5 February 2013.

Cardinale, I. and Scazzieri, R. (2016) 'Structural Liquidity: The Money-Industry Nexus', *Structural Change and Economic Dynamics*, 39 (December), pp. 46–53.

Cardinale, I. and Scazzieri, R. (2017) 'Beyond "Austerity vs. Expansion": Elements for a Structural Theory of Liquidity Policy', *Revue d'économie industrielle*, 160 (4), pp. 107–136.

Cardinale, I. and Scazzieri, R. (2018a) 'Political Economy: Outlining a Field', in I. Cardinale and R. Scazzieri (eds.), *The Palgrave Handbook of Political Economy*. London, Palgrave Macmillan, pp. 1–25.

Cardinale, I. and Scazzieri, R. (2018b) 'Political Economy as Theory of Society', in I. Cardinale and R. Scazzieri (eds.), *The Palgrave Handbook of Political Economy*. London, Palgrave Macmillan, pp. 787–815.

Cardinale, I. and Scazzieri, R. (2019) 'Explaining Structural Change: Actions and Transformations', *Structural Change and Economic Dynamics*, 51 (December), pp. 393–404.

Cerniglia, F. and Saraceno, F. (eds.) (2019) *A European Public Investment Outlook*, Cambridge, Open Book Publishers.

Cesa, M. (2004) *Machiavelli on International Relations*, Oxford, Oxford University Press.

Chandler, A. D. Jr. (1977) *The Visible Hand: The Managerial Revolution in American Business*, Cambridge, MA., The Belknap Press.

Chandler, A. D. Jr. (1990) *Scale and Scope*, Cambridge, MA, The Belknap Press.

Chang, H.-J. (1993) *The Political Economy of Industrial Policy*, London, Palgrave Macmillan.

Chang, H.-J. (2003) *Kicking Away the Ladder: Development Strategy in Historical Perspective*, London, Anthem Press.

Chang, H.-J. and Andreoni, A. (2020) 'Industrial Policy in the 21st Century', *Development and Change*, 561 (1, March), pp. 324–351.

Chaudhuri, K. N. (1985) *Trade and Civilisation in the Indian Ocean: An Economic History from the Rise of Islam to 1750*, Cambridge, Cambridge University Press.

Chochoy, N. (2015) 'Karl Polanyi et l'encastrement politique de l'économie: pour une analyse systémique des rapports changeants entre économie et société', *Revue française de socio-économie*, 1, pp. 153–173.

Coffman, D. (2021) 'François Quesnay, Luigi Pasinetti and the Historical Contexts of Economic Theory', *Structural Change and Economic Dynamics*, 56 (March), pp. 64–73.

Cohendet, P., Ledoux, M.J., and Zuscovitch, E. (eds.) (1988a) *New Advanced Materials: Economic Dynamics and European Strategy. A Report from the FAST Programme of the Commission of the European Communities*, Berlin and Heidelberg, Springer.

Cohendet P., Ledoux M.J., and Zuscovitch E. (1988b) '"Inter-materials" Variety and the Overchoice Phenomenon', in Cohendet, P., Ledoux, M.J., and Zuscovitch, E.(eds.), *New Advanced Materials*, Berlin and Heidelberg, Springer, pp. 74–91, https://doi.org/10.1007/978-3-642-73809-8_8

Collini, S., Winch, D., and Burrow, J. (1983) *That Noble Science of Politics: A Study in Nineteenth-Century Intellectual History*, Cambridge, Cambridge University Press.

Collins, G. M. (2020) *Commerce and Manners in Edmund Burke's Political Economy*, Cambridge, Cambridge University Press.

Collison Black, R. D, Coats, R. W., Crauford D., and Goodwin, W. (eds.) (1973) *The Marginal Revolution in Economics*, Durham, NC, Duke University Press.

Constant, B. (1818–1819) *Collection complète des ouvrages publiés sur le Gouvernement representatif et la Constitution actuelle de la France, formant une espèce de Cours de politique constitutionnelle*, Paris, de l'imprimerie de Mme Jeunehomme-Cremière.

Costabile, L. (2012) 'Scuola Napoletana', in V. Negri Zamagni and P. L. Porta (eds.), *Il contributo italiano alla storia del pensiero. Economia*, Roma, Istituto dell'Enciclopedia Italiana, pp. 240–251.

Costabile, L. (2015) 'Le radici del pensiero economico italiano: Napoli e l'Europa', in L. Costabile G. Lunghini, A. Quadrio Curzio, A. Roncaglia, and R. Scazzieri (eds.), *Gli economisti italiani. Protagonisti, paradigmi, politiche*, Roma, Accademia Nazionale dei Lincei, Atti dei Convegni Lincei n. 290, pp. 25–47.

Costabile, L. (2020) 'La teoria politica della divisione del lavoro', *Rendiconti, Classe di Scienze Morali, Storiche e Filologiche*, Accademia Nazionale dei Lincei, serie ix, vol. xxxi, pp. 225–229.

Costabile L. and Nappi E. (2018) 'The Public Banks of Naples between Financial Innovation and Crisis', in L. Costabile and L. Neal (eds.), *Financial Innovation and Resilience. Palgrave Studies in the History of Finance*, Cham, Palgrave Macmillan, pp. 17–53.

Costabile, L. and Scazzieri, R. (2008) 'Social Models, Growth and Key Currencies', in L. Costabile (ed.), *Institutions for Social Well-Being. Alternatives for Europe*, Houndmills, Basingstoke, Palgrave Macmillan, pp. 126–151.

Coyle, D. (2018) 'Platform Dominance: The Shortcomings of Antitrust Policy', in M. Moore and D. Tombini (eds.), *Digital Dominance: The Power of Google, Amazon, Facebook and Apple*, Oxford, Oxford University Press, pp. 50–70.

Coyle, D. (2019) 'Practical Competition Policy Tools for Digital Platforms', *Antitrust Law Journal*, 82 (3), pp. 835–860.

Coyle, D. (2020) *Markets, State, and People. Economics for Public Policy*, Princeton, Princeton University Press.

Crick, B. (1992) *In Defence of Politics*, 4th edition, Chicago, University of Chicago Press.

Croce, B. (1925) 'Shaftesbury in Italia – con lettere inedite', *La Critica. Rivista di Letteratura, Storia e Filosofia*, 23, pp. 1–27.

Crockett, A. D. (2000) 'Marrying the Micro- and Macro-prudential Dimensions of Financial Stability', Remarks before the Eleventh International Conference of Banking Supervisors, Basel, 20–21 September 2000.

Crouzet, F. (1990) *Britain Ascendant: Comparative Studies in Franco-British Economic History*, Cambridge, Cambridge University Press.

Cudworth, R. (1743 [1678]) *The True Intellectual System of the Universe [...]*, London, printed for J. Walthoe, D. Midwinter, etc.

Cumberland, R. (1672) *De legibus naturae disquisitio philosophica, in qua elementa philosophiae hobbianae cum moralis tum civilis considerantur et refutantur*, London, Flesher.

D'Addio, M. (1954) *L'idea del contratto sociale dai sofisti alla riforma e il "De Principatu" di Mario Salamonio*, Milano, Giuffré.

Daalder, H. (1966) 'The Netherlands: Opposition in a Segmented Society', in R. A. Dahl (ed.), *Political Opposition in Western Democracies*. New Haven, Yale University Press, pp. 188–236.

Dagum, C. (1969) 'Structural Permanence: Its Role in the Analysis of Structural Dualisms and Dependences and for Prediction and Decision Purposes', *Zeitschrift für die Gesamte Staatswissenschaft*, 125, pp. 211–235. (Also published in Hagemann, H., Landesmann, M., and Scazzieri, R. (eds.), *The Economics of Structural Change: Vol. I. Economic Structure and Change: Concepts and Theories*, Cheltenham and Northampton, MA, Edward Elgar, Vol. 2, pp. 377–401.)

Darwall, S. (2006) *The Second-Person Standpoint. Morality, Respect and Accountability*, Cambridge, MA and London, Harvard University Press.

Daunton, M. (2010) 'From Bretton Woods to Havana: Multilateral Deadlocks in Historical Perspective', in A. Narlikar (ed.), *Deadlocks in Multilateral Negotiations: Causes and Solutions*, Cambridge, Cambridge University Press, pp. 47–78.

Daunton, M. (2018) 'International Political Economy', in I. Cardinale and R. Scazzieri (eds.), *The Palgrave Handbook of Political Economy*, London, Palgrave Macmillan, pp. 605–655.

David, P. (1994) 'Why Are Institutions the "Carriers of History"? Path Dependence and the Evolution of Conventions, Organizations and Institutions', *Structural Change and Economic Dynamics*, 5 (December), pp. 205–220.

de Finetti, B. (1979) 'Due lezioni su "teoria delle decisioni"', in *Contributi del Centro Linceo interdisciplinare di scienze matematiche e loro applicazioni*, n. 6, Seminari su La scienza dei sistemi, parte seconda, pp. 643–656.

Deane, P. (1980) *The First Industrial Revolution*, 2nd edition, Cambridge, Cambridge University Press.

Deane, P. (1989) *The State and the Economic System*, Oxford, Oxford University Press.

Deleersnyder, J.-L., Hodgson, T. J., Muller, H., and O'Grady, P. J. (1989) 'Kanban Controlled Pull Systems: An Analytic Approach', *Management Science*, 35 (9, September), pp. 1079–1091.

Di Battista, F. (2007) 'L'economia civile genovesiana e la moderna economia politica', in B. Jossa, R. Patalano, and E. Zagari (eds.), *Genovesi economista. Nel 250° anniversario dell'istituzione della cattedra di 'commercio e meccanica', Atti del Convegno di Studi di Napoli del 5–6 maggio 2005*, Napoli, Istituto Italiano per gli Studi Filosofici, pp. 291–315.

Di Tommaso, M. and Tassinari, M. (2017) *Industria, governo, mercato. Lezioni americane*, Bologna, Il Mulino.

Di Tommaso, M. R., Tassinari, M., Barbieri, E., and Marozzi, M. (2020) 'Selective Industrial Policy and "Sustainable" Structural Change: Discussing the Political Economy of Sectoral Priorities in the US', *Structural Change and Economic Dynamics*, 54 (September), pp. 309–323.

Dobb, M. H. (1973) *Theories of Value and Distribution since Adam Smith: Ideology and Economic Theory*. Cambridge, Cambridge University Press.

Donati, P. (1991) *Teoria relazionale della società*, Milano, Franco Angeli.

Donati, P. (2006) 'Il significato del paradigma relazionale per la comprensione e l'organizzazione della società: una visione "civile"', in P. Donati and I. Colozzi (eds.), *Il paradigma relazionale nelle scienze sociali: le prospettive sociologiche*, Bologna, Il Mulino, pp. 51–113.

Donati, P. (2010) *Relational Sociology: A New Paradigm for the Social Sciences*, London, Routledge.

Donati, P. and Archer, M. S. (2015) *The Relational Subject*, Cambridge, Cambridge University Press.

Doria, P. M. (1724) *Discorsi critici filosofici*, Venezia.

Doria, P. M. (1729 [1709]) *La vita civile, di Paolo-Mattia Doria, con un trattato della Educazione del principe, terza impressione, dall'autore ricorretta, e di molte aggiunzioni adornata*, Napoli, Angelo Vocola a Fontana Medina.

Doria, P. M. (1981 [1740]) *Del Commercio del Regno di Napoli*. Con l'aggiunta di un'appendice. Nel quale s'indagano le cagioni generali e particolari, dalle quali il buono e retto Commercio trae la sua origine. E si fa vedere il rapporto che il predetto Commercio deve avere con gli altri

Ordini, de' quali la Repubblica si compone. Lettera diretta al Signor D. Francesco Ventura, Degnissimo Presidente del Magistrato di Commercio, in P. M. Doria, *Manoscritti napoletani di Paolo Mattia Doria*, vol. I, ed. C. Belgioioso, Galatina, Congedo, pp. 141–208.

Drolet, A. and Suppes, P. (2008) 'The Good and the Bad, the True and the False', in M. C. Galavotti, R. Scazzieri, and P. Suppes (eds.), *Reasoning, Rationality and Probability*, Stanford, CA, CSLI Publications, pp. 13–35.

Dubois, V. (2018) 'The Fields of Policy Making', in I. Cardinale and R. Scazzieri (eds.), *The Palgrave Handbook of Political Economy*, London, Palgrave Macmillan, pp. 29–51.

Dunn, J. (1990) 'Introduction', in J. Dunn (ed.), *The Economic Limits to Modern Politics*, Cambridge, Cambridge University Press, pp. 1–13.

Durkheim, E. (1902) *De la division du travail social*, 2nd edition, augmentée d'une préface sur les groupements professionels, Paris, Alcan.

Duso, G. (1996) 'Sulla genesi del moderno concetto di società: la "consociatio" di Althusius e la "socialitas" di Pufendorf', *Filosofia politica*, x (1, April), p. 5–31.

Edgeworth, F. (1881) *Mathematical Psychics: An Essay on the Application of Mathematics to the Moral Sciences*. London, C.K. Paul & Co.

Ehrenberg, J. (1999) *Civil Society. The Critical History of an Idea*, New York, New York University Press.

El Maraghy, H. and Caggiano, A. (2014) 'Flexible Manufacturing System', in L. Laperrière and G. Reinhart (eds.), *The International Academy for Production Engineering, CIRP Encyclopedia of Production Engineering*, Berlin and Heidelberg, Springer, https://doi.org/10.1007/978-3-642-20617-7_6554

Elazar, D. J. (1998) *Constitutionalizing Globalization: The Postmodern Revival of Confederal Arrangements*, Lanham, Boulder, New York, Oxford, Rowman and Littlefield.

El-Khalil, R. and Darwish, Z. (2019) 'Flexible Manufacturing Systems Performance in U.S. Automotive Manufacturing Plants: A Case Study', *Production Planning and Control*, 30 (1), pp. 48–59.

Fairbank, J. (1941) 'On the Ch'ing Tributary System', *Harvard Journal of Asiatic Studies*, 6 (2, June), pp. 135–246.

Ferguson, A. (1966 [1767]) *An Essay on the History of Civil Society*, Edinburgh, Edinburgh University Press.

Ferguson, T. (1983) 'Party Realignment and American Industrial Structure: The Investment Theory of Political Parties in Historical Perspective', *Research in Political Economy*, 6, pp. 1–82.

Ferguson, T. (1995) *Golden Rule: The Investment Theory of Party Competition and the Logic of Money-Driven Political Systems*, Chicago, University of Chicago Press.

Ferguson, T., Jorgensen, P., and Chen, J (2018) 'Industrial Structure and Political Outcomes: The Case of the 2016 US Presidential Elections', in I. Cardinale and R. Scazzieri (eds.), *The Palgrave Handbook of Political Economy*, London, Macmillan, pp. 333–440.

Ferguson, T., Jorgensen, P., and Chen, J. (2019) 'How Money Drives US Congressional Elections: Linear Models of Money and Outcomes', *Structural Change and Economic Dynamics*, https://doi.org/10.1016/j.strueco.2019.09.005

Ferrannini, A., Barbieri, E., Biggeri, M., and Di Tommaso, M. R. (2021) 'Industrial Policy for Sustainable Human Development in the Post-Covid19 Era', *World Development*, 137 (January), https://doi.org/10.1016/j.worlddev.2020.105215

Ferrarese, M. R. (2015) *Diritto sconfinato. Inventiva giuridica e spazi nel mondo globale*, Bari and Roma, Laterza.

Fidler, D. P. and Welsh, J. M. (eds.) (1999) *Empire and Community: Edmund Burke's Writings and Speeches on International Relations*, Boulder, Westview Press.

Filangieri, G. (1806 [1780]) *The Science of Legislation, from the Italian of Gaetano Filangieri*, London, Thomas Ostell.

Fleischacker. S. (2005) *On Adam Smith's Wealth of Nations: A Philosophical Companion*, Princeton and Oxford, Princeton University Press.

Fligstein, N. and McAdam, D. (2012) *A Theory of Fields*, New York, Oxford University Press.

Galli, C. (2010) *Political Spaces and Global War*, Minneapolis, University of Minnesota Press.

Geertz, C. (1975) *The Interpretation of Cultures: Selected Essays*, London, Hutchinson.

Gellner, E. (1994) *Conditions of Liberty. Civil Society and Its Rivals*, London, Hamish Hamilton.

Genovesi, A. (1962 [1753]) 'Discorso sopra il vero fine delle lettere e delle scienze [Discourse about the true ends of the arts and sciences]' in G. Savarese (ed.), *A.Genovesi, Autobiografia. lettere e altri scritti*, Milano, Feltrinelli, pp. 231–276.

Genovesi, A. (1973 [1766]) *Della diceosina o sia della filosofia del giusto e dell'onesto* [On the Philosophy of the Just and Honest], Milano, Marzorati.

Genovesi, A. (2013 [1765–1767]) *Lezioni di economia civile*, Introduction by L. Bruni and S. Zamagni, edited with textual commentary by F. Dal Degan, Milano, Vita e Pensiero.

Georgescu-Roegen, N. (1969) 'Process in Farming versus Process in Manufacturing: A Problem in Balanced Development', in G. U. Papi and C. Nunn (eds.), *Economic Problems of Agriculture in Industrial Societies*, New York, St. Martin's Press, pp. 497–528.

Georgescu-Roegen, N. (1970) 'The Economics of Production', Richard T. Ely Lecture, *The American Economic Review*, 60 (2, May), pp. 1–9.

Georgescu-Roegen, N. (1976 [1965]) 'The Institutional Aspects of Peasant Communities: An Analytical View', in N. Georgescu-Roegen, *Energy and Economic Myths: Institutional and Analytical Economic Essays*, New York, Oxford, etc., Pergamon Press, pp. 199–231.

Giarrizzo, G. (1981) *Vico, la politica e la storia*, Napoli, Guida.

Gierke, O. (1900) *Political Theories of the Middle Ages*, tr. F. W. Maitland, Cambridge, Cambridge University Press.

Gierke, O. (1973) *Associations and the Law: The Classical and Early Christian Stages*, tr. George Heinrich, Toronto, Toronto University Press.

Gioja, M. (1815–17) *Nuovo prospetto delle scienze economiche*, Milano, G. Pirotta

Gioja, M. (1819) *Sulle manifatture nazionali e tariffe daziarie*, Milano, G. Pirotta.

Godbout, J. T. and Caillé, A. (1992) *L'Esprit du don,* Paris, La Découverte; trans. *The World of the Gift*, tr. D. Winkler, Montreal, McGill-Queen's University Press, 1998.

Godbout, J. T. (2007) *Ce qui circule entre nous. Donner, recevoir, rendre*, Paris, Seuil.

Goitein, S. D. (1967) *A Mediterranean Society: The Jewish Communities of the Arab World as Portrayed in the Documents of the Cairo Geniza. Vol. I; Economic Foundations*, Berkeley and Los Angeles, University of California Press.

Goldoni, M. and Wilkinson, M. (2018) 'The Material Constitution', *The Modern Law Review*, 81 (4), pp. 567–597.

Goody, J. (2004) *Capitalism and Modernity: The Great Debate*, Cambridge, Polity Press.

Green, D. P. and Shapiro, I. (1994) *Pathologies of Rational Choice Theory: A Critique of Applications in Political Science*, New Haven, Yale University Press.

Green, T. H. (1895) *Lectures on the Principles of Political Obligation*, London, Longmans & Co.

Griswold, C. L. (2007) *Forgiveness: A Philosophical Exploration*, Cambridge, Cambridge University Press.

Grossi, P. (2007) *L'Europa del diritto*, Roma-Bari, Laterza.

Grossi, P. (2010 [2007]) *A History of European Law*, Oxford, Blackwell (English translation of Grossi, 2007).

Grossi, P. (2009) 'La legalità costituzionale nella storia del diritto moderno', Atti della Accademia Nazionale dei Lincei, vol. 156 – *Rendiconti delle adunanze solenni*, Accademia Nazionale dei Lincei, 10 (9), pp. 603–621.

Grossi, P. (2018) *Il diritto in una società che cambia*, Bologna, Il Mulino.

Grossi, P. (2021) 'Sistema moderno delle fonti del diritto ed esperienza giuridica posmoderna in Italia', *Rivista internazionale di filosofia del diritto*, 2 (April–June), pp. 155–176.

Guasti, N. (2006) 'Antonio Genovesi's Diceosina: Source of the Neapolitan Enlightenment', *History of European Ideas*, 32 (4), pp. 385–405.

Guizot, F. (1839) *Cours d'histoire moderne*, Bruxelles, Société belge de librairie, etc. Hauman et compagnie.

Guizot, F. (1851) *Histoire des origines du gouvernememt representatif en Europe*, Bruxelles, Société typographique belge.

Haberler, G. (1964) 'Integration and Growth of the World Economy in Historical Perspective', *The American Economic Review*, 54 (2), pp. 1–22.

Hamilton, A., Madison, J., and Jay, J. (2003 [1788]) *The Federalist with Letters of 'Brutus'*, ed. Terence Ball, Cambridge, Cambridge University Press.

Hankins, J. (2019) *Virtue Politics: Soulcraft and Statecraft in Renaissance Italy*, Cambridge, MA, Harvard University Press.

Hanski, I. (2018) 'Time in Population Biology', *Balzan Papers*, I, pp. 91–99.

Harrington, J. (1656) *The Commonwealth of Oceana*, London, Streater.

Hawkins, D. and Simon, H. A. (1949) 'Note: Some Conditions of Macroeconomic Stability', *Econometrica*, 17 (3), pp. 245–248.

Hayek, F. A. (1976) *Law, Legislation, and Liberty: Vol. 2. The Mirage of Social Justice*, Chicago, University of Chicago Press.

Hegel, G. W. F. (1991 [1821]) *Elements of the Philosophy of Right*, ed. Allen W. Wood, tr. H. B. Nisbet, Cambridge, Cambridge University Press.

Heller, A. (1988) 'On Formal Democracy', in J. Keane (ed.), *Civil Society and the State. New European Perspectives*, London and New York, Verso, pp. 129–145.

Hicks, J. (1941) 'Education in Economics', *Bulletin of the Manchester Statistical Society*, April, pp. 1–20.

Hicks, J. (1969) *A Theory of Economic History*, Oxford, Clarendon Press.

Hicks, J. (1973) *Capital and Time: A Neo-Austrian Theory*, Oxford, Clarendon Press.

Hicks, J. (1975) 'The Scope and Status of Welfare Economics', *Oxford Economic Papers,* new series, 27 (3), pp. 307–326.

Hicks, J. (1982 [1976]) 'Revolutions in Economics', in J. Hicks, *Collected Essays in Economic Theory: Vol. III. Classics and Moderns.* Oxford, Blackwell, pp. 3–16.

Hill, P. (1989) *Development Economics on Trial: The Anthropological Case for a Prosecution*, Cambridge, Cambridge University Press.

Hirschman, A. O. (1958) *The Strategy of Economic Development*, New Haven, Yale University Press.

Hirschman, A. O. (1977) *The Passions and the Interests: Political Arguments for Capitalism before Its Triumph*, Princeton, Princeton University Press.

Hirschman, A. O. (1982) *Shifting Involvements: Private Interest and Public Action*, Oxford, Robertson.

Hirschman, A. O. (1985) 'Against Parsimony: Three Easy Ways of Complicating Some Categories of Economic Discourse', *Economics and Philosophy*, 1 (1, April), pp. 7–21.

Hobbes, T. (1647a) 'Epistola dedicatoria' to William Cavendish, Count of Devonshire, in *Elementa philosophica de Cive*, 2nd edition, Amsterdam, apud Ludovicum Elzevirium.

Hobbes, T. (1647b) 'Praefatio ad Lectores', in *Elementa philosophica de Cive*, 2nd edition, Amsterdam, apud Ludovicum Elzevirium.

Hobbes, T. (1998 [1642]) *On the Citizen*, ed. R. Tuck and M. Silverthorne, Cambridge, Cambridge University Press.

Hobbes, T. (1998 [1651]) *Leviathan or the Matter, Forme and Power of a Commonwealth Ecclesiasticall and Civil*, edited with an Introduction and Notes by J. C. A. Gaskin, Oxford and New York, Oxford University Press.

Hobhouse, L. T. (1911a) *Liberalism*, London, Williams and Norgate.

Hobhouse, L. T. (1911b) *Social Evolution and Political Theory*, New York, Columbia University Press.

Hobhouse, L. T. (1922) *The Elements of Social Justice*, New York, Henry Holt and Company.

Holdsworth, W. S. (1903–1972 [1909]) *A History of English Law*, vol. 2, London, Methuen.

Hont, I. (2010), *Jealousy of Trade: International Competition and the Nation-State in Historical Perspective*, Cambridge, MA, Harvard University Press.

Hont, I. (2015), *Politics in Commercial Society: Jean-Jacques Rousseau and Adam Smith*, ed. Béla Kapossy and Michael Sonenscher, Cambridge, MA, Harvard University Press.

Hume, D. (1978 [1739–1740]) *A Treatise of Human Nature*, 2nd edition, edited, with an Analytical Index, by L. A. Selby-Bigge, with text revised and variant readings by P. H. Nidditch, Oxford, Clarendon Press.

Hume, D. (1998 [1751]) *An Enquiry Concerning the Principles of Morals*, ed. T. L. Beauchamp (The Clarendon Edition of the Works of David Hume), Oxford, Oxford University Press, 1998.

Ibbetson, D. (1986) 'Words and Deeds: The Action of Covenant in the Reign of Edward I', *Law and History Review*, 4 (1, Spring), pp. 71–94.

Ibbetson, D. (2001) *Common Law and Ius Commune*, London, Selden Society.

Ibbetson, D. (2006) 'English Law and the European Ius Commune, 1450–1650', in *Cambridge Yearbook of European Legal Studies*, 8, pp. 115–132.

Ibbetson, D. (2016) 'Bologna and England: The Legal Heritage', *Guest Lecture*, Bologna-Clare Hall Anniversary Meeting, 5 December 2016, University of Bologna, Palazzina della Viola.

Kaldor, N. (1967) *Strategic Factors in Economic Development*, Ithaca, New York State School of Industrial and Labor Relations, Cornell University.

Kantorowicz, E. (1957) *The King's Two Bodies: A Study in Medieval Political Theology*, Princeton, Princeton University Press.

Kauffman, S. A. (1990) 'Requirements for Evolvability in Complex Systems: Orderly Dynamics and Frozen Components', *Physica D*, 4, pp. 135–152.

Keane, J. (1988) 'Despotism and Democracy: The Origins and Development of the Distinction between Civil Society and the State 1750–1850', in J. Keane (ed.), *Civil Society and the State. New European Perspectives*, London and New York, Verso, pp. 35–71.

Kindleberger, C. P. (1978) *Manias, Panics and Crashes*, London and Basingstoke, Macmillan.

Kochen, M. (1980) 'Coping with Complexity', *Omega: The International Journal of Management Science*, 8 (1), pp. 11–20.

Kolm, S.-K. (2009) *Macrojustice. The Political Economy of Fairness*, Cambridge, Cambridge University Press.

Krueger, A. O. (1990) 'Government Failures in Development', *Journal of Economic Perspectives*, 4 (3), pp. 9–23.

Kyburg, H. E. and Man Teng, C. (2001) *Uncertain Inference*, Cambridge, Cambridge University Press.

Kyotaki, N. and Moore, J. (1997) 'Credit Chains', www.princeton.edu/~kiyotaki/papers/creditchains.pdf

La Vaissière, E. de (2004) *Histoire des marchands sogdiens*, 2nd edition, Paris, Institut des Hautes Etudes Chinoises.

Lake, D. A. (1999) 'Global Governance: A Relational Contracting Approach', in A. Prakash and J. A. Hart (eds.), *Globalization and Governance*, London and New York, Routledge, pp. 31–53.

Landes, D. (1965) 'Technological Change and Industrial Development in Western Europe, 1750–1914', *Cambridge Economic History of Europe*, Cambridge, Cambridge University Press, vol. VI, pp. 274–310.

Landesmann, M. A. (1986) 'Conceptions of Technology and the Production Process', in M. Baranzini and R. Scazzieri (eds.), *Foundations of Economics. Structures of Inquiry and Economic Theory*, Oxford and New York, Basil Blackwell, pp. 281–310.

Landesmann, M. A. and Scazzieri, R. (1990) 'Specification of Structure and Economic Dynamics', in M. Baranzini and R. Scazzieri (eds.), *The*

Economic Theory of Structure and Change, Cambridge, Cambridge University Press, pp. 95–121.

Landesmann, M.A. and Scazzieri, R. (1993) 'Commodity Flows and Productive Subsystems: An Essay in the Analysis of Structural Change', in M. Baranzini and G. C. Harcourt (eds.), *The Dynamics of the Wealth of Nations*, London, Macmillan, pp. 209–245.

Landesmann, M. A. and Scazzieri, R. (1996) 'Forms of Production Organisation: The Case of Manufacturing Processes', in M. A. Landesmann and R. Scazzieri (eds.), *Production and Economic Dynamics*, Cambridge, Cambridge University Press, pp. 252–303.

Langholm, O. (1983) *Wealth and Money in the Aristotelian Tradition: A Study in Scholastic Economic Sources*, Bergen, Universitetsforlaget.

Lee, K. and Lim, C. (2001) 'Technological Regimes, Catching-Up and Leapfrogging: Findings from the Korean Industries', *Research Policy*, 30 (1), pp. 459–483.

Leibniz, W. G. (1677) *De jure suprematus, ac legationis Principum Germaniae*, published under the pseudonym Furstenerius Caesar, [Amsterdam, D. Elzevier].

Leontief, W. (1928) 'Die Wirtschaft als Kreislauf', in *Archiv für Sozialwissenschaft und Sozialpolitik*, 60, pp. 577–623; English translation: (1991) 'The Economy as a Circular Flow', *Structural Change and Economic Dynamics*, 2 (June), pp. 181–212.

Leontief, W. (1941) *The Structure of the American Economy, 1919–29*. New York, Oxford University Press.

Leshem, D. (2016) 'Retrospectives: What Did the Ancient Greeks Mean by "Oikonomia"?' *Journal of Economic Perspectives*, 30(1, Winter), pp. 225–238.

Leshem, D. (2013) 'Oikonomia Redefined', *Journal of the History of Economic Thought*, 35 (1, March), pp. 43–61.

Lijphart, A. (1969) 'Consociational Democracy', *World Politics*, 21 (2, January), pp. 207–225.

Lijphart, A. (1975 [1968]) *The Politics of Accommodation: Pluralism and Democracy in The Netherlands*, 2nd revised edition, Berkeley, University of California Press.

Lijphart, A. (1977) *Democracy in Plural Societies: A Comparative Exploration*, New Haven, Yale University Press.

Lijphart, A. (2012) *Patterns of Democracy: Government Forms and Performance in Thirty-Six Countries*, 2nd edition, New Haven, Yale University Press.

List, F. (1904 [1841]) *The National System of Political Economy*, London, Longman.

Liu, E. (2019) 'Industrial Policies in Production Networks', *The Quarterly Journal of Economics*, 134 (4, November), pp. 1883–1948.

Locke, J. (1988 [1690]) *Two Treatises of Government*, ed. P. Laslett, Cambridge, Cambridge University Press.

Lohmann, S. (2008) 'Rational Choice and Political Science', in S. Durlauf and L. E. Blume (eds.), *The New Palgrave Dictionary of Economics*, 2nd edition, vol. 6, Basingstoke and New York, Palgrave Macmillan, pp. 866–872.

Lowe, A. (1976) *The Path of Economic Growth*, Cambridge, Cambridge University Press.

Lutfalla, M. (1981) *Aux origines de la pensée économique*, Paris, Economica.

McCormick, J. P. (2007) *Weber, Habermas and Transformations of the European State: Constitutional, Social, and Supranational Democracy*, Cambridge, Cambridge University Press.

Machiavelli, N. (1988 [1532]) *The Prince*, ed. Q. Skinner and R. Price, Cambridge, Cambridge University Press.

Machiavelli, N. (1996 [1531]) *Discourses on Livy*, tr. H. C. Mansfield and N. Tarcov, Chicago, University of Chicago Press.

MacIntyre, A. (2000 [1981]) *After Virtue: A Study in Moral Theory*, London, Duckworth.

McLean I. (1991) 'Rational Choice and Politics', *Political Studies*, 39(3), pp. 496–512.

McNeil, I. R. (1978) 'Contracts: Adjustment of Long-Term Economic Relations under Classical, Neoclassical and Relational Contract Law', *Northwestern University Law Review*, 72 (6, January–February), pp. 854–905.

McNeil, I. R. (1980) *The New Social Contract*, New Haven, Yale University Press.

McNeil, I. R. (1985) 'Reflections on Relational Contract', *Zeitschrift Für Die Gesamte Staatswissenschaft/Journal of Institutional and Theoretical Economics*, 141 (4), pp. 541–546.

McNeil, I. R. (2000) 'Relational Contract Theory: Challenges and Queries', *Northwestern University Law Review*, 94 (3), pp. 877–907.

MacPherson, C. B. (1962) *The Political Theory of Possessive Individualism: Hobbes to Locke*, Oxford, Clarendon Press.

Magni-Berton R. (2014) 'Rational Choice Theory in Comparative Politics', *Revue internationale de politique comparée*, 21 (2), pp. 19–47.

Maifreda, G. (2012) *From Oikonomia to Political Economy: Constructing Economic Knowledge from the Renaissance to the Scientific Revolution*, London, Routledge.

Maitland, F. W. (2003) *State, Trust and Corporation*, ed. D. Runciman and M. Ryan, Cambridge, Cambridge University Press.

Malloy, R. P. (2022) *Law and the Invisible Hand: A Theory of Adam Smith's Jurisprudence*, Cambridge, Cambridge University Press.

Mamalakis, M. (1969) 'The Theory of Sectoral Clashes', *Latin American Research Review*, 4(3), pp. 9–46.

Mamalakis, M. (1992) 'Sectoral Conflicts in the U.S. and the Soviet Union: A Mesoeconomic Analysis', *Eastern Economic Journal*, 18(4), pp. 421–28.

Manent, P. (2013) *Metamorphoses of the City: On the Western Dynamic*, Cambridge, MA, Harvard University Press.

Marcialis, M. T. (1994) 'Legge di natura e calcolo della ragione nell'ultimo Genovesi', *Materiali per una storia della cultura giuridica*, xxiv (2, December), pp. 315–340.

Marcialis, M. T. (1999) 'Antonio Genovesi e la costruzione scientifica dell' economia civile', in M. T. Marcialis (ed.), *Ragione, natura, storia: quattro studi sul Settecento*, Milano, Angeli, pp. 103–134.

Markusen, J. R. and Venables, A. J. (2000) 'The Theory of Endowment, Intra-Industry and Multi-National Trade', *Journal of International Economics*, 52 (2, December), pp. 209–234.

Marshall, A. and Paley Marshall, M. (1879) *The Economics of Industry*, London, Macmillan.

Martin, J. L. (2003) 'What Is Field Theory?' *American Journal of Sociology*, 109 (1), pp. 1–49.

Marzetti Dall'Aste Brandolini, S. (2011) 'Moral Good and Right Conduct: A General Theory of Welfare under Fundamental Uncertainty', in S. Marzetti Dall'Aste Brandolini and R. Scazzieri (eds.), *Fundamental Uncertainty, Rationality and Plausible Reasoning*, Basingstoke and New York, Palgrave Macmillan, pp. 294–330.

Masera, R. (2015) 'Macro Prudential Policy as a Reference for Economic Policies: A Hicksian Perspective', in Accademia Nazionale dei Lincei, *Workshop 'Between Theory and Policy: Political Economy of Crises*, Rome, 27 October 2015.

Masera, R. (2018) 'Political Economy of Liquidity: The European Economic and Monetary Union', in I. Cardinale and R. Scazzieri (eds.), *The Palgrave Handbook of Political Economy*, London, Palgrave Macmillan, pp. 489–528.

Maskin, E. and Tirole, T. (1999) 'Unforeseeen Contingencies and Incomplete Contracts', *The Review of Economic Studies*, 66 (1, January), pp. 83–114, special issue: 'Contracts'.

Matteucci, N. (1994) 'Il filosofo Friedrich A. von Hayek', *Filosofia politica*, 8 (1, April), pp. 65–92.

Mazzucato, M. (2018) *The Entrepreneurial State: Debunking Public vs. Private Sector Myths*, London, Penguin.

References

Melon, J. (1736) *Essai politique sur le commerce*, Amsterdam, François Changuion.

Mercier de la Rivière, P.-P. (1767) *L'ordre naturel et essentiel des sociétés politiques*, London [Paris], Jean Nourse; & se trouve à Paris, chez Desaint.

Migeotte, L. (2009 [2002]) *The Economy of the Greek Cities: From the Archaic Period to the Early Roman Empire*, Berkeley and London, University of California Press.

Milbank, J. and Pabst, A. (2016) *The Politics of Virtue: Post-liberalism and the Human Future*, London, Rowman & Littlefield International.

Mill, J. S. (1965 [1848]) *Principles of Political Economy with Some of Their Applications to Social Philosophy*, London, J.W. Parker; Boston, C.C. Little and J. Bourn.

Milner, H. (1999) 'The Political Economy of International Trade', *American Review of Political Science*, 2, pp. 91–114.

Mises, L. (1949) *Human Action: A Treatise on Economics*. New Haven, Yale University Press.

Montchréstien, A. de (1889 [1615]) *Traicté de l'Oeconomie Politique*, ed. Téophile Funck-Brentano, Paris, Librairie Plon.

Montesquieu, C.-L. de Secondat, baron de la Brède et de (1989 [1748]) *De L'Esprit des Loix, Amsterdam, chez Chatelain*; Trans. *The Spirit of the Laws*, tr. and ed. A. M. Cohler, B. C. Miller, and H. S. Stone, Cambridge, Cambridge University Press.

Moravcsik, A. (2005) 'The European Constitutional Compromise and the Neofunctionalist Legacy', *Journal of European Public Policy*, 12 (2), pp. 349–386.

Morgenstern, O. (1934) *Die Grenzen der Wirtschaftspolitik*, Wien, Springer.

Morishima, M. (1964) *Equilibrium, Stability and Growth: A Multi-Sectoral Analysis*, Oxford, Clarendon Press.

Morris, D. J. and Stout, D. K. (1985) 'Industrial Policy', in D. J. Morris (ed.), *The Economic System in the UK*, Oxford, Oxford University Press, pp. 851–894.

Mortati, C. (1998 [1940]) *La Costituzione in senso materiale*, reprinted with preface by G. Zagrebelsky, Milano, Giuffrè.

Mutz, D. (2002) 'The Consequences of Cross-Cutting Networks for Political Participation', *American Journal of Political Science*, 46(4), pp. 838–855.

Mutz, D. (2006) *Hearing the Other Side: Deliberative versus Participatory Democracy*, Cambridge, Cambridge University Press.

Myrdal, G. (1939) *Monetary Equilibrium*, London, Edinburgh, and Glasgow, William Hodge and Company.

Nagel, T. (1986) *The View from Nowhere*, Oxford, Clarendon Press.

Nakhimovsky, I. (2011) *The Closed Commercial State: Perpetual Peace and Commercial Society from Rousseau to Fichte*, Princeton, Princeton University Press.

Nikaido, H. (2014) 'Hawkins–Simon conditions', in S. N. Durlauf and L. E. Blume, *The New Palgrave Dictionary of Economics*, 2nd edition, Basingstoke, Palgrave Macmillan, accessed 28 August 2018, www.dictionaryofeconomics.com/article?id=pde20 08H00002710.1057/9780230226203.0708

Noble, D. F. (1986) *Forces of Production: A Social History of Industrial Automation*, New York and Oxford, Oxford University Press.

North, D. C. (1990) *Institutions, Institutional Change and Economic Performance*, Cambridge, Cambridge University Press.

North, D. C. (2005) *Understanding the Process of Economic Change*, Princeton and Oxford, Princeton University Press.

North, D. C., Wallis, J. J., and Weingast, B. R. (2010) *Violence and Social Orders: A Conceptual Framework for Interpreting Recorded Human History*, Cambridge, Cambridge University Press.

O'Mahony, P. O. (2019 [2013]) *The Contemporary Theory of the Public Sphere*, Bern, Peter Lang.

Oakeshott, M. (1975) *On Human Conduct*, Oxford, Oxford University Press.

Ohmae, K. (1993) 'The Rise of the Region State', *Foreign Affairs*, 72 (2), pp. 78–87.

Olson, M. (1971 [1965]) *The Logic of Collective Action: Public Goods and the Theory of Groups*, Cambridge, MA, Harvard University Press.

Olson, M. (1982) *The Rise and Decline of Nations: Economic Growth, Stagflation, and Social Rigidities*, New Haven, Yale University Press.

Ornaghi, L. (1984) 'Introduzione', in L. Ornaghi (ed.), *Il concetto di "interesse"*, Milano, Giuffrè, pp. 4–81.

Ornaghi, L. (1990) 'Economic Structure and Political Institutions: A Theoretical Framework', in M. Baranzini and R. Scazzieri (eds.), *The Economic Theory of Structure and Change*, Cambridge, Cambridge University Press, pp. 23–44.

Ornaghi, L. and Cotellessa, S. (2000) *Interesse*, Bologna, Il Mulino.

Ozdagli, A. and M. Weber (2017) 'Monetary Policy through Production Networks: Evidence from the Stock Market', National Bureau of Economic Research, Working paper n. 23424, doi: 10.3386/w23424

Pabst, A. (2011) 'The Paradoxical Nature of the Good: Relationality, Sympathy, and Mutuality in Rival Traditions of Civil Economy', in A. Pabst (ed.), *The Crisis of Global Capitalism: Pope Benedict XVI's Social Encyclical and the Future of Political Economy*, Eugene, OR, Wipf and Stock, pp. 173–206.

Pabst, A. (2014) 'The Constitutional vs. the Contractualist Tradition: A Foundational Divide in Political Economy', *Paper presented at the Cambridge Research Seminar in Political Economy*, Emmanuel College, Cambridge, 6 February 2014.

Pabst, A. (2016) 'Is Liberal Democracy Sliding into "Democratic Despotism"?', *The Political Quarterly*, 87 (1, January–March), pp. 91–95.

Pabst, A. (2017) 'Political Economy and the Constitution of Europe's Polity' in I. Cardinale, D. Coffman, and R. Scazzieri (eds.), *The Political Economy of the Eurozone*, Cambridge, Cambridge University Press, pp. 183–215.

Pabst, A. (2018a), 'The Political Economy of Civil Society', in I. Cardinale and R. Scazzieri (eds.), *The Palgrave Handbook of Political Economy*, London, Palgrave Macmillan, pp. 289–331.

Pabst, A. (2018b) 'Political Economy of Virtue: Civil Economy, Happiness and Public Trust in the Thought of Antonio Genovesi', *European Journal of the History of Economic Thought*, 25 (4, October), pp. 582–604.

Pabst, A. (2019) *The Demons of Liberal Democracy*, Cambridge, Polity Press.

Pabst, A. (2020) 'The "Body Politic" and Political Economy', *Rendiconti, Classe di Scienze Morali, Storiche e Filologiche*, Accademia Nazionale dei Lincei, serie ix, vol. xxxi, pp. 231–238.

Pabst, A. and Scazzieri, R. (2012) 'The Political Economy of Civil Society', *Constitutional Political Economy*, 23 (4, December), pp. 337–356.

Pabst, A. and Scazzieri, R. (2016) 'The Political Economy of Constitution', *Oeconomia: History, Methodology, Philosophy*, 6 (3), pp. 337–362.

Pabst, A. and Scazzieri, R. (2019) 'Virtue, Production, and the Politics of Commerce: Genovesi's "Civil Economy" Revisited', *History of Political Economy*, 51 (4, August), pp. 703–729.

Pack, H. and Saggi, K. (2006) 'Is There a Case for Industrial Policy? A Critical Survey', *The World Bank Research Observer*, 21(2), pp. 267–297.

Palladini, F. (1978) *Discussioni seicentesche su Samuel Pufendorf. Scritti latini: 1663–1700*, Bologna, Il Mulino.

Pasinetti, L. L. (1973) 'The Notion of Vertical Integration in Economic Analysis', *Metroeconomica*, 25 (1), pp. 1–29.

Pasinetti, L. L. (1977) *Lectures on the Theory of Production*, New York, Columbia University Press.

Pasinetti, L. L. (1980 [1973]) 'The Notion of Vertical Integration in Economic Analysis', in L. L. Pasinetti (ed.), *Essays on the Theory of Joint Production*, London and Basingstoke, Macmillan, pp. 16–43.

Pasinetti, L. L. (1981) *Structural Change and Economics Growth: A Theoretical Essay on the Dynamics of the Wealth of Nations*, Cambridge, Cambridge University Press.

Pasinetti, L. L. (1993) *Structural Economic Dynamics: An Essay on the Economic Consequences of Human Learning*, Cambridge, Cambridge University Press.

Pasinetti, L. L. (2007) *Keynes and the Cambridge Keynesians: A 'Revolution in Economics' to Be Accomplished*. Cambridge, Cambridge University Press.

Pasinetti, L. L. (2019) 'Causality and Interdependence in Econometric Analysis and in Economic Theory', *Structural Change and Economic Dynamics*, 49 (June), pp. 357–363.

Passmore, J. A. (1990 [1951]) *Ralph Cudworth: An Interpretation*, Bristol, Thoemmes.

Pasten, E., Schoenle, R., and Weber, M. (2020) 'The Propagation of Monetary Policy Shocks in a Heterogeneous Production Economy', Federal Reserve Bank of Cleveland Working Paper Series, Paper n. 19_25R https://papers.ssrn.com/sol3/papers.cfm?abstract_id=3488078#

Pearl, J., (2000) *Causality: Models, Reasoning, and Inference*, Cambridge, Cambridge University Press.

Pelligra, V. (2007) 'The Not-so-Fragile Fragility of Goodness', in L. Bruni and P. L. Porta (eds.), *Handbook on the Economics of Happiness*, Cheltenham and Northampton, MA, pp. 290–317.

Perez, C. and Soete, L. (1988) 'Catching Up in Technology: Entry Barriers and Windows of Opportunity', in G. Dosi (ed.), *Technical Change and Economic Theory*, London, Pinter Publishers, pp. 458–479.

Perna, M. L. (1999) 'Genovesi, Antonio', in *Dizionario Biografico degli Italiani* (Gelati-Ghisalberti), Roma, Istituto della Enciclopedia italiana, vol. 53, pp. 148–153.

Persson, T. and Tabellini, G. (2000) *Political Economics: Explaining Economic Policy*, Cambridge, MA, MIT Press.

Persson, T. and Tabellini, G. (2005) *The Economic Effects of Constitutions*, Cambridge, MA, MIT Press.

Petracca, M. P. (1991) 'The Rational Choice Approach to Politics: A Challenge to Democratic Theory', *The Review of Politics*, 53 (2), pp. 289–319. JSTOR, accessed 13 January 2021, www.jstor.org/stable/1407756

Pii, E. (1973) 'Filosofia ed economia in Antonio Genovesi', *Il pensiero politico*, 6 (3), pp. 439–447.

Pizzorno, A. (1986) 'Some Other Kind of Otherness: A Critique of "Rational Choice" Theories', in A. Foxley, M. S. McPherson, and G. O'Donnell (eds.), *Development, Democracy, and the Art of Trespassing: Essays in Honour of Albert O. Hirschman*, Notre Dame, IN, University of Notre Dame Press, pp. 355–373.

Pocock, J. G. A. (1987) *The Ancient Constitution and the Feudal Law: A Study of English Historical Thought in the Seventeenth Century*, 2nd edition, Cambridge, Cambridge University Press.

Polanyi, K. (1957a) 'Marketless Trading in Hammurabi's Time', in K. Polanyi, C. M. Arensberg, and H. W. Pearson (eds.), *Trade and Market in the Early Empires: Economies in History and Theory*, Glencoe, IL, The Free Press, pp. 12–26.

Polanyi, K. (1957b) 'The Economy as an Instituted Process', in K. Polanyi, C. M. Arensberg, and H. W. Pearson (eds.), *Trade and Market in the Early Empires: Economies in History and Theory*, Glencoe, IL, The Free Press, pp. 243–270.

Polanyi, K. (2001 [1944]) *The Great Transformation: The Political and Economic Origins of Our Time*, Boston, Beacon Press.

Poni, C. (1997) 'Standard, fiducia e conversazione civile: misurare lo spessore e la qualità del filo di seta', *Quaderni storici*, 32, (3, December), pp. 717–734.

Poni, C. (1998) 'Mode et innovation. Les strategies des marchands en soie de Lyon au XVIII siècle', *Revue d'histoire moderne et contemporaine*, 45 (3, July–September), pp. 589–625.

Poni, C. (2001) 'Comparing Two Urban Industrial Districts: Bologna and Lyon in the Early Modern Period', in P. L. Porta, R. Scazzieri, and A. Skinner (eds.), *Knowledge, Social Institutions and the Division of Labour*, Cheltenham and Northampton, MA, Edward Elgar, pp. 199–225.

Porta, P. L. and Scazzieri, R. (2003) 'Accounting for Social Knowledge: The Relevance of Adam Smith's Framework', in S. Rizzello, ed., *Cognitive Developments in Economics*, London, Routledge, pp. 107–132.

Prebisch, R. (1951) 'Theoretical and Practical Problems of Economic Growth', Economic Commission for Latin America, Fourth Session, Mexico D. F. (28 May 1950), mimeo.

Pufendorf, S. (1668) *De statu imperii germanici ad Laelium fratrem, dominum Trezolani*, liber unus, published under the pseudonym of Severinus de Monzambano Veronensis, Veronae, apud Franciscum Giulium.

Pufendorf, S. (1672) *De iure naturae et gentium libri octo*, Lund, Adam Junghans.

Quadrio Curzio, A. (1967) *Rendita e distribuzione in un modello economico plurisettoriale*. Milano, Giuffrè.

Quadrio Curzio, A. (1986) 'Technological Scarcity: An Essay on Production and Structural Change', in M. Baranzini and R. Scazzieri (eds.), *Foundations of Economics. Structures of Inquiry and Economic Theory*, Oxford and New York, Basil Blackwell, pp. 311–338.

Quadrio Curzio, A. (1990) *Rent, Distribution and Economic Structure: A Collection of Essays*, Milan: CNR-IDSE.

Quadrio Curzio, A. (1996) 'Production and Efficiency with Global Technologies', in M. Landesmann and R. Scazzieri (eds.), *Production and Economic Dynamics*, Cambridge, Cambridge University Press, pp. 105–126.

Quadrio Curzio A. (2017) 'Eurobonds for EMU Stability and Structural Growth', in I. Cardinale, D. Coffman, and R. Scazzieri (eds.), *The Political Economy of the Eurozone*, Cambridge, Cambridge University Press, pp. 395–434.

Quadrio Curzio, A. and Pellizzari, F. (1999) *Rent, Resources, Technologies*, Berlin, Springer.

Quadrio Curzio, A. and Pellizzari, F. (2018) 'Political Economy of Resources', in I. Cardinale and R. Scazzieri (eds.), *The Palgrave Handbook of Political Economy*, London, Palgrave Macmillan, pp. 657–704.

Quadrio Curzio, A. and Scazzieri, R. (1986) 'The Exchange-Production Duality and the Dynamics of Economic Knowledge' in M. Baranzini and R. Scazzieri (eds.), *Foundations of Economics: Structures of Inquiry and Economic Theory*, Oxford and New York, Basil Blackwell, pp. 377–407.

Quadrio Curzio, A. and Silvani, A. (2020) 'Research and Development in European Union Politics', in *Oxford Research Encyclopedia of Politics*, Oxford, Oxford University Press, https://doi.org/10.1093/acrefore/9780190228637.013.1050

Quesnay, F. (1972 [1759]) *Quesnay's Tableau Économique*, ed. M. Kuczynski and R. L. Meek, London and New York, Macmillan.

Rae, D. W. and Taylor, M. (1970) *The Analysis of Political Cleavages*, New Haven, Yale University Press.

Ranky, P. (1983) *The Design and Operation of FMS: Flexible Manufacturing Systems*, Bedford, IFS Publications Ltd.; Amsterdam, New York, Oxford, North-Holland.

Raphael, D. D. (2007) *The Impartial Spectator*, Oxford, Clarendon Press.

Raphael, D. D. and Macfie, A. L. (1976) 'Introduction', in A. Smith, *The Theory of Moral Sentiments*, eds. D. D. Raphael and A. L. Macfie, vol. I of *The Glasgow Edition of the Works and Correspondence of Adam Smith*, Oxford, Clarendon Press, pp. 1–52.

Ratcliffe, S. (2008) *On Sympathy*, Oxford, Clarendon Press.

Rathmill, K. (ed.) (1986) *Proceedings of the 5th International Conference on Flexible Manufacturing Systems*, Bedford, IFS Publications.

Rawls, J. (1971) *A Theory of Justice*, Cambridge, MA, Harvard University Press.

Reggiani, A. (2013) 'Network Resilience for Transport Security: Some Methodological Considerations', *Transport Policy*, 28 (July), pp. 63–68.

Reinert, E. (1995) 'Competitiveness and Its Predecessors: A 500-Year Cross-National Perspective', *Structural Change and Economic Dynamics*, 6 (March), pp. 23–42.

Reinert, E. (1999) 'The Role of the State in Economic Growth', *Journal of Economic Studies*, 26 (4/5), pp. 268–326.

Ricardo, D. (1951 [1817]) *On the Principles of Political Economy and Taxation*. Vol. I of *The Works and Correspondence of David Ricardo*, ed. Piero Sraffa with the collaboration of Maurice H. Dobb, Cambridge, Cambridge University Press.

Richelet, P. (1785) *Dictionnaire de la langue française ancienne et moderne*, Basel, Brandmüller.

Riley, P. (1986) *The General Will before Rousseau: The Transformation of the Divine into the Civic*, Princeton, Princeton University Press.

Robertson, D. H. (1915) *A Theory of Industrial Fluctuation*, London, P.S. King and Son.

Robertson, J. (2005) *The Case for the Enlightenment: Scotland and Naples, 1680–1760*, Cambridge, Cambridge University Press.

Romagnosi, G. D. (1827) 'Quesito. Il modo usato da alcuni scrittori di oggidì nel trattare le Dottrine economiche è forse plausibile?' *Annali Universali di Statistica*, 13 (July), pp. 23–30.

Romagnosi, G. D. (1835) 'Ordinamento della economica dottrina', in G. D. Romagnosi, *Opere*, vol. X, Firenze, Piatti, pp. 21–40.

Romagnosi, G. D. (1848) *Scienza delle costituzioni*, Milano, Volpato.

Roncaglia, A. (2005), *The Wealth of Ideas*, Cambridge, Cambridge University Press.

Rosenfeld, S. (2011) *Common Sense: A Political History*, Cambridge, MA, Harvard University Press.

Rosenstein Rodan, P. N. (1943) 'Problems of Industrialization of Eastern and South-Eastern Europe', *The Economic Journal*, 53 (June–September), pp. 202–211.

Rothschild, E. (2001) *Economic Sentiments: Adam Smith, Condorcet and the Enlightenment*, Cambridge, MA and London, Harvard University Press.

Rothschild, E. and Sen, A. (2006) 'Adam Smith's Economics', in *The Cambridge Companion to Adam Smith*, ed. K. Haakonssen, Cambridge, Cambridge University Press, pp. 319–365.

Rotstein, A. (1970) 'Karl Polanyi's Concept of Non-Market Trade', *The Journal of Economic History*, 30 (1, March), pp. 117–126.

Rousseau, J. J. (1923 [1755]), *The Social Contract and Discourses by Jean-Jacques Rousseau*, tr. with an Introduction by G. D. H. Cole, London and Toronto, J.M. Dent and Sons.

Rousseau, J. J. (1997 [1762]) *The Social Contract and Other Later Political Writings*, tr. and ed. Victor Gourevitch, Cambridge, Cambridge University Press.

Rubinelli, L. (2019) 'Costantino Mortati and the Idea of Material Constitution', *History of Political Thought*, 40 (3, Autumn), pp. 515–546.

Rubinelli, L. (2020) *Constituent Power: A History*, Cambridge, Cambridge University Press.

Sainsbury, D. (2020) *Windows of Opportunity: How Nations Create Wealth*, London, Profile Books.

Samuelson, P. A. (2004) 'Where Ricardo and Mill Rebut and Confirm Arguments of Mainstream Economists Supporting Globalization', *Journal of Economic Perspectives*, 18 (3, Summer), pp. 135–146.

Sassen, S. (2001) 'Global Cities and Global City-Regions: A Comparison', in Allen J. Scott (ed.), *Global City-Regions: Trends, Theory, Policy*, Oxford, Oxford University Press, pp. 78–95.

Scazzieri, R. (1990) 'Vertical Integration in Economic Theory', *Journal of Post Keynesian Economics*, 13 (1), pp. 20–46.

Scazzieri, R. (1993) *A Theory of Production: Tasks, Processes, and Technical Practices*, Oxford, Clarendon Press.

Scazzieri, R. (1997) 'A Theory of Resilient Flow-Fund Linkages', in K. Mayumi and J. M. Gowdy (eds.) *Bioeconomics and Sustainability. Essays in Honour of Nicholas Georgescu-Roegen*, Cheltenham (UK) and Northampton (MA), Edward Elgar, pp. 229–256.

Scazzieri, R. (1998) 'Hierarchy of Production Activities and Decomposition of Structural Change: An Essay in the Theory of Economic History', in H. D. Kurz and H. Hagemann (eds.), *Political Economics in Retrospect: Essays in Memory of Adolph Lowe*, Cheltenham and Northampton, MA, Edward Elgar, pp. 195–207.

Scazzieri, R. (1999a) 'Modelli di società civile', *Filosofia politica*, 13 (3, December), pp. 363–378.

Scazzieri, R. (1999b) 'A Theory of Resilient Flow-Fund Linkages', in K. Mayumi and J. M. Gowdy (eds.), *Bioeconomics and Sustainability: Essays in Honor of Nicholas Georgescu-Roegen*, Cheltenham and Northampton, MA, pp. 229–256.

Scazzieri, R. (2003a) 'A Theory of Framing and Coordination: Hayek and the Scottish Tradition', *Rivista Internazionale di Scienze Economiche e Commerciali*, 50 (3, September), pp. 323–349.

Scazzieri, R. (2003b) 'Experiments, Heuristics and Social Diversity: A Comment on Reinhard Selten', in M. C. Galavotti (ed.), *Observation and Experiment in the Natural and Social Sciences*, Dordrecht, Kluwer, pp. 85–98.

Scazzieri, R. (2003c) 'Teoría económica de la sociedad civil global', in J. V. Beneyto (ed.), *Hacia una socieded civil global*, Madrid, Taurus, pp. 119–138.

Scazzieri, R. (2006) 'A Smithian Theory of Choice', in Vivienne Brown (ed.), *The Adam Smith Review*, vol. 2, pp. 21–47.

Scazzieri, R. (2008) 'Context, Congruence and Co-ordination', in M. C. Galavotti, R. Scazzieri, and P. Suppes (eds.), *Reasoning, Rationality and*

Probability: CSLI Lecture Notes n.183, Stanford, CSLI Publications, pp. 187–207.

Scazzieri, R. (2012a) 'Paolo Mattia Doria', in P. L. Porta and V. Zamagni (eds.), *Il contributo italiano alla storia del pensiero. Economia*, Roma, Istituto della Enciclopedia italiana, pp. 326–331.

Scazzieri, R. (2012b) 'The Concept of "Natural Economic System": A Tool for Structural Analysis and an Instrument for Policy Design', in R. Arena and P. L. Porta (eds.), *Structural Dynamics and Economic Growth*, Cambridge, Cambridge University Press, pp. 218–240.

Scazzieri, R. (2014a) 'A Structural Theory of Increasing Returns', *Structural Change and Economic Dynamics*, 29 (June), pp. 75–88.

Scazzieri, R. (2014b) 'L'illuminismo delle riforme civili: divisione del lavoro, commercio, produzione della ricchezza', in P. L. Porta and R. Scazzieri (eds.), *L'illuminismo delle riforme covili: il contributo degli economisti lombardi*, Milano, Istituto Lombardo di Scienze e Lettere, pp. 13–38.

Scazzieri, R. (2014c) 'Foreword to Albert Aftalion's Essay', *Economia Politica*, 31 (1, April), pp. 89–92.

Scazzieri, R. (2015) 'The Medium-Term Approach to Economic Crises: A Framework', unpublished mimeo, Accademia Nazionale dei Lincei, Workshop *'Between Theory and Policy: Political Economy of Crises'*, Rome, 27 October 2015.

Scazzieri, R. (2017) 'Liquidity Architectures and Production Arrangements: A Conceptual Scheme', in I. Cardinale, D. Coffman, and R. Scazzieri (eds.), *The Political Economy of the Eurozone*, Cambridge, Cambridge University Press, pp. 155–182.

Scazzieri, R. (2018a) 'Political Economy of Economic Theory', in I. Cardinale and R. Scazzieri (eds.), *The Palgrave Handbook of Political Economy*, London, Palgrave Macmillan, pp. 193–233.

Scazzieri, R. (2018b) 'Structural Dynamics and Evolutionary Change', *Structural Change and Economic Dynamics*, 46 (September), pp. 52–58.

Scazzieri, R. (2019) 'Between Theory and History: The Structural Dynamics Tradition', in A. Sinha and A. M. Thomas (eds.), *Pluralistic Economics and Its History*, Abingdon and New York, Routledge, pp. 136–159.

Scazzieri, R. (2020a) 'Ripensare l'economia politica. Strutture analitiche e contesti', *Rendiconti, Classe di Scienze Morali, Storiche e Filologiche*, Accademia Nazionale dei Lincei, serie ix, vol. xxxi, pp. 175–210.

Scazzieri, R. (2020b) 'Remembering, Forgetting, and the Construction of Identity', *Balzan Papers*, 3, pp. 155–160.

Scazzieri, R. (2021) 'Complex Structures and Relative Invariance in Economic Dynamics', in A. Reggiani, L. A. Schintler, D. Czamanski, and R. Patuelli (eds.), *Handbook on Entropy, Complexity and Spatial Dynamics: A Rebirth of Theory?* Cheltenham and New York, Edward Elgar, pp. 274–289.

Scazzieri, R. (2022) 'Decomposability and Relative Invariance: The Structural Approach to Network Complexity and Resilience', *Networks and Spatial Economics*, vol. 22, special issue 'Resilience, Vulnerability and Complexity in Socioeconomic Systems', pp. 635–657.

Scazzieri, R. and Quadrio Curzio, A. (2022) 'Introduzione. Sulla complessita' teorica e storica dell'economia politica', in A. Quadrio Curzio (ed.), *Economia, complessita', sviluppo. Scritti vari*, Atti della Accademia Nazionale dei Lincei. Memorie, pp. 13–37.

Scazzieri, R. and Zamagni, S. (2008) 'Between Theory and History: On the Identity of Hicks's Economics', in R. Scazzieri, A. Sen, and S. Zamagni (eds.), *Markets, Money and Capital: Hicksian Perspectives for the Twenty First Century*, Cambridge, Cambridge University Press, pp. 1–37.

Sen, A. K. (1977) 'Social Choice Theory: A Re-Examination', *Econometrica*, 45 (1, January), pp. 53–89.

Sen, A. K. (1999a) *Reason before Identity, The Romanes Lecture for 1998*, delivered before the University of Oxford on 17 November 1998, Oxford, Oxford University Press.

Sen, A. K. (1999b) 'The Possibility of Social Choice', *The American Economic Review*, 89 (3, June), pp. 349–378.

Sen, A. K. (2002) 'Positional Objectivity', in *Rationality and Freedom*, Cambridge, MA and London, The Belknap Press of Harvard University Press, pp. 463–483.

Sen, A. K. (2006) 'What Do We Want from a Theory of Justice?', *The Journal of Philosophy*, 103 (5), pp. 215–238.

Sen, A. K. (2009) *The Idea of Justice*, New Delhi, Penguin Books Ltd.

Sen, A. K. (2017 [1970]) *Collective Choice and Social Welfare*, 2nd expanded and updated edition, London, Penguin.

Serra, A. (2011 [1613]) *A Short Treatise on the Wealth and Poverty of Nations*, tr. by Jonathan Hunt, ed. and with an introduction by Sophus A. Reinert. London and New York, Anthem Press (Original title: *Breve trattato delle cause che possono far abbondare li regni d'oro e argento dove non sono miniere, con applicazione al Regno di Napoli*, Naples, Scorriggio).

Seton, F. (1992) *The Economics of Cost, Use, and Value: The Evaluation of Performance, Structure, and Prices across Time, Space, and Economic Systems*, with a foreword by Jan Tinbergen and a special annex and appendix contributed by A. E. Steenge. revised and expanded edition, Oxford, Clarendon Press.

Seton, F. (2000) 'Scissor Crises, Value-Prices, and the Movement of Value-Prices under Technical Change', *Structural Change and Economic Dynamics*, 11 (July), pp. 13–24.

Shaftesbury, A. A. [Anthony Ashley Cooper, Earl of] (1790 [1699]), 'An Inquiry Concerning Virtue and Merit', in *Characteristics of Men, Manners, Opinions, Times*, Basil, J.J. Tourneisen and J.L. Legrand, pp. 1–145.

Shepsle, K. A. (1989) 'Studying Institutions: Some Lessons from the Rational Choice Approach', *Journal of Theoretical Politics*, 1 (2, April), pp. 131–147.

Sidgwick, H. (1891) *The Elements of Politics*, London and New York, Macmillan.

Simmel, G. (1955 [1922]) 'The Web of Group-Affiliations', in *Conflict; The Web of Group Affiliations*, Glencoe, IL, The Free Press.

Simon, H. A. (1962) 'The Architecture of Complexity', *Proceedings of the American Philosophical Society*, 106 (6, December), pp. 467–482.

Simon, H. A. (2002) 'Near Decomposability and the Speed of Evolution', *Industrial and Corporate Change*, 11 (3), pp. 587–599.

Simon, H. A. and Ando, A. (1961) 'Aggregation of Variables in Dynamic Systems', *Econometrica*, 29 (2, April), pp. 111–138.

Sinha, A. (2019) *Essays on the Theory of Value in the Classical Tradition*, London, Routledge.

Skinner, Q. (1983) 'Machiavelli and the Maintenance of Liberty', *Politics*, 18 (2), pp. 3–15.

Skinner, Q. (1998) *Liberty before Liberalism*, Cambridge, Cambridge University Press.

Skocpol, T., Evans, P., and Rueschemeyer, D. (1985) *Bringing the State Back In*, New York and Cambridge, Cambridge University Press.

Smith, A. (1976 [1759]) *The Theory of Moral Sentiments*, D. D. Raphael and A. L. Macfie (eds.), Oxford, Clarendon Press.

Smith, A. (1976 [1776]) *An Inquiry into the Nature and Causes of the Wealth of Nations*, general eds. R. H. Campbell and A. S. Skinner, textual ed. W. B. Todd, Oxford, Clarendon Press.

Smith, A. 1978 [1762–1762, 1766]) *Lectures on Jurisprudence*, ed. R. L. Meek, D. D. Raphael, and P. G. Stein, Oxford, Clarendon Press (report dated 1766).

Smith, A. (1980 [ms. circa 1777]) 'Of the Nature of That Imitation Which Takes Place in What Are Called the Imitative Arts', in W. P. D. Wightman and J. C. Bryce (eds.), *Essays on Philosophical Subjects*, Oxford, Clarendon Press, pp. 176–213.

Smith, V. (2008) *Rationality in Economics. Constructivist and Ecological Forms*, Cambridge, Cambridge University Press.

Soudek, J. (1952) 'Aristotle's Theory of Exchange: An Inquiry into the Origin of Economic Analysis', *Proceedings of the American Philosophical Society*, 96 (1, February), pp. 45–75.

Sraffa, P. (1960) *Production of Commodities by Means of Commodities: Prelude to a Critique of Economic Theory*, Cambridge, Cambridge University Press.

Sraffa, P. (1998 [1925]) 'On the Relations between Cost and Quantity Produced', in L. Pasinetti (ed.), *Italian Economic Papers*, Oxford, Oxford University Press and Bologna, Il Mulino, vol. III, pp. 323–363.

Stahl, H. H. (1939) 'Organizarea socială a țărăânimii' [Social Organization of Peasantry], *Enciclopedia României*, vol. I, pp. 559–576.

Steenge, A. E. (2011) 'On the Evolution of Multi-Sectoral Models; Optimality and Beyond', in M. Ciaschini and G. C. Romagnoli (eds.), *L'economia Italiana: metodi di analisi, misurazione e nodi strutturali; Saggi per Guido M. Rey*, Milano, Franco Angeli, pp. 92–114.

Stein, P. (1999) *Roman Law in European History*, Cambridge, Cambridge University Press.

Stigler, G. (1951) 'The Division of Labour Is Limited by the Extent of the Market', *Journal of Political Economy*, 59 (3), pp. 185–193.

Stone R. (1962), 'Multiple Classifications in Social Accounting', paper presented at a meeting of Institut International de Statistique, Paris, 1961, *Bulletin de l'Institut International de Statistique*, 39, pp. 215–233.

Strathern, M. (1988) *The Gender of the Gift: Problems with Women and Problems with Society in Melanesia*, Berkeley, Los Angeles, and London, University of California Press.

Strathern, M. (2004) *Partial Connections*, updated edition, Oxford, AltraMira Press.

Strathern, M. (2018) 'Acceptance Speech', *Balzan Prizes 2018*, Milano, Fondazione Internazionale Premio E. Balzan 'Premio'.

Strathern, M. (2020) *Relations: An Anthropological Account*, Durham, NC, Duke University Press.

Streeck, W. (2019) 'Reflections on Political Scale', Adam Smith Lecture in Jurisprudence, University of Glasgow, 30 May 2018, *Jurisprudence: An International Journal of Legal and Political Thought*, 10 (1, April), pp. 1–14.

Sugden R. (2005a) 'Correspondence of Sentiments: An Explanation of the Pleasure of Social Interaction', in L. Bruni and P. L. Porta (eds.), *Economics and Happiness: Framing the Analysis*, Oxford, Oxford University Press, pp. 91–115.

Sugden, R. (2005b) 'Fellow-Feeling', in B. Gui and R. Sugden (eds.), *Economics and Social Interaction: Accounting for Interpersonal Relations*, Cambridge, Cambridge University Press, pp. 52–75.

Szirmai, A. (2012) 'Industrialisation as an Engine of Growth in Developing Countries, 1950–2005', *Structural Change and Economic Dynamics*, 23 (December), pp. 406–420.

Tinbergen, J. (1952) *On the Theory of Economic Policy*, Amsterdam, North-Holland.

Tocqueville, A. de (1856) *L'Ancien Régime et la Révolution*, Paris, Michel-Lévy frères.

Tocqueville, A. de (1969 [1835–1840]) *Democracy in America*, tr. G. Lawrence, New York, Doubleday.

Tocqueville, A. de (2005 [1847–1848]) 'Question financière', in A. de Tocqueville, *Textes économiques*, Anthologie critique par J.-L-. Benoît et É. Keslassy, Paris, Pocket, pp. 184–189.

Torrini, M. (1983) 'Le passioni di Paolo Mattia Doria: Il problema delle passioni dell'animo nella "Vita Civile"', *Giornale critico della filosofia italiana*, 62 (1, January–April), p. 129–152.

Trakman, L. E. (2003) 'From the Medieval Law Merchant to E-Merchant Law', *The University of Toronto Law Journal*, 53 (3), pp. 265–304.

Tribe, K. (2017) *Governing Economy: The Reformation of German Economic Discourse, 1750–1840*, 2nd rev. edition, Newbury, Threshold Press.

Tuck, R. (1993) *Philosophy and Government, 1572–1651*, Cambridge, Cambridge University Press

Tuck, R. (2016) *The Sleeping Sovereign: The Invention of Modern Democracy*, Cambridge, Cambridge University Press.

Tugan Baranovsky, M. I. (1894) *Promyshlennye krizisy v sovremennoi Anglii* [Industrial Crises in Great Britain], St. Peterburg, Tip. I. N. Skorochodova.

von Tunzelmann, G. N. (1995) *Technology and Industrial Progress: The Foundations of Economic Growth*, Aldershot and Brookfield, VT, Edward Elgar.

Tuomela, R. (2007) *The Philosophy of Sociality: The Shared Point of View*, Oxford and New York, Oxford University Press.

Turchin, P. (2016) *Ages of Discord: A Structural-Demographic Analysis of American History*, Chaplin, CT, Beresta Books

Vanberg, V. J. (2005) 'Market and State: The Perspective of Constitutional Political Economy', *Journal of Institutional Economics*, 1 (1, June), pp. 23–49.

van Schendelen, M. P. C. M. (ed.) (1984) 'Consociationalism, Pillarization and Conflict-Management in the Low Countries', Special issue of *Acta Politica*, 19 (1), pp. 7–178.

Venkatachalam, R. and Kumar, S. M. (2021) 'Economic Structures and Dynamics: A Morphogenetic View', *Structural Change and Economic Dynamics*, https://doi.org/10.1016/j.strueco.2021.02.003

Vico, G. B. (1709) *De nostri temporis studiorum ratione dissertatio*, Naples, Mosca.

von Hermann, F. B. W. (1832) *Staatswirthschaftliche Untersuchungen*, München, A. Weber.

von Sonnenfels, J. (1765) *Grundsätze der Polizey, Handlung und Finanzwissenschaft*, Wien, Kurzboeck.

von Stein, L. (1878) *Die Volkswirtschaftslehre*, Wien, Braumüller.

von Strigl, R. (2012 [1934]) *Capital and Production*, tr. from the German by M. R. Hoppe and H. H. Hoppe; ed. with an introduction by J. G. Hulsmann, Auburn, Mises Institute.

Wakefield, E. G. (1835–1843) 'Commentary', in L. L. D. Adam Smith, *An Inquiry into the Nature and Causes of the Wealth of Nations*, with a commentary by the author of 'England and America', London, Charles Knight.

Wamba, S. F., Akter, S., Edwards, A., Chopin, G., and Gnanzou, D. (2015) 'How "Big Data" Can Make Big Impact: Findings from a Systematic Review and a Longitudinal Case Study', *International Journal of Production Economics*, 165 (July), pp. 234–246.

Wang, H. (2014) *China from Empire to Nation-State*, Cambridge, MA and London, Harvard University Press.

Weaver, W. (1948) 'Science and Complexity', *American Scientist*, 36 (4, October), pp. 536–544.

Weber, M. (1947 [1922]) *Wirtschaft und Gesellschaft*, Tübingen, Mohr (Paul Siebeck); trans. *The Theory of Social and Economic Organization*, New York, The Free Press of Glencoe.

Weingast, B. R., and D. A. Wittmann (eds.) (2006) *The Oxford Handbook of Political Economy*, Oxford, Oxford University Press.

Whately, R. (1831) *Introductory Lectures on Political Economy*, London, B. Fellowes.

Williamson, J. (2000) 'What Should the World Bank Think about the Washington Consensus?' *World Bank Research Observer*, 15 (2, August), pp. 251–264.

Willinger, M. (1989) 'Industrial Development of Composite Materials: Towards a Functional Appraisal', *Composites Science and Technology*, 34 (1), pp. 53–71.

Yongjin, Z. and Buzan, B. (2012) 'The Tributary System as International Society in Theory and Practice', *The Chinese Journal of International Politics*, 5 (1, Spring), pp. 3–36.

Young, A. (1928) 'Increasing Returns and Economic Progress', *The Economic Journal*, 38 (December), pp. 527–542.

Zadeh, L. (2011) 'Generalized Theory of Uncertainty: Principal Concepts and Ideas', in S. Marzetti Dall'Aste Brandolini and R. Scazzieri (eds.), *Fundamental Uncertainty. Rationality and Plausible Reasoning*,

Basingstoke, Hampshire, and New York, Palgrave Macmillan, pp. 104–150.

Zamagni, S. (2004) 'Towards an Economy of Human Relations: on the Role of Psychology in Economics', *Group Analysis*, 37 (1, March), pp. 17–32.

Zamagni, S. (2015) 'Development, Capabilities and Institutions', in M. Baranzini, C. Rotondi, and R. Scazzieri (eds.), *Resources, Production and Structural Dynamics*, Cambridge, Cambridge University Press, pp. 259–278.

Name Index

Subject Index

acquisition point of view (in a supply chain), 162
action-choice correspondences (Aoki), 178
actions
  of the collective type, 16, 29, 120, 131
  coordination of, 62
  and dispositions, 4, 5, 38, 181
  hierarchical arrangement of, 16
  instrumental, 194
  and interpersonal association, 8
  in the material sphere, 40
  of the means-ends type, 15
  multidimensional structure of, 57
  mutual fitting of, 45
  of the purposive type, 16
  and the pursuit of objectives, 23
  and time horizon, 186
  by a sovereign actor, 15
  and structures, 2, 16, 177, 180, 182
  and systemic interest, 175
activities
  classification of, 167
  as 'instruments of action (Aristotle),' 73
  as 'instruments of production (Aristotle),' 73
administered trade, 116, 117
Adriatic and Ionian Region (EUSAIR), 160
aggregation, 2, 6, 7, 14–16, 25, 26, 31, 35, 36, 57, 58, 64, 67, 69, 70, 82, 97–99, 101, 103, 106, 112, 126, 128, 145, 162, 170, 189–191, 196, 201, 207, 210, 213, 214
analytical map of institutional relations (Georgescu-Roegen), 157
argumentative reasoning, 217
association, 126, 127, 136, 137
  of capabilities, 44, 63
  and cooperation, 63, 65
  as defined by Max Weber (*Verein*), 21
  and dispositions, 44
  and division of labour, 64, 67, 118
  and mutual exchange (Althusius), 64
  and patterns of interdependence, 62
  and production regimes, 63, 64, 68, 72, 80, 81
  and proportionality conditions, 63, 70, 71
  and social structures, 64
  and structural change, 64, 85, 89
  of 'virtues,' 43
Association of Iron Ore Exporting Countries (APEF), 162, 208
association, mode of, 64, 65, 81, 86, 88, 89, 97, 99–103, 105, 108, 117–121, 188

Babbage's 'law of multiples'
  and division of labour, 66–68, 70
body politic, ix, 1, 7, 9, 18, 31, 43, 44, 58, 114–116, 125–128, 133–136, 139, 144, 149, 153–156, 181, 191, 193, 194, 209, 217, 219, 220

capabilities, 2, 6–8, 14, 24, 36, 39, 45, 46, 62–64, 67–69, 71–84, 86–93, 98, 99, 103, 104, 106–109, 117–121, 130, 140, 161, 162, 164, 194
capability matrix, 82–84, 89, 90
catallactics (Hicks), 32, 128
catallaxy (Hayek), 34
circular flow economy, 58, 84, 85, 88, 100, 163, 170, 172
civil association as defined by Oakeshott, 21–23

Printed in the United States
by Baker & Taylor Publisher Services